NATIVE AMERICAN ARTS AND CRAFTS

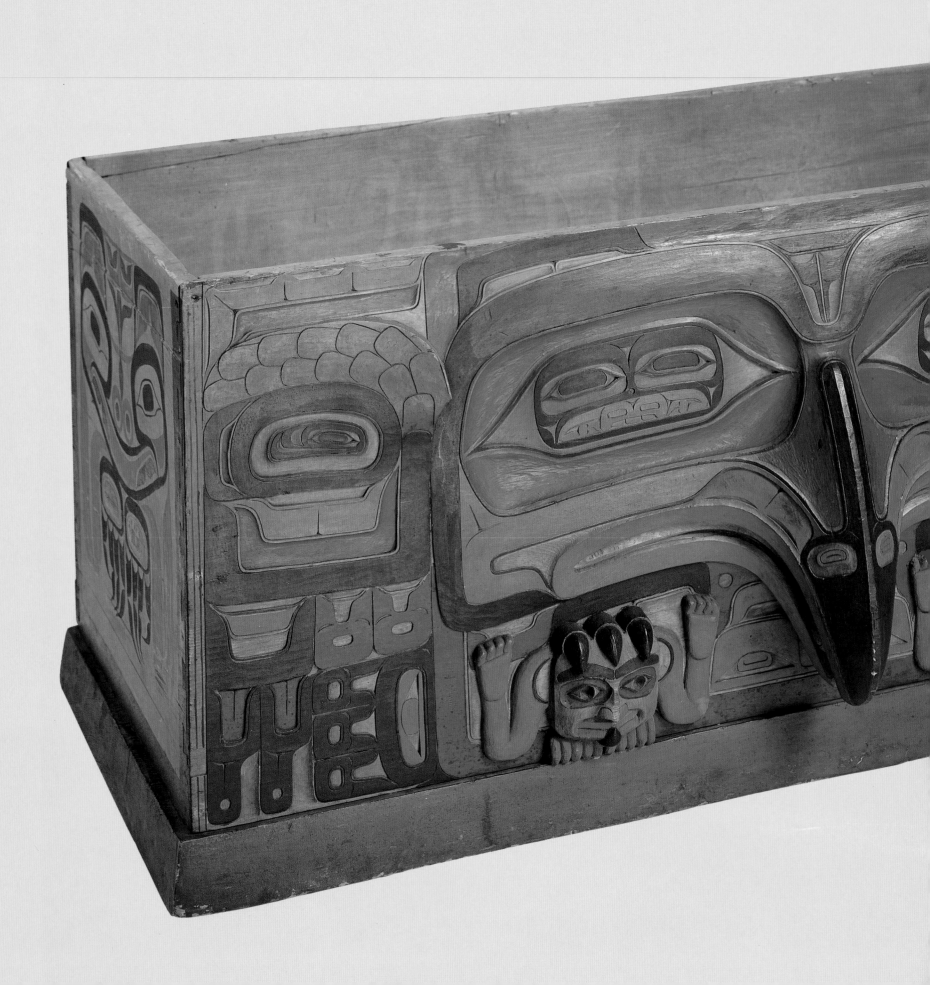

NATIVE AMERICAN ARTS AND CRAFTS

✦

EDITORIAL CONSULTANT
COLIN F. TAYLOR Ph.D

SMITHMARK

This edition published in 1995 by SMITHMARK Publishers Inc., 16 East 32nd Street, New York, NY 10016.

 2 3 4 5 6 7 8 9

SMITHMARK books are available for bulk purchase for sales promotion and premium use. For details write or call the manager of special sales, SMITHMARK Publishers Inc., 16 East 32nd Street, New York, NY 10016; (212) 532-6600.

Produced by Salamander Books Ltd
129-137 York Way
London N7 9LG
United Kingdom

ISBN 0-8317-6756-1

Printed in Italy

CREDITS
Project Editor: Christopher Westhorp
Designer: Mark Holt
Color photography: Don Eiler, Richmond, Virginia (© Salamander Books Ltd)
Editor: Joyce Willcocks
Map: Janos Marffy (© Salamander Books Ltd)
Filmset: SX Composing Ltd, England
Color reproduction: Pixel Tech Ltd, Singapore

Page 1: A Hopi kachina known as *Poli Mana* or Butterfly Maiden. This kachina dates from 1910 and is painted with natural pigments. Dressed in traditional pueblo dress this kachina brings in the growing season.

Pages 2/3: This Haida chest represents Eagle or Thunderbird. The family crest, Grizzly Bear, adorns the sides. Some people believed the box (used chiefly to hold costumes and ritual paraphernalia) contained the spirit of the supernatural creature depicted on its sides. The applied decoration of such chests was sophisticated, enigmatic and one of the most difficult to decipher of all Northwest Coast art.

Page 5: A Chippewa (Ojibwa in Canada) woven bead bag from the Great Lakes region. Characterized by large, loom-woven bead panels with attached fringed tabs and floral beaded extension, these bags were suspended on wide shoulder straps notable for their distinctively different patterns on each half. The panel here is framed by a repetitive geometric motif usually identified as 'otter tail'.

CONTRIBUTING AUTHORS

Colin F. Taylor Ph.D (Introduction, The Plains, and Editorial Consultant) is a Senior Lecturer at Hastings College of Art and Technology, Hastings, England. He is acknowledged as a leading expert on Plains Indian culture and his previous books include *Native American Myths and Legends* and Smithmark's highly successful *The Native Americans*.

Robbie Ethridge (The Southeast) is a doctoral candidate in Anthropology at the University of Georgia in Athens, Georgia. Her specialities are Southeastern Indian ethnohistory and the historic Southeastern Indians. She is currently writing a social history of the late-18th century Creek Indians.

Ellen Bradbury (The Southwest) was brought up near the Tewa pueblo of San Ildefonso. She is a graduate in American Art History from the University of New Mexico. Previously Director of the Museum of Fine Arts, Museum of New Mexico, she now runs an educational, non-profit organization called Recursos de Santa Fe, that specialises in artistic, historical and anthropological tours of the southwest region.

Allen Chronister (Plateau and Basin) is a lawyer based in Helena, Montana, who has developed an extensive interest in the tribes and cultures of the western Plains and the Plateau and Basin regions. The interest has become an expertise and Allen has consulted with, among others, the Montana Historical Society, the US National Park Service, and the Buffalo Bill Historical Center.

Craig D. Bates (California) is Curator of Ethnography at Yosemite National Park in California. He has worked with California's Native Americans over many years and has published numerous books about their culture and beliefs.

Carol Sheehan (The Northwest Coast) has a degree in anthropology from the University of British Columbia. She is now a freelance writer and consultant, having worked previously as a lecturer at the University of Calgary in Alberta, and as the Assistant Curator of Ethnology at the Glenbow Museum. She is the author of *Pipes That Won't Smoke; Coal That Won't Burn: Haida Argillite Sculpture*, has contributed to a number of other books, including *Native American Myths and Legends*, and written many articles and papers on ethnographic subjects.

Marion Wood (The Subarctic) is a graduate of the University of St. Andrews and was for many years the Assistant Curator of Anthropology at the Horniman Museum in London. She is now a freelance writer and curator with the Northeast Fife District Museum Service in Scotland. She has written a number of books on Native American subjects, including *Ancient America: Cultural Atlas for Young People* and *Spirits, Heroes and Hunters in North American Indian Mythology*.

Bernadette Driscoll-Engelstad (The Arctic) has an MA from Johns Hopkins University in Baltimore, Maryland, where she is presently studying for her doctorate in Anthropology. As a curator at the Winnipeg Art Gallery (Canada), she gained considerable expertise in the field of contemporary Inuit art. She has lectured extensively and written numerous articles for museum catalogues, art journals, and ethnographic publications.

Cath Oberholtzer (The Northeast) is based in Ontario where she teaches anthropology as well as native art and architecture of the Americas at Trent University. Her specific interest is the Cree of the eastern Subarctic, with whom she has done fieldwork, as well as the more general one of native cultures in the Northeast and Subarctic regions.

CONTENTS

INTRODUCTION

A Chippewa (Ojibwa) dish used in rice-making, collected at the White Earth Reservation by the ethnologist Frances Densmore before 1913, exemplifies the practical use of birch bark, a highly popular natural material from the northern woodlands. Here, the birch bark has been cut, folded and sewn at the corners with strips of the inner bark of basswood, to form an oblong dish. Birch bark was always used with the inner or brown side out and could be decorated by scraping away the thin layer of dark bark around the design. Seams could be made watertight by sealing them with a type of pitch made from the gum of an evergreen tree and mixed with charcoal from cedar chips which was pounded to a fine powder.

THE DIVERSIFIED AND NUMEROUS abilities of the North American Indian are reflected in the great skills in arts and crafts which are the subject of this book. Since, however, in one volume it is impossible adequately to cover the wide variety of arts and craft skills practiced in the nine cultural areas of North America, the approach here has been to select some of the finest of their work from the Historic Period and, in several instances, to bring it up to the present day. In all cases the attempt has been both to elucidate and illustrate the craft and artistic endeavors of the indigenous people of North America. A combination of inherited skills born of economic, social and spiritual existence, they illustrate the innate artistry of the Indian and underline the Indian's place as the creator of North America's indigenous folk art – although, as one respected scholar has pointed out, to the individual tribesman 'art for art's sake was incomprehensible'.[1]

Nevertheless, crafts were not limited purely to the material conditions of their lives, techniques being developed so that the esthetic sense was satisfied and the art became ancillary to both ceremonial and social institutions. In all these endeavors, the North American Indian maximised the use of the mineral, animal and vegetal wealth around him, it being developed and modified to match environmental requirements of the particular culture area.

Thus, for example, waterproofing and extensive use of animal hides and fur for clothing and transportation were vital for survival to the Inuit, while technically fine baskets, which could be used for winnowing and even carry water, were essential to the lives of the Southwestern tribes, such as the Hopi and Navajo. All this developed over a period of many thousands of years and, in consequence, it should be recognized that the products of their labors which now repose in the museum collections of the world generally represent the best of the arts and crafts of 'The People' reflecting the efforts of countless generations who by trial and error achieved, by inheritance, an end product which not only satisfied practical and physical needs but often esthetic and spiritual ones as well.

Unfortunately, not all is well-represented in the ethnographical collections, much being destroyed at the instigation of zealous missionaries, such as occurred among the Nez Perce[2] or by brutal army campaigns waged against the Plains tribes. Typical is Bourke's report on the aftermath of an attack on Dull Knife's village in the winter of 1876, when the troopers of the 3rd and

4th cavalry 'toiled and burned, wiping off the face of the earth many products of aboriginal taste and industry which would have been gems in the cabinets of museums'.[3]

Nevertheless, much has been saved and reconstructed and by good fortune, amazing 'gems' of sources have from time to time been discovered, such as in the case of Ishi, the sole noble survivor of the Yahi of California. Ishi spent the last five years of his life, from 1911 to 1917, at the Museum of Anthropology of the University of California, where he demonstrated the intricate craft skills of his tribe, all of which were systematically recorded for posterity by the anthropologists, Kroeber and Waterman.[4] It was to the credit

Collecting reeds for mat making (left) was an occupation not only of the Indians of the woodlands but also of the Plateau. In both areas the mats served various purposes, including both floor and dwelling covering. This Yakima woven bag (below) shows one of the wide variety of bags made in the Plateau region. The decoration was often by 'false embroidery', the designs appearing only on the outside of the bag.

An Aleutian fisherman's eyeshade of bent wood (above) collected in Alaska prior to 1892. Wooden visors from this region invariably display two flat ivory or bone plaques, one at each side. The upper end was carved in the form of a scroll and the lower end tapered like the beak of a bird. This one is embellished with ivory attachments carved in the form of walruses and seals referring to hunting magic.

A *Yeibichai Ye'ii* dancer of the Navajo (right), one of the impersonators of the supernatural beings, displays much of Navajo arts and crafts – hard-soled moccasins, wolf mask, featherwork and silver conchas with turquoise, all typical of the tribe.

of such scientists, who in the late-19th century were mindful that dynamic, enviable cultures were fast vanishing in North America, that a program of 'salvage' anthropology was instigated. Thus, august institutions such as the Smithsonian Institution in Washington,[5] the American Museum of Natural History in New York, the Field Museum in Chicago and the Brooklyn Museum in New York, sent the young anthropologists Wissler, Lowie, Dorsey, Kroeber, Cushing and Culin and others into the field to document and collect the remnants of the destroyed cultures.

Typical of such activities were the expeditions led by R. Stewart Culin,[6] a founder member of the American Anthropological Association. A close colleague of Culin's was George A. Dorsey, a Harvard-trained anthropologist who became curator of anthropology at the Field Museum in 1897. Between them they organized expeditions in the field to the Southwest, California, Northwest Coast and Oklahoma. From these four cultural areas they collected a wide range of objects which illustrated the range and wide diversity of the arts and crafts of the indigenous inhabitants. Such artifacts as Kachina dolls – carved from one

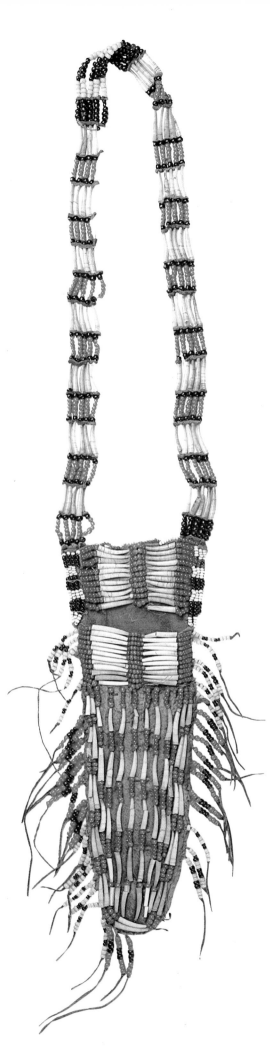

Aho Jeobe (left), a Choctaw Indian, photographed in 1909. He is wearing a typical Choctaw shirt of the period made from trade fabric, which by this time had virtually replaced garments of dressed deerskin. The shoulder sash, however, is an early Choctaw style and, in particular, the scroll-like beadwork pattern, a marked feature of Choctaw male costume which was first pictured by George Catlin in the 1830s.

piece of wood – were collected from the Hopi; hand-spun garments from the Zuni; and coiled baskets from the Western Apache[7] as well as superb examples of bowls and pitchers representing an earlier culture of the region – the Anasazi and Sikyatki – dating from the 15th century or earlier. From California came the superbly woven basket hats of the Hupa, carved horn spoons of the Yurok, seed flails of the Pomo and dance capes and headbands of eagle, hawk and red-shafted flicker feathers. From the Northwest Coast were collected impressive carvings – figures, house-posts, totem poles, kerfed chests, spoons and rattles of cedar wood, all elaborately painted with abstract designs typical of the area.

Similar expeditions were those made by Wissler, Lowie, Dorsey and Spinden to the Plains and Plateau regions in the period 1890-1915, when superb examples of art and craft work in feathers, beads and quills – even skin-painted tipis – were obtained.

Their legacy, however, superb anthropological studies and systematically collected objects representing the best of tribal arts and crafts, was – together with the artifacts collected in an earlier era – all but ignored for more than half a century,

A knife sheath (far left) collected from the Han, a tribe of the Subarctic Athapaskans. Such sheaths were worn around the neck and hung on the chest. This one is made of heavy, tanned caribou skin embellished with dentalium shells in combination with red, white and blue trade beads. The dentaliums were very highly prized shells which were first obtained from the Northwest Coast tribes; later, white traders imported large quantities into the Subarctic region where they were used in profusion, adorning the hair, worn as earrings, and used to embellish various items of costume such as shirts, leggings and mittens.

A spruce-root hat (above) made by the Haida of Queen Charlotte Islands in British Columbia, was collected by J. G. Swan at Masset in 1883. Some 2ft (60cm) in diameter, it is painted with designs in black, red and blue and displays the crest of the wearer. These hats were generally worn on ceremonial occasions when the family's honors were displayed, consistent with rank and the structure of Haida society. The crown itself is strengthened by an inner wooden framework and leather straps tie under the chin to hold the large hat on the head.

except by the dedicated scholar and perceptive connoisseur.[8]

The 1950s saw a resurgence of interest in the material culture and decorative craftsmanship of American Indians,[9] and in the last two decades[10], scholars have become increasingly aware that many of the artifacts produced by Indians, from whatever cultural area, exhibit those attributes used to evaluate any work of craftsmanship or art – formal structure, expressiveness, virtuosity and transcendence[11] – and that an ensemble of North American Indian material can, if the effort is made to interpret, give deep insights into the ethos and culture that produced it.[12]

The following pages will demonstrate that materials found naturally and in rich supply in a particular culture area – wood, bone, ivory, furs and hides, shell, stone and feathers – were used by the (largely) unnamed craftsmen and women[13] to produce impressive objects which were functional and essential to the life of the people. In addition, they demonstrate that the western concepts of artistic propriety were frequently crossed and recrossed without concern; little was rendered directly from life but more from memory or through mystic communication, and stunning emblems not infrequently made visible the invisible.

Thus images – those of the Northwest Coast or the Plains for example – were painted and rendered as if they floated and all animal images were flatly generalized as if caught on the move.

Sculptures too – be they from shell of the Southeast, catlinite from the Great Plains, wood or steatite from the Northwest Coast or the clever ivory miniatures from the Arctic or Subarctic regions – made both religious and social comment, while traditional beadwork, quillwork, painted pottery and the like, not infrequently reflected abstract and subtle metonymic thought.

The legacy is a tribute to a strong and remarkable people who, despite great suppression, tenaciously maintained their values and beliefs. The wonder of it all is, given the profound anomic state of most tribes in all the cultural areas during the second half of the 19th century, that they retained and produced so many things of beauty. This is a theme which not infrequently continues in the creations of present-day Native Americans,[14] many of whom draw inspiration from their heritage; however, as Spinden observed: 'The ideas of beauty which arise in the red man's consciousness move with the times, and the spiritual forces behind them are not held to the trail of the vanished buffalo'.[15]

The arts and crafts
discussed in this volume
embrace the nine major
cultural areas of North
America (above). The
boundaries are, of course,
fluid rather than rigid
and the map thus serves
to delineate them
approximately. They are:
Southeast (1), Southwest
(2), Plains (3), Plateau
and Basin (4), California
(5), Northwest Coast (6),
Subarctic (7), Arctic (8),
and Northeast (9).

THE SOUTHEAST

> *'Our best road to understanding their artistic and recreational forms is to view them as the outward expressions of their belief system. Only in this way can we come to understand truly the feeling and care they lavished on their pottery, basketry, and stonework.'*
>
> CHARLES HUDSON, 1976[1]

THE STORY of Southeastern Indian arts and crafts is different from that of other Native Americans. When Europeans first penetrated the Southeast in the early-16th century, the Indians had reached a social, political, and religious development more akin to the grand civilization of the Mesoamerican Aztecs than to other North American Indian groups. Between about AD 1000 to AD 1540, the Mississippian Period, the Southeastern Indians' political order consisted of large and small chiefdoms presided over by a priestly elite who could command the construction of large temple mounds and other impressive earthworks. This system was supported by intensive riverine corn agriculture and maintained through warfare.

The Mississippian way of life suffered swift deterioration after European contact. European diseases, to which the Southeastern Indians had no natural immunity, were deadly foes causing a sharp population decline, the destruction of the chiefdom political order, and social dislocation as people relocated and reorganized. During this time, the better-known historic Southeastern Indian groups such as the Cherokee, Choctaw, Catawba, Creek, Chickasaw, and Seminole formed out of the wreckage of the chiefdoms. Their societies bore little resemblance to the past.

Following on the heels of the introduction of disease, an equally profound force for change occurred when the Southeastern Indians were incorporated into the European economic system through trading deerskins. Throughout the 17th and 18th centuries, the Southeastern Indians regularly encountered, lived among, were dependent upon, intermarried with, and, occasionally, fiercely resisted whites. By the 19th century the cotton agriculture and the plantation economy came to dominate the Old South. Unlike the deerskin trade, the plantation economy did not need the Indians; it needed their land. No longer necessary to the market system, the Indians became an obstacle, and this ultimately led to Removal, when almost all of the southern Indians were forcibly relocated to western territories.

Southeastern Indian art reflects their history. The highest artistic achievements of the Southeastern Indians undoubtedly occurred during the Mississippian Period. The people who lived during the Mississippian Period displayed a pageantry and rich ceremonial life unparalleled anywhere in Native North America. Mississippian accoutrements are lavish, eloquent, and highly crafted. Mississippian art is explicitly iconographic. Design motifs, although varying stylistically, are elements in what is termed the Southeastern Ceremonial Complex. These motifs include the bi-lobed arrow, the falcon-man, the forked-eye design, sun circles, crosses and swastikas, winged serpents, and animals with mythological or social significance such as the bear, woodpecker, raptorial bird, and rattlesnake.

This artistic expression, so closely tied to ceremony and elite authority, declined along with the

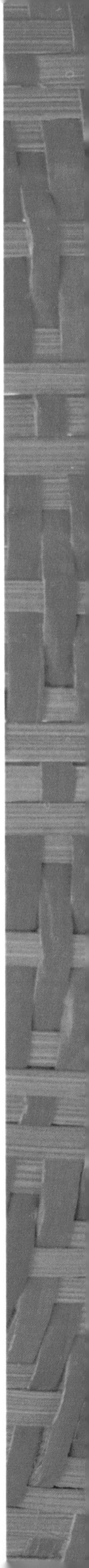

The pieces shown here (main picture) illustrate the Southeastern Indian's penchant for color and rectilinear and curvilinear designs. The beaded sash, made by the Koasati of Alabama, is made from red and black stroud onto which the beadwork is embroidered. The basket was made by the Chitimacha of Louisiana, the most famous of Southeastern Indian basket makers, in the early-20th century. The chain effect of connecting diamonds, shown in the close-up (right and far left), is a typical design motif for Southeastern Indian basketry. The shirt is a man's big shirt made by the Seminoles of southern Florida. The swastika design is an ancient motif found also on Mississippian Period objects. The Seminole fan (above left), made of turkey tail feathers sewn to buckskin, was used for everyday purposes, such as fanning fires.

13

This pipe (below) was made by the Catawba of North Carolina around 1910. The pipe probably was made from a mold in which clay is pressed between halves of a ceramic, hand-modeled, double pipe mold. After molding, the pipe is removed, polished, the facial and feather lines incised, and then dried.

This picture (right), taken in the late-19th century, shows two Cherokee potters at work. The potter shapes her wares in her lap, outdoors, and in the company of others. The woman on the left is coiling a fillet of clay with one hand, and pinching the coils together and smoothing the seams with the other hand.

chiefdoms after European contact.[2] In the Ceremonial Complex, art was inextricably associated with religious, social, or political life. During the Historic Period, Southeastern Indian ceremonial life took a more egalitarian turn and did not require the trappings of a priestly elite. In the Historic Period, European trade provided most of the material items of daily life.

Ceramics

Southeastern Indian ceramic art during the Mississippian Period was unsurpassed in North America. Southeastern Indians did not possess the potter's wheel, and women, who were the masters of this medium, used coiling and hand modeling to fashion their wares. Although there are no descriptions of Mississippian potters at work, contemporary Catawba potters still practice a variant of the coiling method, and it is reasonable to suppose that Mississippian women followed similar procedures.

In the coiling technique, lumps of clay are rolled on a board until they form rounded fillets of uniform thickness and length.[3] Each piece of rolled clay is pinched together to form one long, continuous fillet which is then wound around and up to form the rough shape of the vessel.[4] The ware is then smoothed and further shaped and the walls thinned with a spoon-shaped gourd rind or mussel shell.[5] After allowing the ware to air dry, Catawba potters finish the surface by using a smooth mussel shell or kitchen knife to scrape the inside and outside of the ware and to cut and smooth the rim.[6] Handles, spouts, lugs, pedestals, legs, necks, and so on are hand-molded and attached separately. Before fire-drying, the potter polishes the surface with a worn, smooth pebble.[7] Catawba women prize their polishing stones; the more worn and smooth ones are considered irreplaceable and are often handed down from generation to generation.

Mississippian ceramics were made in an interesting array of forms. Utilitarian wares, usually undecorated, vary from small bowls to cooking

and storage pots that hold up to six gallons. Ceremonial and mortuary objects have elaborate decorations and forms. Some of the most outstanding ceremonial forms are the human and animal effigy bottles and bowls, especially the noticeable 'dead-head' effigies which obviously represent a dead person.[8] The bottles were shaped into full figures of animals or into a usually kneeling human form. The bowls have miniature ceramic human or animal heads attached to the rim.[9] Other ceremonial bottles are globular bottles with relatively long necks and decorated with geometrical or curvilinear incising or polychrome painting. Many of the ceremonial containers are incised or painted with Southeastern Ceremonial Complex motifs such as the sun circle, the hand and eye motif, and the winged serpent.[10] All of the archeological and ethnohistorical evidence points to a drastic decline in ceramic art after the arrival of Europeans and, especially, after the Indians had access to metal pots, pans, bowls, cups, and dishes. The historic groups continued to make ceramic utilitarian wares, but not in such quantities, and certainly without the mastery of their ancestors. Ceremonial ceramic wares further ceased being made. Around the turn of the 20th century, with an increase in

tourist trade and collector interest, Catawba and Cherokee women returned to ceramic manufacturing as an art form.[11]

Stonework

The stonework of the Southeastern Indians, like their ceramic art, reached its height during the Mississippian Period. Stone working was almost certainly a man's domain. Mississippian men knew the attributes and limitations of a vast variety of stone for sculpting and chipping. Men quarried local stone sources such as chert, steatite, greenstone, shale, quartz, granite, diorite, slate, hematite, limestone and marble.[12] Especially valued high grade stone was traded throughout the Southeast.

The primary techniques in stonework were chipping and grinding. The chipping technique was used mostly in the manufacture of cutting tools. Flakes were struck from the stone being shaped with another stone or a piece of deer antler to give it the desired form and thinness. Smaller flakes were removed by applying pressure with smaller tools to refine the shape and sharpen the edges.[13] In the grinding technique, the stone to be worked was simply pecked and ground into shape and then polished with sand mixed with oil or water.[14] To fashion the more intricate stone objects such as effigy pipes, men used a soft, easily carved stone such as steatite, and then used stone chisels, drills, and scrapers to carve highly detailed forms

with deeply incised lines.[15] The pipe holes were then drilled and the pipe polished.

Although many tools for daily life were made of stone, stonework became a true art form in the production of ceremonial and religious objects. Chipped stone war clubs, blades and batons are so finely crafted, delicate, and unmarred, that they could not have been used in actual hand-to-hand combat. Grinding produced some marvelously sculpted objects, the most noteworthy being the kneeling-human mortuary figures carved out of limestone, sandstone or marble. These figures, which may have represented mythical or real ancestors, were kept in the charnel houses which were the repositories of the elite dead; some were interred in high-status burials.[16]

The chunky game, played well into the Historic Period, required a ground-stone gaming piece or chunky stone. These pieces are discoidal stones, sometimes with concave centers on both sides; the finer ones are highly polished and perfectly round. Chunky stones, although probably used frequently, are works of art in themselves, showing a gracefulness of line and beautiful symmetry.

After European contact there was a dramatic decline in stonework.[17] Southeastern Indians readily replaced stone tools with European-made

Mrs. Edna Welch, one of the most skillful and famous Cherokee potters of her time, crafted this ceramic duck effigy bowl (left) in the 1930s. Mrs. Welch used the coiling technique to fashion the body; the head was hand-modeled and attached separately. She then incised the feathers and eyes after polishing. Mrs. Welch was known to copy archeological specimens, and she may have fashioned the duck effigy bowl after Mississippian Period animal effigy bowls.

This Mississippian Period monolithic ax (left), recovered near Ballground, Georgia, is carved from a single piece of stone. The handle is etched with Southeastern Ceremonial Complex motifs associated with warfare. The design shows two human heads with forked-eye designs, a hand, a long bone, and a scalp attached to a hoop.

Historic Period Cherokee pipes, like those above, are typically 'elbow' pipes with the bowls at right angles to the stems. They commonly have an animal effigy in full relief carved on the stem. Frogs and bears, as shown on these pipes, are common Historic Period animal motifs. The tomahawk effigy pipe was also a popular design form. The stem is a piece of hollowed-out wood.

This shell gorget (right) was found at Spiro Mound in Oklahoma, one of the largest Mississippian Period ceremonial and political centers. The gorget is broken in half; the missing half would be a mirror image of the surviving half. The man probably represents a warrior, holding in his right hand a bow. The raised arms and slightly bent knees impart a sense of movement, in this case, perhaps a warrior dance.

metal tools and weapons. Men continued to make stone tools, but these did not have the same attention to detail and craftsmanship as those from the Mississippian Period. After all, the flintlock gun was now the weapon of choice.

Men, however, never completely lost the artistry of grinding and carving. Chunky stones from the Historic Period are as finely crafted and beautiful as those from the Mississippian Period. Tobacco pipes played an important role in Historic Period Southeastern Indian ceremonial life, and a great deal of care and attention went into the artistry of Historic Period steatite pipes.[18] The Cherokee were famous for their fine tobacco pipes. Historic Period pipes are usually carved with an animal effigy on the stem. Animal figures on the pipes are often bears, although panthers and frogs are also common. Pipes occasionally have a reclining human carved on the stems or, reportedly, even men and women in explicit sexual poses.[19]

Metal and Shellwork

During the Mississippian Period, shell and metal, primarily copper, were scarce in the southeast, and that which was available was traded throughout the area. Traders brought copper from the Lake Superior region and from the Tennessee Valley, and shells from the coastal areas were commonly traded to interior peoples.

The techniques used in copperwork were fairly simple. The coppersmith placed a copper nugget on a piece of buckskin laid over a hard surface, and hammered out the nugget with a hammer stone and then cut it into shape.[20] A smooth cobble or piece of stone was then used to smooth further the surface on both sides. Shellwork was usually done on large conch shell (*Busycon perversum*). The conch shells were hollowed out for use as cups or dippers, or the smooth interior portions of the shell were cut into circles for use as gorgets which were worn around the neck, over the breast or collarbone.

Shell and copper objects are almost all ornaments – beads, necklaces, hairpins, masks, gorgets, earspools, headdress emblems, and so on. Except for the jewelry, these ornaments were used as part of ceremonial or religious dress or as grave offerings to accompany the elite dead. Sheet copper, laminated over celts, axes, earspools, or other stone and wood objects, have been discovered in elite burials. Sheet copper also was cut into silhouettes of war clubs, bi-lobed arrows,

or feathers that were worn in the ceremonial headdresses of the elite.[21] Coppersmiths devoted special skill and time embossing figures of men in various poses and dances on copper sheets. The most prominent of these are the copper plates from the Etowah site in Georgia in which a falcon-man is depicted in full ceremonial regalia and brandishing a war club. These plates appear to have been intended only as grave offerings to the elite dead.[22]

On gorgets, designs were incised on the smooth interior using sharpened stone awls and needles. Shell cups and dippers usually were engraved on their outside portions. Some shell gorgets and cups have incised designs representing human figures like those on the copper plates but most of them represent rattlesnakes, woodpeckers, spiders, or mythological beings such as the under-water panther and the winged serpent.[23] Gorgets may have been worn as political or military insignia. For instance, the Citico gorget, which depicts a coiled rattlesnake-like being, is only found in those Mississippian Period archeological sites that once comprised the chiefdom of Coosa.[24] The shell cups and dippers were probably used to serve black drink, a herbal tea drunk as a sacrament at political and religious events.[25]

With the abrupt disruption of the Mississippian ceremonial and political life, copper- and shellwork virtually ceased.[26] Historic Period Southeastern Indians appreciated fine metals and purchased trade ornaments such as crescent-shaped gorgets, hairpins, arm bands, turban bands, earrings, and rings. The Southeastern Indians continued to drink black drink throughout the Historic Period, but shell cups and dippers were replaced by European metal ones.

Basketry

Southeastern Indian basketry is perhaps the only craft that continues from the prehistoric past until the present.[27] River cane (*Arundinaria tecta* and *A. macrosperma*) is the preferred material for basketry.[28] Despite the difficulty in cutting and processing river cane splints, the women never forfeited the distinct shiny gloss of river cane for easier material. The sheer abundance of river cane also probably contributed to its popularity, since a woman would not have had to search far for her supplies.[29]

To prepare cane splints, a stalk is split lengthwise, usually into four splints. The shiny outer material is then pulled from the coarse inner fiber. The inside of the splint is then scraped of any remaining inner fiber and trimmed along the edges to a uniform width. The famous Chitimacha basketry has distinctively narrow, delicate cane splints, a technical feat in itself.

The women employ primarily two types of weaving techniques – checkerwork and twilling – both of which were used in prehistoric times.[30] In checkerwork, a number of splints are placed side

During the Historic Period, the Southeastern Indians acquired silver from white traders and fashioned accessories by hammering the silver into shape, and incising, piercing, or stamping designs on the finished object. This Choctaw silver headpiece (left) was worn probably as a turban band or as a comb with men's fancy dress.

The most difficult task in basketry is form, and Southeastern Indian women are masters in achieving symmetrical and proportional forms as shown in this double-lidded Cherokee split-cane basket (below) made around 1900. This particular basket form is a modern style.

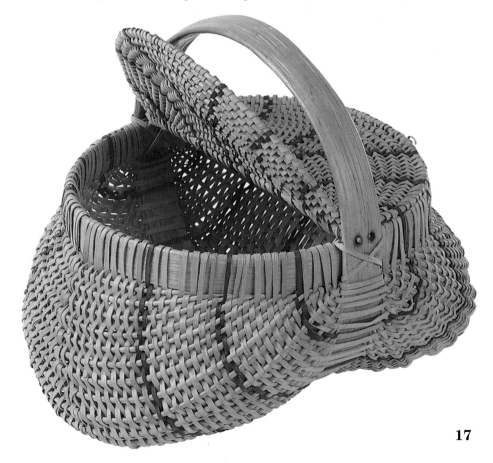

This cow or bull nose basket (right) was made around 1980 by the Choctaw of Louisiana. Cow or bull nose baskets are remarkably similar to the pouches depicted in the Southeastern Ceremonial Complex motifs. Today, these baskets are used as wall hangings or for storage. The central design is made with cane dyed with commercial dyes, which many women use today in addition to natural dyes. The background is the natural color of cane splints.

These Chitimacha baskets (below) are a typical Southeastern basket form of twilled, double-weave baskets with a square base, rounded sides, and slip-on lids. The curvilinear designs and color bands are distinctly Chitimacha.

by side to make the warp; weft splints are woven in one at a time, over and under, at right angles, until a mat base is formed. Then all the splints are turned up to form the warp of the sides.[31] Twilling is a diagonal weave in which each element of the weft is woven over two or more warp splints at an oblique angle.[32] The most difficult and skillful twilling technique is the double-weaved twill, in which the weave is doubled over at the rim and continued inside the basket. In this way so-called double weave baskets are made.

Southeastern Indian basketry is noted for its mastery of color and design. Cane splints are colored with vegetable dyes made from black walnut and butternut for a deep brown or black, puccoon root for a red or orange, bloodroot for a redbrown, broom sedge for a burnt orange, and yellowroot for a deep yellow.[33] A variety of geometrical and curvilinear designs are formed by varying the width and color of cane splints and the number of over and under turns. Because of their intricate designs, the most famous basket makers in the Southeast are the Chitimacha women of southern Louisiana and the Cherokee women of North Carolina. Chitimacha women weave distinct, colorful design bands that criss-cross or curve over the whole of the basket.[34] Cherokee women prefer simple geometric lines forming squares, triangles, diamonds, and crosses over the whole basket.[35]

Women make small baskets with handles, sieves for sifting hominy, hampers, and mats for sitting, sleeping, or as wall hangings.[36] The most striking basket form of the Southeastern Indians is the burden basket. These are large, sturdy baskets with a flared opening. They were carried on the back with a leather tump-line attached to the sides and placed across the chest or forehead. Choctaw, Chitimacha, and Creek women fashion 'cow nose' or heart-shaped baskets, which are small, triangular baskets remarkably similar to the pouches of the Ceremonial Complex.[37]

Fabrics and Clothing

Daily clothing for Southeastern Indian men and women was a simple affair. Women wore knee-length skirts and men wore breechclouts, and both usually went without upper garments. They wore leggings which are long, wide pieces of single cloth wrapped around each leg and suspended by garters from a belt. In cold weather, men and women wore 'matchcoats' which were cloak-like garments worn draped over the shoulders. Europeans often compared textiles from the late-Mississippian Period through most of the Historic Period to finely-made European fabrics.

During the Historic
Period, the Southeastern
Indians decorated their
military-style shirts with
applique strips along the
hems and necks. After
removal, the Seminoles
who remained in Florida
elaborated on applique
design by sewing
applique designs over
most of the shirt, as
shown in the Seminole
shirt to the immediate
left. After the sewing
machine became
available, applique gave
way to the more intricate
patchwork design, and
Seminole women created
distinctive and
characteristically
Seminole fabrics (far left).
The shirt style is also
particular to the
Seminole. These are
Seminole men's big shirts
which are derived from
the military-styled shirts
popular among
Southeastern Indian men
during the Historic
Period. Seminole big
shirts are blousy, open,
all-over garments
reaching to just above the
knees. Seminole men
wore patchwork big shirts
well into the 20th
century. Nowadays, these
shirts are worn for
special occasions and sold
on the tourist market.

These textiles were made from various types of animal fur, grasses, and bark, particularly the inner bark of the mulberry tree which produced a fine, pliable cloth similar to linen.[38] Animal skins from deer, bison, bear, and smaller animals were used to fashion moccasins and matchcoats.[39] Handmade textiles were either dyed with vegetable dyes or painted with mineral paints. Skin matchcoats were sometimes painted with geometric designs, animals, or military exploits.

As soon as European textiles became available in any appreciable quantity, men and women substituted them for handmade textiles.[40] Buckskin continued to be used through most of the 18th century for moccasins, but the Southeastern Indians soon preferred European woolens for their matchcoats. Men eschewed European-style pants until the 19th century; but they quickly adapted the knee-length, military-style European jackets and shirts and began wearing these blousy, open shirts as part of their daily and fancy wear.[41] These shirts were decorated with colorful applique strips along the bottom, and often they were covered with various ornaments of beads, silver, ribbon, and so on. Women began using European textiles for their skirts and began

wearing calico bodices in the late-18th century. Both skirts and bodices were fully ornamented with beads, bells, rattles, and ribbons.

After Removal, most Southeastern Indians began wearing American-style dress, except for the Seminoles. Those Seminoles who escaped Removal moved into the Florida Everglades where they remained isolated for a long time. American-style clothing was not readily available to them, and Seminole women made ankle-length skirts, bodices with capes, and military-style men's shirts into the 20th century.[42] After the manual sewing machine became available, applique gave way to the patchwork garments which have become the national dress of the Seminole.[43]

In Seminole applique, single strips of printed cloth are sewn directly onto the garment. In patchwork, patterned cloth is first torn into long strips which are then sewn together to produce a band of striped cloth. The band is then snipped into several pieces which are arranged side by side or offset and sewn together into a long band. This technique allows for an astonishing variety of designs, and a woman usually uses several bands of varying designs in making one

This Koasati sash (above) was made around 1930 by embroidering bead designs on red and black stroud. Bead embroidering in curvilinear designs is characteristic of the Western style area. The Eastern style area sashes are hand woven with interwoven beading in geometric designs. The scroll design, often seen on prehistoric Southeastern Indian pottery, is a basic motif of the Western style area. The Choctaw beaded collar (below) is a modern innovation using pan-Indian beadworking designs. This collar, made around 1940, was worn around the neck of a dress shirt as a substitute for a man's tie.

garment.[44] The bands are then sewn together, to form a whole piece of cloth that can be cut into patterns and sewn. The final product is a very colorful patchwork garment, with a variety of intricate, detailed designs.[45]

Beadwork and Featherwork

Except for the delicate feather wands and fans, beads and feathers were used as clothing decorations or for personal adornment. Southeastern Indian women produced finger-woven, tasselled sashes, belts, and garters, and they did so in the Mississippian Period as evidenced by the engraved figures on shell gorgets and copper plates. Sashes and belts constituted part of their clothing throughout the Historic Period as well, and to the present day the Choctaw and Creek are noted for their beaded belts.[46]. Sashes were worn over one or both shoulders, crossing diagonally or criss-crossing across the chest and tied at the waist with tassels and cords hanging down, often below the knees. In the late Historic Period, belts worn about the waist served to fasten the button-less military-style shirts. Women also made finger-woven garters with which to fasten leggings and the fancy, beaded, men's pouches (their clothing usually did not have pockets).

In finger-weaving, yarns are attached to a single bar and the threads are intertwined by the fingers alone.[47] This technique only allows for the manufacture of relatively narrow strips of cloth, hence the predominance of sashes and belts made with this technique. With beaded sashes and belts, beads are slipped onto the threads during the weaving process. Designs are constructed by varying the color of threads and weave. In examining the design motifs of belts and sashes, two style areas emerge. The Eastern style area, typified by the Seminole and Yuchi, is characterized by simple, all-over geometric designs of diamonds, Vs, Ws, and crosses. In the Western style area, comprising the Choctaw, Chickasaw, Koasati, and Alabama (the latter two were both historic Creek groups), curvilinear designs are laid out in a panel against a monochrome background.[48]

Without doubt, feather matchcoats were the finest featherwork products from the Southeast.[49] Basically, these were made of woven or mulberry cloth nets into which hundreds of feathers were twisted or tied. Turkey feathers, which have opalescent brown, red, purple, and blue hues were the preferred feathers. The feather down, of course, made these cloaks particularly good outerwear during cold weather.[50]

Finally, feather wands and fans were made from the Mississippian Period through the Historic Period. These wands were usually made of eagle feathers arranged fan-like and fastened at the quills with a leather handle or attached to a fan frame or a carved sourwood rod.[51] The eagle was a revered emblem of peace, and eagle feather

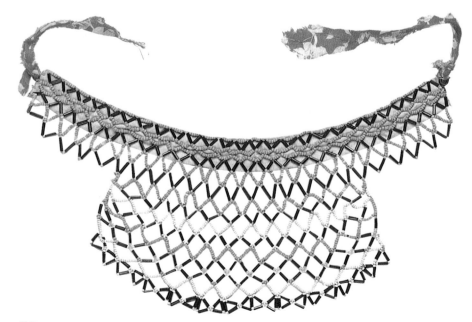

fans were frequently used during ceremonial occasions and dances.[52] Fans made from other feathers such as turkey apparently were used as everyday fans.

Woodwork

Because wood preserves poorly in the acidic Southeastern soils, one can only estimate the importance of this medium to the Southeastern Indians. Although some wooden artifacts have been found elsewhere, the largest cache of Mississippian wooden artifacts are from the Key Marco site in Florida, from which many utilitarian and ceremonial wooden objects have been recovered from the saltwater marsh muck. Of these, the painted masks and tablets, animal figurines and naturalistic animal heads are the most noteworthy.

Masks and figurines were carved and chiseled from a single piece of wood using shell chisels, sawfish-tooth blades, and stone scrapers and drills. They were then smoothed with sand or sharkskin to remove all traces of tool scars.[53] Wooden animal heads sometimes were made of several pieces. For instance, a deer head has detachable ears and an alligator has a separate lower jaw that articulates with the upper jaw. These wooden pieces are painted, incised, and inlaid with shell.

How the people of Key Marco understood or used the animal figurines and heads is unknown since, for the most part, these are not representative of the Southeastern Ceremonial Complex. However, masks were worn by Southeastern Indians in various dances and ceremonial affairs from the Mississippian Period through the Historic Period. Some were used as decoy masks for hunting, in which a hunter donned an animal skin and mask and mimicked, with astonishing fidelity, the movements of his prey. Some decoy masks also were used in performing hunting dances.

Masks also were used to impersonate mythical beings, other humans, or to characterize esteemed personal traits such as bravery and fierceness in war.[54] The falcon-man motifs of the Southeastern Ceremonial Complex clearly depict masked creatures. The rattlesnake-dance masks of the Cherokee reportedly indicate the dancer's bravery since he would be obviously unconcerned about the rattlesnake carved on the forehead.[55]

Historic Cherokee masks are the most well-known. Cherokee masks may seem crude in comparison to those from the northwest coast or from the northeast. Certainly the detail is missing. However, the Booger Dance masks show a finesse in caricature that is truly artistic. The Booger Dance was a burlesque dance performed by the Cherokee of North Carolina that re-enacted the arrival of white people. The Boogers wore masks representing what the dancers perceived as grotesque attributes of white men.[56] These masks were carved with grimaces and leering smiles and topped by shaggy, unkempt hair and mounds of facial hair. One mask, made in the mid-20th century by Will West Long, depicts in perfect caricature a quite distressed Indian.

The Cherokee also make masks out of gourds, such as the child's Booger Dance mask of a 'funny' buffalo (above). The horns and nose are gourd necks stuck through cut-out holes. For the painted features, the mask maker uses a dye made from black walnut or charcoal (for black) and applies the paint with his fingers. Other Southeastern Indian dances require their own special paraphernalia. The photograph (left) shows some things early-20th century Cherokee needed to perform the Eagle Dance. Eagle feather wands (shown hanging on the wall) were integral to the performance, and the ritual collection of eagle feathers for the wands initiated the Eagle Dance.

'O our Mother the Earth, O our Father the Sky,
Your children are we, and with tired backs
We bring you the gifts that you love.
Then weave for us a garment of brightness;
May the warp be the white light of morning.
May the weft be the red light of evening.
May the fringes be the falling rain,
May the border be the standing rainbow . . .'

TEWA SONG[1]

The American Southwest has one of the most harsh and difficult climates of any area on the North American continent, yet for thousands of years it has supported a culturally active and spiritually integrated Native American population. The arid climate has naturally produced religions which are fixed upon water, control of water, and water in its many various forms: snakes, frogs, clouds and long cotton tassels on white dance sashes which evoke the rain falling from the high clouds.

The greater part of this area is arid or semi-arid, with extreme variations from high forested mountain ranges, from which springtime run-off of the heavy winter snows provides an important part of the waters of the Rio Grande, the Colorado and the Pecos. A major part of the area is plateau, steep-sided sandstone mesas, deep canyons with intermittent streams and scattered clumps of piñon and juniper trees. The southern half of the area is marked by broad areas of nearly level, hot, dry desert separated by steep, rocky mountains of limited extent which break up the flat land.

This varied Southwestern habitat offered its prehistoric occupants – the Anasazi, Hohokam and Mogollon, Basketmakers and Mimbres cultures – an enormous variety of resources, many of them to be found only in very restricted zones. This encouraged the development of greatly differing lifestyles, each adjusted to the resources available and taking advantage of several different micro-environments. To take advantage of this diversity, the peoples of the Southwest were knit together by interlocking networks of economic and social relationships.

These ancient cultures all produced pottery, basketry, weaving, carving in wood, and some small carvings in shell and stone, some of them very beautiful and sophisticated. The study of the Southwest and its arts and crafts is influenced by the knowledge that the present Indians are the descendants of those who made the great cities in the desert such as Chaco and Mesa Verde. In the Southwest it is possible to observe in use the same loom that was used prehistorically, the same sash, the same basket . . . and this also gives insight into the meaning of these things within their original culture.

Crafts in the Southwest have maintained their high standards, techniques and esthetic vision, and are still an important source of income for Native American people. Many of them sell their arts and crafts to supplement their income. There is an artisan in almost every home, and the importance of their arts and crafts is appreciated. Until this century the finest objects were made for ceremonial purposes, for the gods, and to ensure the continuation of human life. Today often the very best of their arts and crafts are most frequently destined for collectors or museums.

Although their lives often reflect the stress of living in two cultures, the Indians of the Southwest maintain their traditional way of life, and it is possible to glimpse the way these people

The bright colors and skilled workmanship of the Southwest are represented by the beautiful black, green and red woven woman's manta from San Juan pueblo (main picture, right and far left) and the eyecatching silver and green turquoise Navajo necklace (main picture). Both are items from crafts for which the region is renowned – jewelry and weaving.

Ceremonial aspects were never neglected either and many things were made with rituals, dances, etc specifically in mind. The buckskin hat with beadwork decoration (above left) was bought from the Apache, among whom it belonged to a war shaman for use in the Gun Ceremony when amulets were given protective powers.

lived 500 years ago. A quiet moment at a ceremonial dance, with the drum beat which has gone on and on all day, and the long lines of dancers stretch back to earliest days of the Anasazi, when the plaza dancers heard the same songs and drums. The past is not distant here; there is an occasional pot shard, a broken bit of flint, or the discovery of a ruin, tucked away in a cliff to remind us that there were people here long ago.

The arts are one of the strongest and most visible links to this past. The bestselling articles are made in the old traditional ways. Everything is done by hand, and with materials which are available if one knows how to pray for them, where to find them, how to process them, and to respect them.

Ceramics

Of all the arts of the Southwest, pottery may be the most definitive. It is still made using the same methods that have been used for thousands of years, and ceramics of great beauty and sophistication have been produced. The pottery of the Mimbres, Anasazi, Hohokam and the historic and contemporary pueblos are some of the best known of the crafts of the American Indian. There is a clear stylistic link between the present and the past in Pueblo pottery, and prehistoric designs are often reused; for example, the Mimbres-influenced pottery designs of Lucy Lewis in Acoma. It has always been a central feature of the Pueblo world, serving both utilitarian and ceremonial functions and tying social life to the natural environment in a fundamental way. And Pueblo pottery accounts for probably 90 per cent of all Southwestern pottery and thus typifies the region.

In centuries past, many vessels were hand-painted with elaborate designs, and simple kitchen items – storage jars, pitchers, and ladles, canteens, seed jars, and serving bowls – were executed with the care and creative genius that characterize works of art. Like many traditional craftspeople, Pueblo potters have a remarkable ability to instill in a common household object a life and spirit of its own, and the so-called utility

wares are exemplars of this quality.[2] Traditionally, pottery has also been viewed as possessing power and the ability to take on the attributes of the substance it holds. Thus water, a sacred element, transfers its power to the pottery vessel that holds it: 'Water contains the source of continued life. The vessel holds the water; the source of life accompanies the water, hence its dwelling place is in the vessel with the water.'[3]

Potters have a respected place in contemporary Pueblo society, apart from the economic role. The ability to make a pot is an integral, even a sacred, part of everyday life:

'Despite the changes which have engulfed the Pueblo world, there remains the underlying world view that recognizes a spiritual dimension to every phase of life, to all common objects and everyday activities. This world view is expressed by the still vital ceremonial calendar and is embodied in items fashioned by hand from the materials provided by the earth.'[4]

Pottery for sale to outsiders very quickly became an important part of the economy of the pueblos. The created wares were sold while displayed in simple fashion by their makers. These Tewa women from Santa Clara are fairly typical of the 1940's period, busy shaping their hand-coiled ceramics while looking after a child but still prepared for customers. Polished red pottery and red polychrome are made in traditional style in the pueblo to this day.

To make a pot (or a figurine, spindle whorl, charm or fetish), an Indian woman goes to her traditional clay source, which every pueblo has, and then to her own part of the source and digs out as much clay as she needs. She then dries it and puts it through a sieve or screen to get rid of the rocks and roots. After the clay is clean, she will add some sort of temper, old pot shards, volcanic earth or ground mica, which keeps the clay from expanding too fast and cracking, and then add water so that the clay is workable. Pots are made not on a wheel but by coiling ropes of clay one on another, and then pinching them together. The clay is then smoothed, often with a piece of gourd, so that no joints are visible. The clay is then sanded and smoothed again. This may end the process or, at this point, the slip, or a paint made from clay and usually of a different color, is applied, and quickly the burnishing begins. The slip is a fine clay dissolved in water so that it is really like a paint. Slips can be of red or white clay. Production methods differ little between pueblos; the temper of the clays may differ but the main visible difference is in the decoration and thickness of the walls of the pots.

Polishing pottery is a long and tiresome process. Small polishing stones, sometimes dinosaur gizzard stones frequently found in the arroyos or dry stream beds, are used to press and stroke the surface of the new pot until it begins to gleam. These small, smooth stones are treasured and passed down from generation to generation. Once the polishing is started it cannot be stopped, so the effort required to polish a large pot takes a small team of people. If the pot is to be painted, then it is not polished. Before firing it will be covered with a slip and it can then be decorated and polished.

The pot is then fired. Sheep manure provides a good fuel, burning evenly and slowly. The ashes retain their initial form and hold the heat of the fire. Some potters today in very windy locations like Acoma, high on a mesa, are using electric kilns which are easier to control. Firing is the most delicate part of the potting process, and pots are usually fired in the morning when there is little wind.

There were no glazes in the Southwest but the lack of a glaze was not considered to be very important. It was understood that the pottery would let the water evaporate slowly. The clay gives the water a sweet taste, and many Pueblo people think that the best water comes from these pots, called ollas, which keep the water cool and tasty.[5] There are, as mentioned, many decorative variations in the Pueblo pottery of the Southwest. If a black ware is desired, the fire is smothered after it has burned down, and covered with sheets of tin or any fireproof material so that the heat and smoke are held in the fire and forced into the body of the pottery. Today this black ware is made in New Mexico by San Ildefonso and Santa Clara pueblos, but prehistorically this sort of pottery was more widespread. This black ware is burnished to a metallic sheen and had almost disappeared but was revived by Maria Martinez of San Ildefonso, and today her lustrous black pottery is

Black on black burnished pottery is strongly identified with the late Maria Martinez of San Ildefonso pueblo and it was she who manufactured the classic piece seen here (below). Maria made the pots and her husband decorated them, achieving the delicate patterned effect clearly visible here. This piece was made in the late 1940s.

This Laguna woman (above) epitomizes the Pueblo relationship with clay, standing by her adobe home with a jar that will be used to carry water – the essential for life. This Zuni bowl (below) has dragonflies and frogs as symbols of water and fertility – dragonflies are said always to know where to find water.

in charge of religion they may have produced and painted all the pottery for *kiva* use, or, as Dillingham suggests, occasionally it was made by a woman who had been struck by lightning and lived, thus qualifying her to make *kiva* pottery.[7]

The shapes of pots have evolved gradually. The olla, or water vessel, was designed to be balanced on the head of a woman carrying water from a stream or spring to her house. It generally has a shoulder, which spreads the weight of the water, and a narrow neck, to keep the water from spilling and evaporating. Other types of pottery produced continuously are seed jars, small globe-like pots with very narrow openings, canteens, which were introduced by the Spanish and, occasionally, effigy jars. Prehistorically the Anasazi produced mugs and pitchers, but those shapes, like the black pottery, had disappeared until these forms were revived for tourists.[8] A later, unintended effect of the popularity of the pueblo pottery was that the pottery library at the pueblos was depleted by institutions such as the Smithsonian who purchased enormous amounts of material and shipped it into museums. In cultures where innovation is not greatly valued, this produced more changes than might have occurred otherwise, since it removed the collective memory bank of the potters of a pueblo.[9]

The Pueblos share a way of life, a world view, and a landscape, but they speak half a dozen languages and live in more than 30 villages. Although several pueblos may share a language, internally they may have different societies and clan structures, so that they are not alike in organization. There are, naturally, several distinct styles of pottery.

Down along the Rio Grande the Tewa pueblos of San Ildefonso and Santa Clara are known today for their black and red wares. San Ildefonso, the home of Maria Martinez, produces mostly black pottery, but earlier this century when Maria was a young woman, she produced a fine black on white ceramic ware. Today no one in San Ildefonso makes the black on white pottery which was once so common. Maria's switch to

highly prized by collectors. Maria and her husband Julian, who decorated her pots when she began to make pottery for sale, became the best known of many teams of potters whose production was designed for the market.

The relationship between market desires and the potter's designs is recurrent; tourist tastes have strongly influenced pottery designs: for example, the decorative use of floral motifs which have been incorporated into pueblo designs, particularly those of the Southern pueblos, Acoma, Laguna, Zuni, Zia, Santa Ana, San Felipe and Cochiti. Many of the designs which now seem traditional may have been adapted from things which the 19th century potters saw on imported crockery – flowers, parrots, and bands which separated areas of the pot – in order to make the pottery more saleable to outsiders.[6] More traditionally, the decoration was distinctive if a pot was to have some role in an internal ceremony, often including water symbols, frogs, tadpoles and clouds. Since men were

The Keresan pueblos to the south of Santa Fe make a thinner walled ceramic which is slipped white and decorated with black and red. This is called polychrome because it has several colors. The Keresan-speaking pueblos of Cochiti, Santo Domingo, Santa Ana, Zia, Laguna and Acoma all produced large bowls and ollas. Their pots all have a red band at the base, then a design area which is white with black and red designs, often birds and flowers. The top band is either a continuation of the middle panel or geometric.

In Cochiti Helen Cordero invented, or more accurately revived, a figure called a story-teller. She remembered her grandfather singing to his children and began to produce sitting figures with open mouths and many small children sitting and listening to the story or song. Helen Cordero, like Maria Martinez and the Hopi Nampeyo, has opened many economic doors for the pueblo

Pots varied greatly in size, shape and color, although combinations of these are usually enough to enable the pueblo of manufacture to be identified, both today and historically. This large black jar (left) is from Santa Clara earlier this century, black wares being typical of the Tewan Rio Grande pueblos. The slipped white jar with red and black decor (below) is from Cochiti in the 19th century or earlier, its polychrome design being typical of the Keresan-speaking pueblos.

black on black, a reduction-fired clay which is burnished and then painted which leaves certain areas matte, has become the standard for San Ildefonso. Similarly, no white-slipped pottery is made at neighbouring Santa Clara.

The Tewa pueblo of San Juan produced pottery which was mostly undecorated; today's new style is really a reinterpretation of ancestral shards, combining incised lines in unslipped tan on a middle band between a polished top and bottom. In northern New Mexico the Tiwa speaking pueblos of Taos and Picuris are the home of an unslipped micaceous ware which usually comes in the form of a lidless beanpot. This is used for cooking stews and beans, and the clay is thought to impart a special, delicious flavour.

In the early part of this century potters from the Tewa pueblo of Tesuque made pottery which was black on white and looked like that being made at the same time in San Ildefonso. In the 1940s and '50s it produced a lot of low fired work painted in unfired, bright commercial tempera paint to appeal to tourists visiting nearby Santa Fe. Paradoxically, it remains a conservative pueblo maintaining a rich ceremonial life.

Black on white designs, harking back to the ancient Mimbres, such as this graceful water jar from Acoma (right) are very representative of the westernmost Keresan-speaking pueblos and their Zuni neighbors. Note the fine hatched lines and the decoration of flowers and parrots.

In modern-day Zuni many artistic items are produced for sale to tourists, much of it beautifully designed and crafted, drawing inspiration from traditional forms. Ceramic owls similar to this one (above) are popular with today's buyers; this particular piece, however, was collected by the Hayden Survey in the 1870s.

potters. Story-telling figurines are changing rapidly and may be considered folk art. Very popular, they have been copied extensively.

Santo Domingo is a few miles south of Cochiti and it is a very conservative pueblo. Even recent designs are likely to be variations of designs which were popular in the 1700s. These designs are described as simple geometric. Santo Domingo leaders forbid the representation of the human figure and other designs are not allowed on pottery for sale. Santo Domingo pots continue to be used on feast days and in the *kivas*, but today's production is limited.

To the west were, and are, more great potters, in the three Keresan-speaking pueblos of Zia, Laguna and Acoma, and in Zuni. These have much in common; all use white slip and black and red decorations. The clay around Acoma is special, dark and dense, and it has a tendency to pit, which has made some modern Acoma potters resort to commercial clay. The pottery of Acoma has been especially enhanced by looking at the designs of their ancestors in the Mimbres valley. Prehistorically the potters of this western part of New Mexico excelled at black on white designs, and the tradition is carried on today. In the past 20 years Acoma has developed this distinctive style, and the distinguished potter Lucy Lewis and her descendants have inspired a younger group of potters to continue their traditions and innovations.

Zuni is a separate language although Zuni pottery appears to be closely related to the Keresean model. Historical Zuni-related pottery is called Tularosa Black on White and St. Johns Polychrome, although at other sites there are polychrome pieces which have a glaze decoration. After the Pueblo Revolt in 1680, the Zunis consolidated in one pueblo which is called Zuni. Historical Zuni ware has a white slip and three bands of design. The Zuni designs of this century have concentrated on the rosette and deer with what is called a heart line, from the mouth to the heart of the deer. Zuni ceramics were in decline earlier this century, but are currently being revived and young Zunis are making pottery again, although most today make jewelry.

Hopi pottery from about 1300 was not distinct, but there was an artistic explosion in the 1450s which produced black on white and black on orange wares. These early Hopi designs are characterized by sweeping curvilinear motifs, birds, animals and human representations. The free designs are different from all other pottery designs in the Pueblo world, with the possible exception of the Mimbres in western New Mexico.[10] The Hopi have always used coal to fire their pottery and are the only group to do so, although it crops up all over the Pueblo world.

The Hopi pottery renaissance is partly due to a woman named Nampeyo who lived a century ago in the Hopi village of Hano and was extremely skilled at making symmetrical vessels. In 1890 Nampeyo saw some of the pot shards from the excavation of black on yellow pots being excavated at Sikyatki and was inspired to reproduce these fragments as pots. Sikyatki Polychrome uses unbalanced design areas, dynamic color fields, stippling, engraving and other textures. Nampeyo was a Tewa whose ancestors moved to Hopi as a result of Spanish pressure in New Mexico in the 17th century, so her pottery is Hopi/Tewa. Today the Hopi pottery she revived is characterized by its golden slip and polychrome decoration, elements derived from Sikyatki. Nampeyo's great fame came from her elegant

Arguably the greatest Hopi potter, and certainly one of the best known in the region, was Nampeyo from Hano. This large jar (left) is 16.5in (41cm) deep and shows her sense of form and great decorative skill. the designs are derived from older forms found as shards at Sikyatki ruins. It is a classic example of geometric polychrome design elements. Her descendants still make excellent pottery today.

design sense, which took elements of the past and reused them on contemporary pottery. Today there are many potters at Hopi who have been inventive and produced very simple variations of the traditional designs.

Other pottery in the Southwest is not as well known. The Athapaskan Navajo and Apache did make some early pottery but it is impossible to identify today.[11] Although the Pueblos continue to dominate pottery today, there is an increasing production of some unslipped, pinched rim pottery made by the Navajo. The Navajo are also making low-fired ceramic figurines of Navajo going about their daily life. These figures are very lively and appealing and are being sought by folk art collectors. Apaches, too, have produced some ceramics, but their efforts so far have been limited to undecorated pieces, red slipped canteens and other small pieces.

The Pima and Papago of Arizona produced a red ware pottery using the paddle and anvil and the coil technique, although they are much better known for their basketry. Their neighbors the Maricopa made a red and black were using coils. Maricopa ware shows some Mexican influence; they paint black designs around the necks of the pots in unbanded designs. The Maricopa, and the other Rancheria tribes including the Yuma, the Cocopa and Mojave also make clay figurines which wear clothes and beads.

Jewelry

The work of Navajo silversmiths was very elegant and often quite stunning in its beauty and skill; it is even better appreciated when it is considered how very basic were the tools used and the surroundings worked in. The smith pictured here (right) in 1915 is working on a small anvil set up temporarily on a blanket in a small dwelling. His tools are clearly visible. The concha belt was one of the best products of the smith's labors; that seen here (above) is decorated with large decorative plates of silver, derived from Spanish silver buttons, by which the belt can be recognized instantly.

Among humans the urge to ornament is universal. In the Southwest, body paint was probably the most common ornament in the past, with jewelry scarce but popular. Most of this jewelry was made of stone or shell, the latter obtained by travel or trade which contributed to a wide distribution of marine shell varieties. The only non-marine shell used was the terrestrial snail (gastropod). All other shells were worked to some extent; the most common use was to make beads from the small olivella shell. Shell was made into beads, rings and bracelets by abrading it against a harder surface. Objects of ornaments are rare before AD 500 and become more popular in later periods. In the southern parts of the area there are some copper bells which were probably traded up from Mexico. By 900-1200 there was an increase in jewelry in the Southwest, stone and bone rings, copper bells, turquoise, jet and stone pendants, stone and shell beads and shell bracelets. In both the Hohokam and later in the Anasazi/Chaco area there was beautiful mosaic inlay. Shell was cut into the shape of birds and animals, and acid and wax etching was done on shell pendants.

Turquoise was the favorite stone of all Southwestern Indians and has many variant colors, from green to robin's egg blue, depending on the mine and the mineral composition. Because of this demand, it was traded over great distances; turquoise from the Cerrillos mines in New Mexico – controlled today by Santo Domingo Indians[12] – went into the inlaid Aztec masks from Tenochtitlan. The Santo Domingo Indians have a myth that when their people emerged from the underworld two other groups came with them, and that before they parted to go their individual ways, the Santo Domingo promised to make beads for the other Indians. To this day, they love to trade and whole families are engaged in the production and distribution of turquoise and beads of other materials.

The manufacture of these beads, called *hishi*, is still a very important skill. The shaping of turquoise, and other materials like shell or stone, into beads is done by rolling it on tufa or sandstone to smooth all the edges. The beads are then assembled into graduated necklaces or *jaclos*, a very old and simple necklace form that has been unchanged since prehistoric times. Beads found in the Anasazi burials at Chaco Canyon are indistinguishable from beads made now. Beads and amulets were holed in the center by the use of a pump drill; the string of rough beads was then rolled on a wet slab of sandstone. This time-consuming technique is still used because it produces beads which fit together in a comfortable way.

When the Spanish first came into the Southwest looking for gold, the Indians did not have a word for metal. They were, however, quick to appreciate the bright and enduring qualities of it, and small pieces began to appear as necklaces or rings, or as additions to a shirt although it was not worked until the middle of the last century.[13]

The Native Americans had to learn to work metal in the most primitive of conditions. The early techniques for silversmithing were very simple. Some coals were taken from the fire, and a torch was used to heat the silver. The coals caught the heat and acted as a small furnace melting the metal. As soon as the metal was hot, it was placed on an anvil and pounded into shape. As it cooled, it was reheated with bellows and reworked. The tools needed were an anvil, a hammer, several die stamps for decoration, some silver, some solder and a fire.[14]

The original Navajo bellows were made of goat hide and served to keep the coals glowing.[15] Decoration was added after the piece was shaped. Often differently shaped dies were stamped into the silver. If the die was cut too deep, it could slice through the silver, so the artist had to be careful. Many of these dies were originally made in Spain or Mexico to stamp Mexican leather saddles, bags and costumes. The Navajo discovered that the dies worked beautifully as silver decoration but they also learned to make their own dies using files to cut designs. The early Navajo silver work was very straightforward, and is characterized by its pure sense of design.

The influence of Mexicans who occupied New Mexico and Arizona was strong, their love of ornament being adopted by the Navajo. This is evident in several examples: the concha belt, the squash blossom necklace, the naja and the use of ornamental buttons were all related to the Mexicans. The Navajo found that coins pounded into a domed shape and with a loop soldered to the back made both a decoration and a purchase at the trading post. The conchas, which means shells in Spanish, were originally round or oval silver plates which were larger than buttons and were attached by straps. These were used to decorate belts, spurs, or a jacket, and the shape and design of the concha belt were fixed as early as 1880: 'The grand prize of the dandy Navajo buck is his belt . . . this is of leather completely covered by immense elliptical silver plaques.'[16] Navajos owned concha belts long before they learned to make them. The Utes, Comanches, Kiowas and other Southern Plains Indians with whom the Navajo feuded wore belts strung with plaques of copper, brass, or German silver (a non-ferrous alloy of copper, nickel and zinc), and a Navajo might take a belt from a slain enemy or, in peacetime, obtain it in trade. Even before their capture and exile in the 1860s at the Bosque Redondo, the rich Navajos wore concha belts. White influence has reduced the size of the conchas and other forms alternate with traditional ones. Today these belts are very popular both with the Native Americans and the visitors to the area.

Another design element which the Navajo borrowed from the Mexican is the naja which is a crescent-shaped ornament used to decorate the centre of a horse bridle. It appeared on Navajo horses about the same time as concha belts became common. The naja may derive from the Moorish crescent moon, or another Moorish symbol, the hands of Fatima. Crescent-shaped figures were also popular with the Plains Indians, and the Navajo may have found it in their hunting

Spanish and Mexican influences were strong in the southwest of the United States and were reflected in the culture and crafts of many tribes, but particularly the Navajo. This silver naja (below) was made in 1893, an ornament appearing among the Navajo from the Mexicans who obtained it from the Spanish who, in turn, received it from the Moors of North Africa who had occupied Spain for centuries. It forms part of every squash blossom necklace (see overleaf).

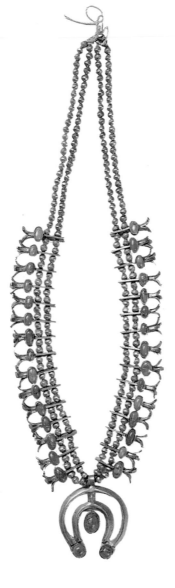

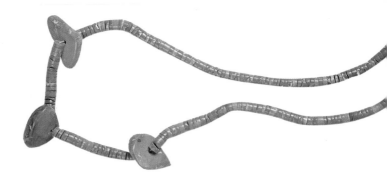

and raiding there. The design of the naja occurs all over the world, but the most likely source for the Southwest is the Spanish/Moorish route. The naja was a popular pendant and for the Navajo was used almost exclusively, although the cross was also used, sometimes in combination with a naja, the cross symbolizing the morning star.

In addition to decorating the horse bridle, the naja is part of every squash blossom necklace. The squash blossom is a fertility symbol for the Pueblo people, and the name has become associated with this necklace although the actual flower in the necklace is a pomegranate blossom, which is also a fertility symbol. The pomegranate was a popular bead shape on Mexican trouser and jacket ornaments and has been a favorite Spanish decorative motif for centuries. The combination of pomegranate shaped ornaments with a naja, spaced with shaped silver beads has a hybrid beauty. This design, along with the concha belt, has come to be thought of as distinctively Navajo.

By the 1890s the Navajo had begun to add turquoise to their jewelry and were setting turquoise in simple bezels. Some of the first traders to the Navajo even imported turquoise for their silversmiths. The trader Lorenzo Hubbell at Ganado was selling fine Persian turquoise to the Navajo in 1890.[17] Hubbell also often supplied the Navajo with Mexican pesos which were pure silver and easy to work as in 1890 there was a prohibition against defacing United States coins which had previously supplied the silver necessary to make jewelry. The Navajo silversmiths were supplied partly by the traders and partly by their old trading partners in the Pueblos.[18] In addition to making and selling jewelry, the Navajo love to wear jewelry which they make. The display of wealth in the form of necklaces, belts, bracelets, rings, earrings, buttons, and silver-decorated horse bridles was, and is, important to the Navajo culture.

Among all the pueblos, the pueblo of Zuni is most noted for its jewelry. The Zuni probably learned to make jewelry from the Navajo. In 1880 they were making simple forms but by 1910 they

had evolved the style which is recognizably Zuni. In contrast to the Navajo, the Zuni generally had more modern jewelry tools, which they got from their trader C. J. Wallace. Their work is more intricate and uses more and smaller stones than that of the Navajo. The tools included fine pliers which are essential to make the small bezels for the small turquoise stones which characterize Zuni jewelry in the style known as Needlepoint. The other important tools were the vise and the emery wheel, which makes polishing turquoise and silver much easier. The small rows of turquoise stones in Zuni bracelets may be inspired by rows of kernels of blue corn (a crop with sacred significance). Zuni jewelry is usually lightweight and the silver serves as a base to hold the turquoise rather than as an important design element. Commercial from an early stage, the sale of their jewelry has made a big difference to the economic well-being of Zuni.

Turquoise is sacred stone with potent powers, among which are good fortune and love. These modern Navajo pieces combine it with silver in traditional design forms, the squash blossom necklace (above) and the bracelet (right). The stones are from Nevada. The Zuni necklace (above right) is much older, its small pieces having been drilled and strung.

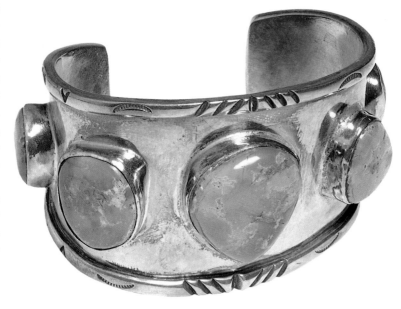

In the late 1930s the Hopi began to make jewelry, but there were not many silversmiths until after 1946. The work done before that is not distinctive from that of the Zuni or Navajo. The best-known Hopi jeweler was Charles Loloma from Hotevilla. He used secret settings of different stones, turquoise, coral, sugulite and obsidian to make colorful bands inside the curves of his rings and bracelets, so that they could only be seen by the wearer. His design sense was very strong and clear and today many of the Hopis make jewelry which is inspired by Loloma and his teachings. Other pueblos make some jewelry, but most of the production is from Zuni, Hopi, Santo Domingo and, of course, the Navajo Nation.

Weaving

Prehistorically textiles were made by a number of ingenious processes from whatever suitable plant or animal fibers came to hand. After cotton was introduced these processes were still retained. Non-loom techniques can be divided into two categories: finger-weaving of the single element which requires no tools or only simple devices; finger-weaving using netting and looping, and coil without foundation, or warp-weft weaves involving two sets of elements worked at right angles to each other. It is interesting to note that knots had great ceremonial and cultural importance, and are carefully rendered in the murals of the *kivas* at Pottery Mound and Kuaua.

Surprisingly large and complex textiles can be made with these simple processes. Non-loom warp-weft weaves are made without a loom with heddles. These were favored by the basketmakers to make narrow bands, sandals, soft bags and fur or feather robes. This process involved winding a sturdy yarn continuously around two supports. The yarn between these loops was separated and treated as warps. More complicated weaves such as tapestry weaves were employed by the Anasazi Basketmakers for apron fronts, tump-lines and other bands. The Anasazi and Mogollon sites also produce warm, weft-twined blankets of fur or feather cord. In these the warps are established

by winding one continuous fur or feather cord back and forth. Pueblo weaving on looms goes back to at least AD 700 when cotton first began to appear in the Southwest. The loom was introduced from Mexico, and by 1100 vertical looms were found all over the Southwest. The vertical loom of the Pueblos was used exclusively with cotton yarns, a medium in which the Hopi excelled, creating a distinctive form known as Beautiful Design which consists of embroidered colors on a white cotton background.

There was a division of labor between the Pueblo men and women in weaving, the men producing most of the weaving. Men wove on their

A ceremonial sash forms part of the full dress of this Hopi flute priest (above left) pictured at Oraibi in 1901. Woven by men, the sash he wears is of the same typical embroidered design as pieces worn as girdles (above) or breechcloths. It is thought that the patterns might represent the mask of one of the guardian kachinas, with diamonds for eyes and zig-zags for bared teeth.

Woven mantas, from the Spanish for blanket, were worn as both dresses and shawls by Pueblo women in the mid- to late-19th century. This example (right) is from San Juan, the black background is embroidered on opposite sides in a green and red pattern, with tassels in each corner.

A newly married Pueblo woman was presented with a wedding sash, along with other textile items, which had been woven by male relatives of her husband. These were treasured until death. This gray-white sash (below) with the long tasseled fringe is from Jemez and dates from 1890. It is patterned with interlaced striped and diamond designs.

looms in the *kivas* (although they also made non-loom ceremonial belts and tump-lines). A Hopi groom's male relatives were expected to weave his bride's wedding dress. Groups of women working together made fur and feather blankets, which were non-loom weaving. The use of the upright loom with heddles has now almost died out in the pueblos, but there is still non-loom weaving, now done by men.

The Navajo probably learned to weave from the Pueblo Indians no more than 300 years ago – although they weave wool rather than cotton using women rather than men – and today they are the best-known weavers. The Navajo textiles are closely related to Pueblo cultures in their use of balanced formal designs; indeed the distinctive banded design style of Pueblo blankets and shawls is an obvious influence on much Navajo work. The loom which they use, an upright loom, is related to the loom used by Pueblo men. The interchange between Pueblos and Navajo is hard to trace, but the twill and diamond designs appear in Pueblo weaving from long ago and the Navajo may have learned from the Pueblos and then later given the technique back. The woman's dress, or manta, for both Pueblo and Navajo is black wool with a red border, but blue at Zuni. It is woven in two pieces, joined at the side and fastened over one shoulder. Today the women wear a cotton calico undergarment, but on feast days the garment is worn as it was prehistorically. It may be that the diamonds in the weaving represent the different worlds in which the

Indians lived and passed through to arrive in this, the world of living people.

The Navajo loom is made from any wood which is at hand. The main supports are two posts which are set upright in the ground. A set of beams is then lashed horizontally at the top and bottom forming a roughly rectangular frame.[19] Usually a woman weaves outside her home or *hogan*, in the shade of a tree. She weaves when there is time, when the baby is asleep, when the sheep are not demanding care, or when the meal is over. It is a stop and start process. Navajo weaving is characterized by the use of what are called lazy lines. These are breaks in the weaving which are the result of a sitting woman weaving only as far as she can reach, then scooting over and weaving another section. They are so-called because they save energy for the weaver who is sitting in the shade, and not working her entire loom.

The Navajo value weaving highly and say that they learned to weave as a gift from Spider Woman. Baby girls are prepared with a special ritual for their future as weavers. In Navajo legend it is said: 'When a baby girl is born to your tribe you shall go and find a spider web which you must take and rub on the baby's hands and arms. Thus when she grows up she will weave and her fingers and arms will not tire from the weaving.'[20] In deference to such origin stories the women used to leave a hole at the center, like a web, but traders stamped out the practice and a 'spirit outlet' replaced it; this is a thin line or flaw from the center to the edge.

Early Navajo blankets were banded and serrated with limited amounts of red used carefully as a color accent. These are the early blankets which are woven to be worn with the stripes around the body. They are woven with a very tight weave, which makes them somewhat waterproof, and warm; the colors derived from various hues in the wool (white, black, gray) and vegetable dyes (yellow, red, indigo). Because the Navajo were nomadic and far-flung in their remote region, we know little about the chronology of their weaving but it appears that by 1863 the level of technical sophistication in Navajo weaving was very high.[21]

Navajo women wove from the bottom up on easy to erect looms such as those seen here (center) out in the open, allowing the sheep to be watched. Despite these simple methods their work was very often superb. This Mexican-looking Saltillo poncho serape (above) is very tightly woven, colored with native dyes, and dates from 1850.

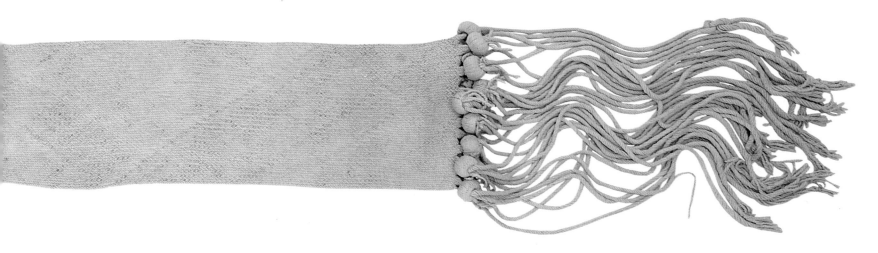

In about 1890 the so-called Germantown yarn was brought into the region in order to upgrade the quality of Navajo wool used in weaving. It can be identified in this zig-zag blanket design (right) by the heavy fringe. The vibrant red background carries diamond pattern designs (indicating 1870 or later) in green, pink, yellow and blue. Red was especially popular with the Navajo.

The categories of First, Second and Third Phase Chiefs' Blankets are somewhat misleading. These handsome blankets were not worn by Chiefs, or even exclusively by men but there is no question that these blankets were valued highly (and ownership lent a connotation of power) and that weaving such a blanket was a mark of prestige. It appears that these Chief blanket patterns were woven concurrently with more complicated design patterns and other weaving which was for internal use and was not as fine.

In 1868 many Navajo were allowed to return to their homes from their imprisonment at Bosque Redondo and a small group of merchants moved onto the reservations to trade the Navajo's manufactured goods (jewelry and blankets) for items the Indians needed in their new economy. In an attempt to help the Navajo two traders, Lorenzo Hubbell and J. B. Moore, and others began to suggest more commercial patterns which the Navajo might weave. They, and traders in other parts of the vast reservation, were responsible for the development and marketing of Navajo crafts, as well as changing the way it looked. Their trading posts were also another way of moving crafts to market and other posts began to appear on the Navajo reservation.

The new designs came from books showing oriental rugs, probably mostly Turkish, thought to be more in keeping with the then tastes of American consumers. The Navajo women looked at the pictures of the oriental rug designs, memorized them and wove them. These designs took the name of their regional trading posts and are called Crystal, Ganado (red, black, gray and white geometric designs), Tuba City (storm designs with lightning), Shiprock (which produced a distinctive *Yei* design of the Navajo gods in long dancing rows), the Two Gray Hills (noted for its very fine tight weave and black, gray and white wool), Wide Ruin (soft, natural colors), and others. There are more than a dozen different areas; the actual design, however, is always different because it is the product solely of the individual weaver. The rugs were more colorful than before and often had a border, an element missing in traditional Navajo weaving. Finally, the Navajo began to weave some of their stories, and occasionally some of their religious ceremonial designs. Navajo sandpaintings, which were used in curing ceremonies, were woven into wall hangings. (These rugs, especially those woven in the 1930s by the great Hosteen Klah, are the core of the collection at the Wheelright Museum of the American Indian, and are quite rare – only a medicine man could weave them.)

Today many copies of old Navajo rug and blanket designs are being produced in Mexico, using cotton weft or inferior wool, but following Navajo colors and designs. These copies of Navajo rugs sell very well, since the cost of a fine Navajo rug has gone up, and fewer young weavers are entering the market. The traditional Navajo way of life, the language, tending sheep and living in isolation, and the importance of ceremonies are all under stress as the modern world makes more inroads on the reservation. There are signs of a weaving revival, but the time and patience required to produce a rug are not easily assimilated into the life of today's teenage Navajo. For the Navajo, the two skills of making jewelry and weaving blankets and rugs have formed the basis of present day Navajo arts and crafts. These are both arts which appeal to the nomadic soul, are useful and portable. In the Pueblos, however, weaving has almost stopped. The pueblos of Acoma and Zuni were weaving wool mantas, which are used to make dresses and can also act as heavy shawls, until after 1900, but the availability of ready-made clothes at the trading post hurt the Pueblo weaving trade. The fine diamond weave designs on mantas with embroidered borders which were done for ceremonial use and are still used for dances are handed down as ceremonial heirlooms.

Basketry

Baskets represent a vital aspect of American Indian life from the standpoint of survival as well as artistic expression. Along with the working of stone and bone, basket making was probably a basic technical skill of the first occupants of the North American continent. Because basketry materials are so perishable not many relics survive, but in the dry climate of the Southwest, especially in caves, many baskets and basket fragments have been preserved, with some radiocarbon dates going back more than 10,000 years.

There was a large prehistoric group in the Southwest called the Basketmakers during the period from 100 BC to AD 700. The technical level of their baskets is unsurpassed. From this period there are large storage baskets, sandals, aprons, and mats, and practically every article which they used, which was not stone or bone, was a type of basketry. The extensive reliance on basketry declined with the introduction of ceramics about AD 700, but baskets were still used for washing grain and winnowing and for starting pots.

The earliest basketry technique is twining, where the moving elements, or wefts, twist around the foundation elements, or warps. Several thousand years later the coiling method came into being. In coiling a hard or soft core element, which makes the coil, is wound round and round in a spiral fashion and held in place by thin wrapping elements, the stitches. A third technique is plaiting, where the warps and wefts merely go over and under each other in a particular pattern which varies from simple to complex. Within these three basic groups large regional variations occur and significant differences can be used to identify each region and tribe.

Before any basket can be made, the weaving materials have to be gathered and prepared. This takes a great deal of time and knowledge, not only in the careful selection of choice raw materials such as willow, grass, and reeds, but because the materials have to be gathered seasonally and to have reached a particular point in their growth cycle. Once the materials have been assembled,

This Zuni blanket (left) is recorded as having been made in 1879 by a boy aged 12. The design for it was carried entirely in the boy's head. Because of its Navajo rather than Zuni influences, it is reasonable to conclude that the boy may have been a captive of the Navajo at some point. It is not, however, an authentic Navajo design for it contains an uneven number of design elements; perhaps this was done deliberately so as not to incur bad luck. Whatever the case it is a remarkable work for a supposedly first effort.

Hopi basketry trays or coiled plaques (right) using traditional designs are still produced today by the women of Second Mesa. Made of galleta grass and yucca leaves, the green ones come from the outside of the plant, the other colors come from natural dyes - such as black from sunflower seeds. This plaque was made in about 1895, and its pattern may represent the four corners of the world or may be a whirlwind design.

before weaving can be started there usually has to be some preparation in the form of cleaning, stripping, splitting or treatment by applying heat or liquids. These procedures are complicated and time-consuming. In some cases the roots of plants are specially treated by heat by being buried in hot sand for a day or so in order to make them more pliable and more durable. Occasionally the fibers may be twisted into cordage for warps or wefts. Stems, shoots and twigs are often split, necessitating great skill to produce long and even-sized elements. Colors and dyes have to be prepared, or the materials may be treated directly, for example, by being buried in mud.

When all the materials are prepared, the basket maker makes a decision about the size and decoration of the basket. Working out a design requires concentrated effort. Gathering materials may be somewhat routine, but thinking up the design takes more effort. It must be fitted to the size and shape of the basket; all the elements must work out evenly, so there has to be mathematical proportion and symmetry with accurate calculations. The weaver has to keep in mind all the details of the various elements of the pattern: where they are design elements, how they are placed and their relationship to each other as the

weaving progresses. The variations in length, size and shape of the design and the spaces between require many permutations and intense concentration. In many cases the weaver cannot keep track visually because she (both historically and at the present, most basket weavers are women) cannot see the opposite part of the basket. For true quality work, the weaver cannot begrudge either time or patience. The finished basket is usually a marvel in geometric and mathematical perfection.

Baskets are versatile and are woven in many shapes. Woven water bottles were common all over the Southwest, many of them made by the Paiute and traded to the Hopi, Zuni and Navajo. These woven water bottles are covered with pinion pitch so that they do not leak. It is also possible to cook in a basket, by filling the basket with hot water and food, and dropping hot rocks into the basket. This method of cooking was still used by the Paiutes as late as 1900. The unbreakable and lightweight nature of baskets made them the best choice for portable cookware. Basketry may be the mother of pottery. Today a shallow basket is sometimes used to hold the clay as a pot is first begun. It is possible that the use of coils to make ceramic vessels came from the experience of using coils to make baskets.

The Hopi of Second and Third Mesa are probably the best known contemporary basket makers in the Southwest. (The other Hopi Mesas do not make baskets.) The Hopis weave by coiling or plaiting, using yucca over grass or shredded yucca bundles; they plait baskets either with yucca strips or with rabbit brush wefts and wild currant warps. The flat baskets best serve as trays or sifters – or as well plaques. Deep baskets with flared sides of rabbit brush and Native or aniline-dyed designs are also decorative and useful items for sale to tourists. The Hopi use coiling to make circular trays or plaques and storage baskets in various sizes. Hopi flat trays of wicker are used for carrying the sacred corn meal, and serving the flat piki bread. Some of the best of these come from the village of Old Oraibi.

When a Hopi girl is about to be married, she asks her female relatives to help weave all the baskets which will be required for her dowry. It may take several years to weave all the baskets. The requirement for this skill in a wife shows both the economic and ceremonial importance of basketmaking to the Hopi. Wedding baskets are important for the Navajo too, but they require only one basket for the wedding and it is an important part of the ceremony, not the dowry. This basket is a shallow bowl which is coiled with the basic colors of red, black and natural vegetation color.[22] The material is of sumac stitched over a three-rod willow foundation. This design band is said to illustrate the hills and valleys of this world and the underworld. There is a break in the design which is the path that spirits take between the two worlds. According to tradition the end of the coil must line up with this break: this provides an easy method of locating the opening which must face east during the ceremony.

Many other fine basket-making groups live in the Southwest. The Havasupai are Hokan-speaking Yumans who live in a secluded branch of the Grand Canyon which has beautiful waterfalls. They are known for their weaving which has continued to the present day. The Walapai are close relatives who live in northwestern Arizona, making baskets by coiling and twining. They frequently use sumac twigs since sumac grows all around their reservation. The Hualapais and Yavapais are similarly active.

A much larger group, the Apaches, are close Athabaskan relations to the Navajo and probably came into the Southwest with them. They are well-known for their excellent baskets. These were nomadic peoples who did not want to settle down on reservations; baskets were easy to move and did not break. Today they do live on reservations but their main craft remains basket making, although that skill is not being passed on to the next generation. Apache basketry has been commercial since the 1880s, traditionally crafted from yucca, sumac and mulberry, made to simple and utilitarian designs, and colored with reds, yellows and blues. The three traditional types are round, shallow trays; tall burden baskets; and vessels made watertight with pitch.

There are two principal divisions in the Apache, a result of their nomadic past, each with

This Navajo wedding basket (above) was made in 1890 with natural and dyed sumac over a willow foundation. At that time such baskets were made exclusively by Ute and Paiute girls married into the Navajo. The design break is clearly visible here. As well as being a spirit path it guarded the maker from trapping herself within the object she had made.

The Apache excelled at tightly coiled, well-decorated basketry, as evidenced by this superb set of objects (left) collected from the San Carlos Apache in 1909. These include coiled baskets, shallow baskets, a seed beater and a straw hairbrush. The black coloration for the willow rods comes from a plant called devil's claw.

Of all the Southwestern basketmakers the Pima and Papago number among the very best. Their designs and patterns are similar. This Papago woman (above) is weaving objects almost certainly destined for the tourist trade, but the Papago also maintain many of their traditional ways and continue to make and use baskets for their own domestic functions such as gathering fruit from the giant cactus.

The rawhide saddlebag (bottom right) of the Apache was leatherwork par excellence. Its patterned cut-work decoration reveals the red strouding underneath; and conical metal tinklers and long fringes add further to its distinctive appearance.

several main bands: the Western Apache comprises the San Carlos, White Mountain, Cibecue and Northern and Southern Tonto; to the east are the Mescalero, Jicarilla, and Chiricahua groups. The Western Apache traditionally practiced more farming and were culturally closer to the Navajo, the San Carlos Apache in particular having produced many examples of beautiful basketry.

The Jicarilla still weave some baskets, partly thanks to Lydia Pena, a remarkable weaver who has done a good job in restoring interest in basket-making among the tribes. She teaches classes and sells most of her produce, but it is hard work and it is difficult to price the baskets high enough to cover the time involved.

The work of the Western Apache is mostly coiled trays, large burden baskets and storage baskets. The designs are mostly geometric, but the use of human and animal forms is common. It is interesting to note that these most nomadic of the Southwestern Indians continued making baskets like burden baskets, for practical use in moving materials around, rather than using baskets for ceremonies or specific processing of food as was the case in the pueblos. This survival of baskets in such ceremonial use makes anthropologists think that basketry is very old in the Southwest, since the ceremonial use of objects is usually very conservative.

There are two groups of Indians in southern Arizona who are specially noted for their baskets, the Pima and the Papago. These people live in the very hot and arid desert and their basket work is closely related. Pima baskets are made from willow and devil's claw over a foundation of tule. Since the 1890s the Papago have changed material, and now yucca has replaced willow in Papago work, which makes it easier to distinguish between them. The start of the baskets is also different, the Papago basket start is a cross, and the Pima a plaited knot. Probably the most recognizable Papago basket is the burden basket. Today's Papago probably make more baskets than any other tribe with animal and plant forms as their favorite decorative elements. Since the Papago basket is pounded as it is woven, their baskets tend to be flatter and wider than a Pima basket. Pima baskets are close to Apache baskets in the excellence of their weave. Their designs are usually geometric patterns in swirls or a quadrant layout. Most designs are based on squash blossoms, whirlwinds or a maze. These are frequently shallow baskets which were used for winnowing seeds or ground wheat.

Sculpture and Leatherwork

There has been sculpture in the Southwest since prehistoric times. Soft stones have been carved, and figurines in stone, wood, clay and shell were common throughout the Anasazi times: there is a carved stone Hohokam ram which may have been a palette, or designed for some ceremonial use. One form of carving still much in evidence is the Zuni art of fetish making from minerals and semiprecious stone. The animal figures are very important in regional culture, being used in the hunt societies and as part of medicine bundles. Carved from turquoise or soft stone, the fetishes are usually small for portability and concealment. They often have bundles of sage or feathers tied around them. Today, fetishes have become popular charms for tourists.

One of the most notable losses during the early Spanish period was that the kachinas, the

masked gods, disappeared from the Rio Grande pueblos, although they still appear in Zuni or Hopi. Many small carvings of the sacred kachinas have been made from dried cottonwood by the Zuni and the Hopi for the past few centuries.[23]

In the 19th century Zuni kachinas were often dressed in real cloth and leather, while Hopi kachinas had their clothing carved out of the wood. Zuni kachinas also usually have taller bodies, and their limbs are articulated. Today, the lines between Zuni and Hopi kachinas are somewhat blurred, and the situation is further confused because the Navajo have been making kachinas since 1985 for sale to tourists. The kachinas embody the spirit of many different ideas and things. For the Zuni and the Hopi the kachinas come to bless and to chastise people. It is important to know what kachina you are seeing, and so the dolls are made to teach the children to recognize and to invoke these special beings. This is especially true for girls, since boys will learn to recognize the kachinas in the *kivas*.

Kachina dolls today can be elaborately carved, but a century ago they tended to be simple. They have always been sought by collectors since they

portray the rich religious life of the Pueblos in a tangible way. Simple, wooden kachina dolls were traditionally given to Hopi children as their first toys, the mother kachina, or *Hahay'iwuuti*, being hung over the cradle to bring good health. Today, the technical excellence of all the carvers has increased and most of the production of kachinas is for the market. There are many kachinas, and different ones appear seasonally. Spending half a year with the Hopi, the kachinas bring them rain and prosperity. Each kachina has different attributes and subtle changes in costume. It is important to all the Pueblos that the kachinas do not disappear, and the depiction of the kachinas is one way of reminding people of who the kachinas are, their special functions, and, as important, who the Pueblo people themselves are.

As well as kachinas, gambling and gaming objectives were carved, ceremonial sticks prepared and painted, and figures created to form part of the altar screen in the *kiva*. Tablitas or flat headdresses were also made and painted for women's dances; the Butterfly Dance or the Corn Dance, for instance, may use different tablitas.

Another craft associated with the Apache in the last century was the manufacture of handsome, cut leather shirts and dresses. Whole skins of deer or antelope were tanned, then fringed and pierced with circles or square holes in order to create designs made by the cutaway portions of the skin. The leather might be dyed and ornamented with shells or feathers to add beauty and/or protective medicine. Many fine examples of dresses and saddle bags are held in various museum collections.

Carved fetishes and kachinas were, and are still, among the most typical of Southwestern items. The bear (left) and mole (right) being very popular choices. The attachment of an arrow to the back is traditional. Also here is the wolf in the form of *Kwewu*, an important kachina figure (above) and hunter who will help to secure food.

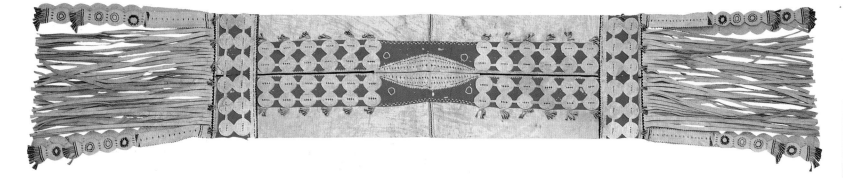

THE PLAINS

> 'Those who have seen the ornamental work of Dakota
> women will admit that much of it is tastefully
> designed and executed. They would admire it if they
> knew the disadvantages which the artists had to labor
> under, working in their dark tents with hands that
> were most of the time employed in the rudest labor,
> which laid down the ax and hoe to take up the needle.'
>
> SAMUEL POND, CIRCA 1830[1]

PERHAPS MORE than any other peoples, the Indians of the Great Plains of North America – the Blackfeet, Sioux, Crow, Kiowa and Comanche to name a few – have captured the imagination of the world. Resplendent in costume, picturesque in appearance and romantic in their customs, these equestrian nomads roamed the prairies and plains living in tipis and hunting the buffalo. The fundamentals of the culture, however, were due largely to two momentous imports of the white man – the horse, which came from the Spanish settlements in the southwest, and the gun from the French in the northeast.

The Plains stretch some 2,000 miles (3386km) from present-day Texas to Alberta and from the Mississippi/Missouri to the base of the Rocky Mountains, and the tribes who dwelt there shared enough traits to be classed together as representing a distinct way of life although some, such as the Mandan and Pawnee, lived in more permanent earth-lodge dwellings. Dominant however, was the dependence on the buffalo which not only provided food but hides for clothing, receptacles and dwellings; during at least part of the year, Plains Indians lived in tipis with a seasonal grouping in a large circle when the scattered groups united for the great ceremonials.

A characteristic of Plains culture was to put great emphasis on the interrelationship between ceremonial, costume, adornment and song – a holistic world view where everything was linked in a complex pattern of mythology and ritual: as one Blackfeet ceremonialist put it 'My clothes are my medicine.'[2] Throughout the region, women displayed a high degree of skill in the preparation of animal hides for use in the fabrication of many household objects, clothing and dwellings. This craft gave a decided common thread to the culture: the emphasis in artwork, however, differed considerably among the areas. Thus, northern and central Plains tribes did some exquisite porcupine quillwork while on the southern Plains such work was almost entirely absent. Later, with the introduction of beads in the early-19th century, definite identifiable area – even tribal – styles were developed. Likewise, skill and emphasis in such fields as carving, pipe-making, featherwork, and pictographs varied from one part of the Plains to the next. Nevertheless, in all cases the end product reflected the concern and skill and dedication of the craftsman or woman to produce an object which was a thing of beauty and in harmony with its environment even though, as the opening quote suggests, the work might be carried out under the most adverse conditions.

Porcupine Quillwork

Although sometimes considered a gastronomic delicacy, the most important use of the porcupine in North America was as a source of material for quillwork. The North American porcupine, *Erethizon dorsatum*, was commonly found on the northern and western Great Plains and the quills

Colorful beadwork and skilled leatherwork of an Arapaho craftswoman, embellish a mirror bag from circa 1890 (main picture). Attached to the bag is a heavily beaded band for passing over the arm, whilst small brass bells, acquired by trade, garnish the lower edge of the bag above the fringe. Pendent from the top are looped buckskin thongs tightly bound with red porcupine quills. Plains Indian skill in carving is displayed by the wooden spoon (main picture) with a turtle effigy as a crest on the handle. Probably the best-known symbol of Plains culture, however, is the feather warbonnet, exemplified here (right and far left) by the coveted immature golden eagle feathers, white with black or brown tips, from a Cheyenne headdress.

A magnificent doll 31in (78cm) high completes the selection of craft items (above). She wears a dress of blue strouding with rows of elk teeth. On the belt is a knife sheath and a beaded cradle.

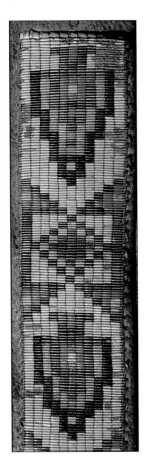

were a significant trade item to those tribes who did not have direct access to the animal.[3] The pelage of the porcupine is a dense woolly undercoat and white-tipped guard hairs and quills on the heads, back and tail. The quills are white stiff hollow tubes with brown to black barbed tips and those used for quillwork range in size from about 2-5in (30mm to 140mm) in length and 1-2mm in diameter. In addition to porcupine quills, bird quills were also occasionally used, particularly by those tribes on the Missouri River, such as the Hidatsa, Mandan and Arikara and, perhaps to a lesser extent, by the Santee and Yankton Sioux and Ojibwa along the upper Mississippi River.[4]

Archeological evidence suggests that porcupine quillwork has long been practiced in North America, the main evidence for this coming from the region of Utah and Nevada where artifacts preserved in caves show the use of quills as a bonding element; such items date to c.500 BC, while moccasins decorated with quillwork and dating from the 13th and 14th centuries have been reported from various archeological sites.[5] It has been suggested that quillwork possibly had its origins in Asia, with examples of woven mats and baskets found in Asia exhibiting the same basic weaving and sewing techniques as used in quillwork in North America.[6]

Highly formalized quillworkers' guilds have been identified among such tribes as the Cheyenne and Arapaho,[7] and these guilds used certain designs which were considered sacred and could only be produced by the initiated women. Similar customs appear to have prevailed among the Blackfeet,[8] whom it has been reported, traditionally at least, put considerable emphasis on the religious significance of quillwork.[9] Guilds appear to have been less formalized among the Siouan tribes such as the Lakota, Mandan, Hidatsa and Crow but several of these tribes – in common with the Plains Algonquian – explain the origin of quillwork in mythological terms.[10]

In preparing the quills for use, they were first softened by the application of moisture, generally by being placed in the mouth, and they were then flattened by being drawn between the teeth or finger nails; while some elaborately carved bone or antler quill flatteners are to be found in the collections, it is probable that they were actually ceremonial in function. In early days, the sources of dye were various roots, berries and mosses, but later, colored trade cloth was used when cloth and quills were boiled together, the color from the cloth penetrating the quills. Commercial dyes obtained from white traders were increasingly used after 1870.

Some 16 porcupine quill techniques were used by the Plains tribes, of which eight were very common and in combination they can frequently be utilized to determine both the tribal origin and age of a particular specimen. The tools used were relatively simple and in addition to the possible use of a quill flattener, a woman quillworker used a bone marker, awl, knife and sinew threads. The marker either simply impressed the surface or was dipped into a colored fluid and then used as a pen. The sinew thread was used to secure the quills to the hide. Wrapping techniques on rawhide strips were common and widely used in the decoration of hair ornaments and pipe-bags,

both being particularly favored by the Sioux. Woven quillwork was used by the Cree and possibly in early days by the Blackfeet and it also occurs on at least one shirt from the Santee Sioux now in the Nathan Jarvis collection in the Brooklyn Museum. The technique is of particular interest since it utilized a small loom, the exquisitely finished work having the appearance of being made from fine cylindrical beads. More specialized methods such as the plaited technique and quill-wrapped horsehair were particularly well-developed by the Crow and appear on shirts, leggings and moccasins and although such work was also found on similar items collected from the Hidatsa, Mandan, Arikara and Nez Perce, in most cases this was probably due to trade with the Crow.[11] With the wholesale introduction of beads to the Plains tribes in the mid-19th century, quillwork was progressively displaced as a decorative

Ta-to'-ka-in'-yanka or Running Antelope (left), Hunkpapa Sioux, during a visit to Washington D.C., in 1872. He wears regalia which displays much of the magnificent art and craftwork so typical of the Lakota for the period, such as decorated feathers and a symbolic arrowhead in his hair, dentalium and abalone shell earrings, large eagle-wing fan and a catlinite pipe, the long wooden flat stem decorated with porcupine quillwork. He wears a buckskin hair-fringed quilled shirt with the hair saved at the extremities.

A superb shirt fringed with buckskin (left) dating from circa 1860. It is identified as 'Sioux' in the museum records but the plaited quillwork technique, displaying the typical line of demarcation running lengthwise through the center of the strip and the complex patterns worked with the technique, suggests that it is of Hidatsa or Crow make, possibly a trade item. The triangular flap at the neck is of red and black cloth and parallel lines in blue paint embellish the body and arms of the shirt, features which are not uncommonly found on Lakota regalia.

A Crow or Hidatsa crupper (right), collected prior to 1850, is fabricated of rawhide and buckskin, heavily fringed at the edges. The loop goes under the horse's tail whilst the bands are tied to the back of the saddle. Decorative, symbolic artwork is in the form of rather large blue and white beads with the addition of red cloth along the outer edges of the bands. Patterns, colors and technique are typical of this so-called pony beadwork period, which bridged the gradual transition from porcupine quillwork to seed beads.

medium. However, fine traditional costumes decorated with quillwork were still being produced in limited quantities as late as the turn of the century on both the central and northern Plains, the Hidatsa in particular excelling in this skill. An exhibition of contemporary Sioux quillwork was assembled in 1974 at the Sioux Museum in Rapid City, South Dakota and since that time, a number of Sioux quillworkers have found a 'ready market for their wares.'[12]

Beadwork

Until approximately 1830, porcupine quillwork predominated over beadwork even though beads were introduced to the Plains tribes in the early 1800s. Thus, when the trader François Larocque traveled to the Crow in the vicinity of the Yellowstone River in 1805, he reported that they already possessed small blue glass beads which had come from the Spaniards in the southwest and probably via Shoshoni intermediaries. The Crow were so fond of these beads that they were willing to give a horse for one hundred of them; in consequence their high value at this time limited their use to the edges of porcupine quillwork strips. This, however, was the beginning of the so-called 'Pony Beadwork' phase on the Great Plains.

Pony beads – so called because they were transported on pony pack trains – were large, somewhat irregular china and glass beads which were made in Venice and were about one-eighth of an inch (3mm) in diameter. The colors were limited, blue being the most popular but white, black and red were also used. By 1840 these beads were being used in great profusion often in combination with a colored cloth and they were applied to pipe-bags, moccasins, leggings, shirts and buffalo robes. On clothing, the beadwork was generally carried out on a separate band, perhaps 3-4in (7cm) wide and then sewn to the shirt or leggings, although on buffalo robes, the bands could be up to 8in (20cm) wide. Patterns consisted of tall triangles, bars, squares and diamonds and often reflected the designs used in earlier quillwork. The pony beadwork period lasted until about

1855 when a smaller type of bead became popular; referred to as 'seed' beads they varied in size from one to three-sixteenths of an inch in diameter and gradually displaced the pony beads as a working medium.[13]

Two main methods of sewing beads to a surface were employed by the Plains tribes, the overlaid or spot stitch which was popular on the northern Plains and the lazy stitch which was much favored by the central Plains tribes. In the overlaid or spot stitch, the technique was similar to that used in quillwork: here, a thread of sinew was strung with a few beads which was then attached to the surface by another thread sewn across it at intervals of every two or three beads. If a broad surface was to be covered, line after line was attached with the lines laid close together. In the lazy stitch, a number of beads were strung on a thread of sinew which had been fastened to the skin, and then a perforation was made to attach the sinew at the end of the row of beads. As in the overlaid stitch, the perforation did not completely pass through the skin but ran just below the surface so that no stitches appeared on the back of the work. The same number of beads were again strung on the sinew which was carried back to the starting point and passed through another perforation adjacent to the first one. Varying colors could be introduced and so arranged as to produce a design.

The tribal differences both in technique and style may be illustrated by reference to the beadwork of the Blackfeet on the northern Plains and that of the Sioux on the central Plains.[14] Almost without exception, the Blackfeet employed the overlaid stitch, patterns being built up of scores of small squares or oblongs which were united to form larger patterns with the borders which were invariably an arrangement of different colored squares or oblongs. The large figures were generally squares, diamonds, triangles or slanted bands with long, stepped sides. The inspiration for this style of beadwork seems, at least in part, to have derived from earlier quillwork designs, particularly in woven quillwork.[15] Floral designs

were also used by the Blackfeet possibly influenced by the Cree and Ojibwa and, with the increased use of seed beads in the late-19th century, floral designs on moccasins became common. As J. C. Ewers has observed, 'Photographs of Piegan Indians in the 1880s indicate that moccasins beaded in flowered patterns were then about as common as ones decorated with geometric designs.'[16] Additionally, floral designs were commonly used on saddles, saddle bags and martingales: less commonly they appear on men's shirts and leggings. In contrast, the Sioux seldom used floral designs – the lazy stitch which they almost exclusively employed in their beadwork tending to restrict the patterns to blocks, crosses, tall triangles and particularly after c. 1880, figures consisting of thin lines, terraced and forked, which were spread out on a white or, less commonly, blue background. The inspiration for this type of work, it has been suggested, came

A Piegan shirt (above) heavily fringed with ermine and some human hair-locks. Collected in 1903, this garment is typical of the style worn by the Blackfeet from about 1880 onwards. Although the shoulder and arm bands are worked in seed beads in the so-called overlaid stitch, the patterns are very similar to those found in quillwork from this tribe at an earlier, pre-Reservation period. Such regalia, often referred to as 'weasel tail' shirts, were regarded as medicine bundles, being cared for and transferred according to rituals.

A beaded warshirt (above) worn by the Miniconjou Sioux leader, Kicking Bear, when he visited Washington D.C. in 1896. Fringed with human hair-locks and eagle feathers, it is replete in Lakota military symbolism. In contrast to the Piegan shirt shown on the previous page, the seed beaded bands are in the lazy stitch – parallel lanes six to eight beads in width. Such 'scalp shirts' were traditionally part of the regalia of the warrior societies and could only be worn by leaders.

from the patterns which appeared on Caucasian rugs brought in by white settlers.[17] About 1890, some craftswomen began embroidering live figures such as men, horses and elk – markedly different to the earlier traditional geometrical designs – and these figures were commonly worked on men's waistcoats and pipe-bags.[18] Crow beadwork is particularly distinctive, the style appearing more massive than that of other tribes with large triangles, hourglasses and lozenges in various combinations. A definite characteristic of Crow beadwork was the outlining of many of the patterns with white beads so setting them off from the background. A similar type of beadwork also prevailed among the Nez Perce and Shoshoni, the inspiration coming, at least in part, from those designs which commonly appeared on

painted parfleches.[19] Men's and women's dress clothing, containers, robes and blankets, moccasins as well as riding gear, were commonly decorated with this distinctive style of beadwork.[20] In marked contrast to those tribes on the central and northern Plains, the beadwork of such tribes as the Kiowa, Comanche and Southern Cheyenne on the southern Plains, was generally restricted to single lanes – perhaps seven or eight beads wide – along the edges of leggings, shirts and women's dresses. The work was always of a high quality, the beads being both small and carefully selected, presenting a neat and expertly finished artifact. Some exceptions were the exquisitely fully beaded bags and awl cases which, particularly among the Kiowa, invariably exhibited a distinctive glassy red bead background.

Carving and Engraving

The large carved house posts, totem poles and the like so common and well-developed by the Indians of the northwest coast of America, found virtually no place in Plains Indian carving, the majority of which was rendered in the miniature. An exception to this was the use of human effigy spirit posts carved by Plains Cree and Ojibwa. These were observed as early as 1799 by the fur trader, Peter Fidler, in the vicinity of the Beaver River in what is now eastern Alberta. The posts were generally life-size and had crudely carved heads being referred to as *Mantokans* which derives from the Algonquian *maniot*, a term used for the mysterious life powers of the universe. Peter Fidler said that they were erected by Indians in the hope that 'the great *Menneto* will grant them and their families health while they remain in these parts'.[21] While the nomadism of most typical Plains tribes does go a long way to explaining the desire for small three-dimensional artwork, even among the semi-sedentary Plains tribes such as the Mandan, Hidatsa and Omaha of the Missouri River, no large carved sculpture was found.[22]

Prior to the arrival of the Europeans, the production of carved artifacts was carried out by the use of stone implements although bone and pieces

The daughters (left) of Comanche chief Quanah Parker photographed in 1891. Both girls wear heavily fringed buckskin dresses with limited beadwork so typical of the southern Plains tribes for this period. Generally, such dresses were made of three deer or antelope skins, one folded lengthwise for the cape, the other two forming the skirt. Moccasins are plain but the leggings of the smaller girl are embellished with German silver conchas and she wears a metal bangle and also necklaces of large metal and glass beads. Her sister's dress is decorated with a broad band of beadwork across the cape in dark pony beads on a white background – a slightly unusual feature for this style of dress.

Typical Crow buckskin and beadwork embellish this superb lance case (left). The case is of rawhide with patterns both incised and painted; additional decoration consists of red and dark blue strouding laced on to the edge of the case with buckskin thongs. The beadwork is almost certainly in the so-called Crow stitch, which is a modified style of the overlaid stitch; note that some of the patterns are outlined in white beads, a distinctive Crow characteristic.

A Cheyenne flageolet (above) collected in 1891. Such carved flutes, together with pipe-stems, rank as the most common articles in wood produced by the Plains tribes and several specimens date back to the early years of the 19th century. This particular six-holed instrument has a wooden stop which appears to be a carved stylized bird-head – a popular effigy on such flutes. The stop covered part of the sound orifice which was an aperture near the top of the flute between the air holes and mouthpiece. This stop could be adjusted to tune the instrument, it being held in place by leather thongs which were wrapped around the middle of the stop and the main body of the flute. Often referred to as courting flutes, the sound produced was adjusted to resemble that of the bull elk whose incredible sexual powers were well-recognized by the Plains tribes.

of copper obtained in trade might have been used. While appearing primitive, they were clearly more efficient in the hands of a skilled craftsman than might be imagined; thus the shaping of lance and flint arrowheads – the so-called Folsom and Clovis points – by early Plains inhabitants, demonstrates that great skill and workmanship was possible without the use of iron tools.

It can only be speculated as to how much wooden carving the early Plains tribes produced since wood rapidly deteriorates in the ground and no archeological sites on the Plains have yielded wooden effigies; however, stone carvings of catlinite (a soft red stone) produced prior to the 15th century, have been found and some of the finest Plains Indian carvings were of catlinite.[23] Additionally, shell and bone effigies which may date as early as AD 1000 have been found in sites associated with the ancestral Mandan.[24]

By the middle of the 19th century, and probably earlier, wooden carved animal effigies were associated with medicine hunts, tree-dweller ceremonials and war medicines. War clubs, courting flutes, pipe-stems, Sun Dance dolls, children's toys and effigy horse figures were also carved and widely distributed across the Plains.[25]

Horse effigies were often depicted on mirror-boards and pipes, but the most elaborate carvings of horses were used in victory dances and were highly symbolic. Thus, when Walter McClintock visited the Blackfeet in 1898, he observed 'One of these dancers named Rides to the Door carried the carved wooden figure of a horse to remind people of his bravery and skill in raiding enemy horses'.[26] Such effigies had wide distribution being used by the Sioux, Crow, Hidatsa, Ute, Blackfeet, Gros Ventre, Blood, Assiniboin, and Cheyenne.[27] A famous carver of horse effigy dance

sticks was the Hunkpapa Sioux, No-Two-Horns and a particularly fine carving (one of several extant) by this man is now in the Medora Museum, North Dakota. It seems to have been made to commemorate an event in the Custer Battle when No-Two-Horns' horse was wounded seven times and died in action. The wounds are indicated on the carved horse by triangular areas of red flowing from a wound at the apex of the triangle. No-Two-Horns was also known to be adept at other types of carving producing dolls and miniature weapons for his grandchildren.[28]

In addition to carving, several items used by the Plains tribes were engraved such as the riding quirts or roach spreaders of elk antler. This was a material which was relatively easy to work and could be shaped and finished with simple tools. When used for quirts, there seems to have been some preference for the prongs which protruded forward on each side of the main rack just above the skull.[29] Such prongs could be made into handles with the minimum of effort; in turn these handles were not infrequently engraved with war exploits, life figures, geometric and curvilinear patterns, the process being carried out by use of an awl or knife point while deeper lines were made with the cutting edge of a knife blade or a file;[30] roach spreaders were engraved in a similar way. Before about 1870, they were usually made of a flat plaque of antler and often displayed military exploits and were carefully shaped matching the contours of the roach base. Later, they were made of wood, metal or rawhide. Roach spreaders had a multifold purpose – to spread the roach farther apart, support the plume holder such that the eagle feathers stood out from the back of the roach, and to beautify the roach further with the engravings which were on it.

Horn spoons with elaborately carved handles displaying effigies of snakes, beaver, bighorn, birds and elk were much favored by the Western Sioux, particularly during the second half of the 19th century and, after the buffalo were virtually exterminated in the 1880s, the effigy spoons were made of cowhorn from those animals slaughtered as rations for Indians on the reservation. Typical is an elk-head spoon of cowhorn on which the handle is bent at the end, the elk head facing the same direction as the bowl of the spoon; the carver has taken pains 'to show the animal's open mouth and lightly incised nostrils and eyes, as well as its spreading horns.'[31] Elk power was associated with sexual prowess by many Plains tribes. As the English sportsman, John Palliser observed in 1847, 'In the breeding season the wapiti chants the most beautiful musical sound in all the animal creation; it is like the sound of an enormous soft flute, uttered in a most coaxing tone.'[32] Thus, in seeking elk power, the Sioux fabricated elaborately carved flutes of cedar wood which not infrequently displayed a carved elk head at one end in the act of calling his mates.

Pipes

The ceremonial use of tobacco was widespread in North America and had supernatural associations; the ritual of smoking was said to lift one's thoughts to the spirits above, linking earthbound man with the sky above. Pipes used by the Plains Indians were made of various workable stones – limestone, steatite and chlorite – but the most favored was a red stone quarried in the area of present-day Minnesota and referred to as catlinite after George Catlin who first visited the quarry in 1835 and who brought a sample of the stone back for scientific analysis. This pipestone was known to the Indians of the region from prehistoric times and prior to c. 1700 was in the territory of the Oto and Iowa. After this time, the Sioux took over the quarry and by the mid-19th century they were its sole owners, the stone rough blanks or finished pipes then being traded to other tribes.[33]

North American Indian pipes have been divided into two major categories depending upon their form; one style is tubular in which the smoke travels in one plane, the other is elbow in

Two spoons (below) exhibit the skills in bending and carving horn, a common craft practiced by most Plains tribes. These two were collected from the Sioux and date from circa 1870. Such spoons were made by boiling the horn so as to make it flexible and then turning it into the required shape, into which position it was held until cooled. The lower spoon is probably made of mountain sheep horn and has a carved effigy representing a loon's head and is decorated with blue, white and red beads along the handle, at the end of which hang pendants of buckskin bound with porcupine quills and terminating in metal cone jingles. Note the turquoise bead eyes.

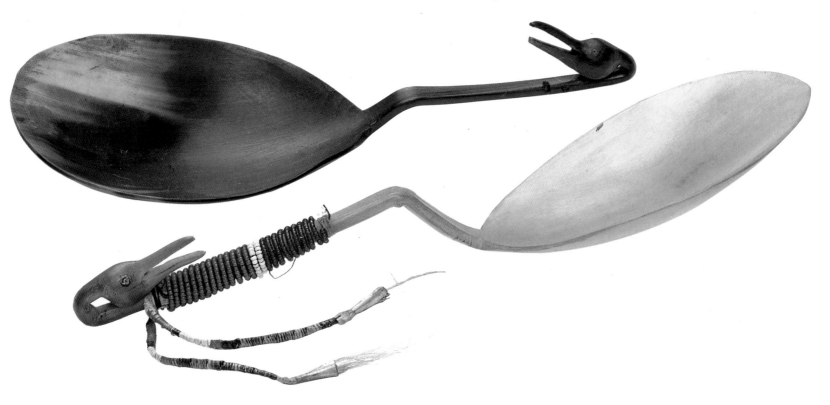

This Sioux pipe (above) is decorated with dyed porcupine quills which have been braided across two threads to produce a continuous string for wrapping around the stem. Additional decoration is in the form of mallard duck feathers, at each end of the quillwork, with a pendant of horsehair. The head is of catlinite. Note the skilled inlay of lead on the shank and bowl.

Also lead inlaid is this magnificent effigy pipe (below), probably Santee Sioux, dating from before 1841. It is typical of pipes used as a medium for social comment; in this case the effect of the liquor trade on Indians. Such intricate carving required infinite patience and care when working on the brittle stone with the most limited of tools.

which it travels in two planes.[34] Both types were found on the Plains in the Historic Period. More recently this classification has been extended to the five most common forms – the tubular or straight pipe, the modified Micmac pipe, elbow pipe, prowed pipe with flaring-bowl, and the calumet or inverted T-shape.[35] A number of these pipes were particularly elaborate exhibiting effigies of animals and humans; some of the finest in the category were made by the Sioux and Pawnee. George Catlin expressed the opinion that the Pawnee were probably the 'most ingenious' of all the Plains tribes in the production of such articles. Effigy bowls were of high artistic quality with imaginative designs, the likenesses of humans and animals usually being carved so that they faced the smoker; some made social comments such as the effects of liquor on Indians.

The carving of a pipe from catlinite or other stone was a formidable task and, before the introduction of steel tools by Europeans, the stone was fashioned using flint or other hard materials, the bowl being drawn on the stone and the excess cut away; the holes for tobacco and stem were a particular problem as Catlin observed: 'the Indian makes the hole in the bowl of the pipe, by drilling into it a hard stick, shaped to the desired size, with a quantity of sharp sand and water kept constantly in the hole.'[36] The bowls were then finally shaped and polished with flint, quartzite and fine sand and buffalo tallow and other animal fats gave the finished piece its polish.

The modified Micmac style of bowl was so named because it was the Micmac of Nova Scotia who were first observed by Europeans using this type of pipe. The style travelled west in trade and was a distinctive shape having a bowl not unlike an inverted acorn upon a keel-like base. The Plains Cree, Crow, Assiniboin and, in particular, the Blackfeet, utilized pipes of this type although there were many variations on the basic style.

Ewers found this modified form of Micmac pipe still being made as late as 1947 and he obtained an example of such a pipe from his Piegan informant and interpreter, Reuben Black Boy, who had fabricated it a short time previously. It resembled a pipe first illustrated by Carl Bodmer more than a century earlier (1833) and was referred to by the Blackfeet as a 'real pipe'. The technique of manufacture had, however, changed markedly – Reuben was now using a pencil to outline the shape of the bowl, a wooden vise to clamp the slab, a hacksaw to rough out the bowl, a carpenter's brace to drill the holes, a wood rasp to get the final shape and the exterior was smoothed with commercial sandpaper. The final blackening of the bowl, however, followed more traditional lines. Reuben built a fire of green buckbrush and, placing a stick in the pipe-stem hole, he held the bowl over the fire for about 15 minutes. After the stone had cooled, he rubbed the surface with his hand, giving it an even, shiny surface.[37]

Most of the pipes so far described had stems which, for ceremonial purposes, could be up to 3-4ft (1-1.3m) in length. The stems were made of

ash, oak, or hickory, the pith in their center being burned out with a hot wire. An alternative was to split the stem lengthwise, scrape out the pith and then glue the pieces together. Flat pipe-stems were most popular on the central Plains while round ones were used on the northern Plains. Some had open work 'puzzle stems' where only the carver knew the true pathway of the smoke as it zig-zagged from bowl to mouthpiece, by-passing the decorative and symbolic designs which were carved on the stem. Other stems were of the spiralling variety where rounds stems were carved with a knife and file, sometimes a double spiral being produced. The stems were not infrequently decorated with porcupine quillwork, generally in the so-called braided technique with additional decoration in the form of horsehair, feathers, beaks and paint. Although both bowl and stem were considered to be endowed with sacred power, the pipe itself was not considered activated until the two parts were brought together and, when not in use, stem and bowl were taken apart and stored in a bag, beautifully embellished with beads and porcupine quills.

Featherwork

As early as the mid-16th century, a crown of feathers came to indicate Indian identity in most of the Americas.[38] Such headdresses generally consisted of a simple band with the feathers of the wild turkey, hawk, heron or eagle attached so that they stood upright around the head. Similar to this early style was the headdress of the Blackfeet of the northern Plains which, by the profuse combination of eagle feathers and ermine skins, turned the ancient and simple headband

Mountain Chief (left), a Blackfeet warrior photographed in 1913, wears a fine straight-up headdress typical of the featherwork of his tribe. Here, the traditional feathers from the immature golden eagle – white with brown or black tips – are set upright in a folded rawhide headband. Each feather is embellished with ermine and hair-locks at the tips and the band profusely decorated with brass studs and ermine fringe. Note also the 'hackle plume' at the center of the headdress; this red colored plume may indicate membership of the Blackfeet military Horns Society. Mountain Chief also carries a carved wooden horse effigy, probably to commemorate his bravery and skill in raiding enemy horses: this is a good example of Blackfeet wood carving. Note the miniature figure of a warrior astride the horse.

A feather bonnet said to have been formerly the property of Stone Calf, a Cheyenne chief. Dating from circa 1880, there are some 40 immature golden eagle feathers attached to the red stroud trade cloth tail and some 30 feathers in the crown. Formerly, each of the feathers was decorated with a lock of horsehair attached to the tip by use of white gypsum. At the base of each feather, as well as attached to the tail, are large eagle 'breath' feathers – perhaps symbolizing communication with higher powers. Along the front of the crown is a tastefully beaded strip worked in white and blue seed beads using the so-called lazy stitch technique, whilst at the sides of the bonnet hang long fringes of ermine, several with the characteristic black tip of the animal's tail. This is a splendid example of the type of featherwork produced by several central and southern Plains tribes, such as the Lakota, Cheyenne and Arapaho, in the period 1870-1910.

style into an imposing form of warrior and society regalia. This style, referred to as a 'straight-up bonnet', was said to have originated with the ancient Bulls Society of the Blackfeet.

Headdresses of this type were made from a piece of thin rawhide or heavy tanned skin six inches (15cm) or so in width and of sufficient length to fit the wearer's head. It was then folded along its long dimension and holes were cut in the edge of the fold through which the eagle feathers were passed.[39] Some 20 to 30 feathers were attached to the band either by cutting the feather quill and tucking it back into itself so as to form a loop or, alternatively, a small wooden pin was pushed into the hollow quill of the feather. The feathers were then fixed in place by the use of a lacing thong which went through the quill loop or over a groove in the wooden pin. A second thong usually passed through the quill about halfway up the feather which held it in place and gave shape to the bonnet. The headdress was then covered with red cloth which was decorated with brass studs or, occasionally, beadwork. Long ermine fringes were hung from the sides and back and additional decoration in the form of narrow strips of rawhide wrapped around with porcupine quills were sometimes attached to the quills of the eagle feathers with small fluffy plumes at the base of each. Finally, the ends of the band were joined by tying them together at the back and carefully adjusting so that it fitted snugly on the head. Such headdresses were worn on ceremonial occasions, in dances and parades. They were also worn in battle but this was considered a particularly brave act since it made the wearer exceptionally conspicuous and a more than likely target for enemy fire.

The use of the straight-up headdress progressively decreased after c.1895 and by the 1940s very few such bonnets were then worn, having been replaced by the Sioux style of flaring bonnet.[40] Elderly Blackfeet explained this by saying that the straight-up bonnet was considered very sacred regalia and that few people had the right to wear it.[41]

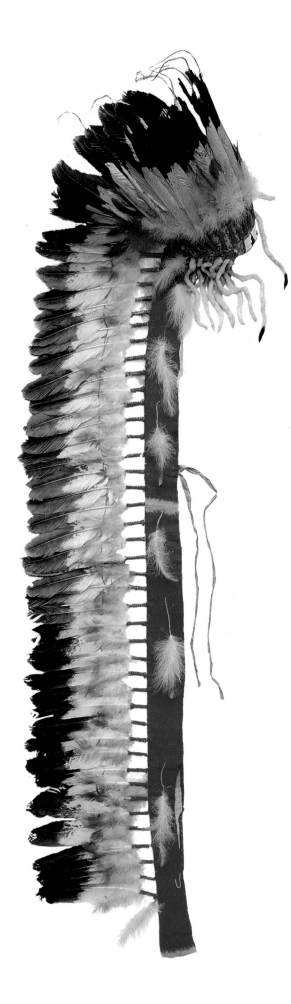

The Sioux-style warbonnet contrasted with the Blackfeet style, having a cap of soft buckskin which fitted loosely to the head. To it were attached feathers to form a circle but unlike the Blackfeet style where the feathers were fixed rigid and upright, the feathers were at an angle, flaring both upward and backward from the wearer's head and having freedom of movement.

The development of the Sioux style flaring bonnet can be traced through early travelers' accounts to the Plains tribes beginning with the French explorer, La Verendrye, to the Mandan in 1738 who referred to feather headbands; while later, in 1811, the English explorer, Brackenridge, refers to Arikara headdresses with the feathers arranged as a kind of crown.[42] It seems that by 1820 the flaring style of warbonnet was well-developed, clustering among tribes who put emphasis on coup designation by the use of eagle feathers, such as the Dakota, Arikara, Pawnee, Hidatsa, Mandan, Crow and Omaha. There were slight variations within the style, but of them all, the Sioux version – where the feathers swept back from the brow and the middle side feathers were approximately 45 degrees to the vertical – typifies the style. Some 30 or more feathers were used, the foundation being a buckskin cap. The feathers were first carefully prepared and most important was the formation of a loop at the bottom of the feather. This was either made by cutting the quill as one would for a pen and tucking the quill back into itself or alternatively leather or rawhide strips were bound to the quill leaving a loop at the bottom. The feathers were further embellished with buckskin or colored cloth at their base together with several fluffy plumes while the tips were decorated with horsehair. The feathers were then laid out in the order that they would appear on the bonnet, the two longest and straightest being at the center. Then they were laced to the cap by running a buckskin thong through the loop and pairs of slits cut in the cap. Another thong was run through the feathers part way up the quill, holding the feathers in place and enabling the bonnet to be set so as to become a balanced

and uniform spread. A 'major plume' was then attached to the center of the cap, originally in the form of a power amulet such as the skin of an animal or bird. In later years – 1870 onwards – it was replaced with a long stripped quill cut and embellished in a certain way to distinguish the owner. The headdress was completed by the addition of a quilled or beaded brow band with rosettes on each side from which were hung ermine and colored ribbons.

Traditionally, the flaring style of bonnet could only be possessed and worn by the consent of a man's fellow warriors – by an individual who had gained both war honors and the respect of the leading men in the community. Among the Omaha each feather stood for a man, the tip of hair fastened to the feather and dyed red, representing the man's scalp-lock. Before a feather could be fastened on the bonnet, a man had to count the war honor which actually entitled him to wear the feather and so enabled him to prepare it for use in decorating the bonnet. When the warrior counted his honors he held up the feathers which were to represent them, saying 'In such a battle I did thus'.[43] Thus, the wearing of a

A Cheyenne warbonnet (above) of immature golden eagle feathers dating from circa 1890. The feathers are attached to the crown of an old felt hat – a favorite base for such headdresses for this period. The method of attachment is by means of a rawhide loop at the base of each feather which has been covered with red trade cloth bound at the top and bottom with white thread. Note the left and right handedness of the feathers either side from the middle of the beaded brow band. Colored ribbons are pendent from the beaded discs which adorn each side of the headdress.

A three-skin dress (below) from the Southern Cheyenne and dating from about 1890 is embellished with elk teeth on the heavily fringed and yellow painted cape. The skirt is decorated with two single lanes of seed beadwork, and an additional scalloped effect pattern at the bottom, below which the buckskin is painted red. Note the cone jingles.

warbonnet by a privileged individual did not refer exclusively to that individual's feats of arms, rather it signified the best warrior and underlined the interdependence of men.

Buckskin Garments

While the most typical garment for Plains Indian women in the mid-19th century was a one-piece sleeveless dress, a closer study of women's costumes indicates that despite this general pattern there were considerable variations in tribal styles. Thus, on the northeastern Plains an early style was the 'strap dress' which consisted of two

long pieces of buckskin sewn at the sides and held up by straps over the shoulders with the addition of separate cape-like sleeves which were connected by thongs across the front and back. Another early style on both the northern and central Plains was the 'side-fold dress' which consisted of a wide rectangular piece of hide folded on one side, the other being sewn with the top turned down to form a type of cape. A hole was made for the arm on the folded side and the dress was sewn or laced at the shoulders. By 1830, however, both these styles of dress were beginning to go out of fashion being replaced by the 'two-skin dress' probably due to influences from the Plateau tribes farther west. This was made by sewing two deerskins together with the hind legs at the shoulders, a few inches – which included the tail – being folded down.[44] Thus, the natural shape of the tanned hide was retained – a good example of how the form of a costume is determined by the material used. Piercing, trimming, additional inserts and mode of decoration on this basic garment were often indicative of tribal origin. On the southern Plains, however, among such tribes as the Southern Cheyenne and Arapaho, Kiowa and Comanche, three skins were used in the construction of a woman's dress. Here, two deerskins were cut straight a few inches below the forelegs, these skins became the skirt of the dress, a third skin being folded lengthwise and sewn to the other two skins at the waist. A hole was cut into the top of the fold to allow the head through. The Southern Cheyenne and Arapaho tended to decorate such dresses with bands of beadwork about 3-4in (7-10cm) wide on both the shoulders and across the chest while the Kiowa and Comanche often painted their dresses and used only a limited amount of beadwork at the edges.

In the fabrication of clothing, a common practice among Plains Indians was maximum use of material at hand with minimum wastage. In this respect, the style of leggings used by men was no exception. Hides from the white or black-tailed deer or prong-horned antelope were commonly used in the manufacture of leggings. An excellent

contemporary account of Plains-style leggings was given in 1805 by the explorers, Lewis and Clark: 'The leggings are generally made of antelope skins, dressed without the hair and with the legs, tail and neck hanging to them. Each legging is formed of the skin entire and reaches from the ankle to the upper part of the thigh and the legs of the skin are tucked before and behind under a girdle around the waist. It fits closely to the leg the tail being worn upwards, and the neck highly ornamented with fringe and porcupine quills, drags on the ground behind the heels. As the legs of the animal are tied round the girdle the wide part of the skin is drawn so high as to conceal the parts usually kept from view, in which respect their dress is much more decent than that of any nation of Indians.'[45]

Such styles of leggings were widely used on the central and northern Plains but farther south tribes such as the Kiowa and Comanche began to make leggings which were more tailored than those used farther north. The most popular form of skin legging in the second half of the 19th century, was the so-called 'tab and fringe' style. Here, the legging was fashioned from a single hide folded lengthwise to form a double flap, after a tailored leg seam had been sewn. The flap was then cut into a fringe leaving a whole portion near the top; referred to as the 'tab' this was generally tastefully decorated with paint and beads.[46]

Embellished buffalo robes, certain styles of headgear, special forms of leggings and, in particular on the central and northern Plains, the ceremonial shirt, were all important ways of communicating an individual's position within the social and political strata. Thus, among the Pawnee, the wearing of the skin shirt was 'one of the outstanding symbols of high status. . . . very few men were privileged to wear them' and even able chiefs might be excluded.[47] The sacred character of a special style of hair-fringed shirt among the Sioux was emphasized by the elaborate rituals developed relating to its conferment and, as late as the reservation period when such shirts were being made for collectors, special rituals were still performed during both its fabrication and transferral.[48] Traditionally, the Sioux ceremonial shirt was made of two deer, bighorn or antelope skins; about one-third of the top was cut off each skin which was then folded to make the sleeves, the lower two-thirds becoming the front and back of the shirt. The head portion from each skin was then used as a decorative flap on the front and back. The sides of the shirt were generally left open and the sleeves sewn from the wrist to the elbow only. Most of these shirts have

Classic southern Plains costume (left) is worn by Kiowa Indians photographed by Hillers in 1894. At the right is *A'piatan* or Wooden Lance, a prominent tribal leader who, in the fall of 1890, was sent by the tribe to see the Paiute prophet *Wovoka* to evaluate the Ghost-dance doctrine; he returned disillusioned. At the center is *Gonkon* or Apache John, a Kiowa Apache sub-chief. All three men wear finely fringed and partially tailored buckskin shirts with sparse beadwork which is so typical of Kiowa and Comanche clothing. *Gonkon* holds an eagle feather fan, the handle of which is embroidered with white and mostly red beads, so characteristic of Kiowa beadwork for the period.

A pair of Kiowa men's leggings (left) dating from the late-19th century. These are made of heavy buckskin which has been stained with yellow earth paint, while the twisted fringes are stained blue. There are brass beads along the sides and glass beadwork on the bottom edges of the leggings. Note the five painted images of the dragonfly painted in blue on each legging – probably symbolic of a hard-to-hit-in-battle warrior.

An engraved drawing on rock of a horse and rider (below) at Joliet, Montana. This magnificent petroglyph, which is probably Crow, dates from the early part of the 19th century and shows many details of accoutrements worn or carried by the horse and rider. The horse is almost certainly reined with a Spanish cheleno bridle and bit – note the chain pendent from the head which is virtually diagnostic of this style of horse equipment. The rider carries a war axe and bow lance and has a long scalp-lock. He is *not* riding side-saddle, the artist simply showing what he knows to be there, rather than as it appears to the eye.

quilled or beaded bands over the shoulders and often two – generally narrower – bands down the arms. These were invariably, although not exclusively, worked separately on a leather base and then sewn to the shirt. Human hair fringes were attached to the edges of these shoulder and arm bands which represented the war deeds – or perhaps a mark of allegiance – of the members of the Chiefs' Society or individuals who sanctioned the wearing of such garments by outstanding leaders.[49] A typical garment in this class was worn by the Oglala leader, Red Cloud, and others when they visited Washington in the 1870s.[50]

Petroglyphs and Pictographs

The communication of ideas by means of petroglyphs and pictographs is of ancient origin in North America. Petroglyphs have been defined as pictures 'upon a rock either in situ or sufficiently large for inference that the picture was imposed upon it where it was found'.[51] Pictographs, on the other hand, were pictures upon skins, bark, pottery and later on woven fabrics such as linen cloth and muslin as well as paper, the latter producing, in the late-19th century, a proliferation of so-called ledger book art.[52]

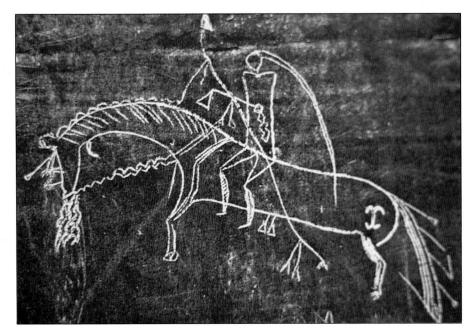

Recent studies of Plains petroglyphs – now popularly referred to as Rock Art – have identified two major styles, Ceremonial and Biographic, the first being of considerably greater antiquity than the second.[53] A variety of techniques were employed in producing the petroglyphs but most commonly the rock surface was scratched or alternatively the surface was pecked with a small sharp-edged stone, both methods removing the darker weathered surface.[54]

Pictographic work on hides was generally carried out using 'brushes' made of the spongy, porous part of the buffalo's leg bone, one edge of which was sharpened to make narrow lines while the flat side was used to spread color over larger surfaces.[55] Colored earth and clay and some vegetable materials were used for paints, these being ground into a powder and mixed with a gluey substance which was obtained from boiling hide scrapings or the tail of a beaver. As with petroglyphs, painted art work on skins was both geometric and representational; generally, the former was done by women and the latter by men.

One of the most popular geometric designs used by women was the so-called 'box and border' and much favored by the Sioux and Arapaho. This exhibited two distinctive features – a continuous border which surrounded all four sides of the hide together with an enclosed rectangular, decorated field, usually located just above the center of the hide and always elongated horizontally. An associated style was the 'border and hourglass' pattern; here, the central pattern tended to be variable in detail but its essential form was always broad at the ends and constricted in the middle – a form suggestive of an hourglass.[56] It is suggested that such designs were stylized representations of the buffalo showing its internal structure as Hail has observed, 'It was easy for the people of hunting cultures to visualize internal organs, as they were accustomed to butchering their kills and distributing the parts. This is true especially of women, since they were responsible for cutting up the meat that the hunters brought in. The joys of a full stomach and relief from the fear of starvation for her children would be part of her pleasure in drawing these designs'.[57]

The earliest documented painted robe showing extensive detail of inter-tribal warfare among the Plains tribes and obviously in the category of an autobiographical treatise, was collected by Lewis and Clark from the Mandan in 1805. It was reported that the pictographs depicted a battle fought about 1797 between the Mandan and Minnetaree against the Sioux and Arikara.

Analysis of robes of this type leads to the conclusion that the subject matter of early Plains Indian representative painting was overwhelmingly that of humans and horses, while the episodes recorded put emphasis on the stealing of horses or the counting of coup on the enemy.

Horses were represented in a variety of ways, a stick-like leg with a hooked hoof – actually representing a hoof print – being typical of hide painting done prior to 1850. Later, horses are shown in a more realistic way, the eyes, phallus, tail and sometimes the mane being depicted while the running horse was conventionalized to forelegs extending forward and hind legs backward.[58] Early depictions of human figures were knob-like heads which were generally devoid of features although hair-styles were not infrequently shown. Arms and legs were stick-like with simple triangular and rectangular bodies. There were several notable exceptions to this early style – in particular the work of the Mandan chief, *Matotope* (c. 1833) whose pictograph technique was possibly influenced by white artists.[59] In the second half of the 19th century, there was considerable refinement of human proportions, an abundance of detail, increase in richness of colors, some experimentation with spatiality and the appearance of new themes and subject matter.[60]

Rawhide

Rawhide has great strength and versatility and because of these qualities it was highly prized by Plains Indians and used in a variety of ways.

The preferred hide for making rawhide was that of the buffalo and although elk, moose and

domestic cattle hides were used, particularly during the reservation period, buffalo was considered to be more elastic and fibrous and 'long use of a piece of buffalo rawhide made it somewhat like heavy, firm cloth'.[61] There were considerable variations in the production of rawhide but the end product was always the same – a clean hide devoid of fleshy material and hair which, on drying, was white and opaque. A widespread technique was to stake the hide out by putting pegs through slits cut around its edge and to use a chisel-like bone (later metal) tool called the 'deflesher' to remove fat and tissue from the inner part of the hide.[62] The hide was then turned over and with an adze-shaped tool, the hair was carefully scraped away. Finally, it was thoroughly washed and left in the sun to dry and bleach.

While rawhide was used in the fabrication of such items as shields, drums, knife sheaths, saddles, cruppers, horseshoes, burden straps, hats, doors of tipis, mortars, decorative and symbolic

A painted buffalo robe (above), probably Lakota and dating from before 1840. This is a superb example of early Plains Indian pictography which in dramatic graphic form documents the war exploits of the owner and his followers. Details of costume and accoutrements, such as pipes, headgear, weapons, hair styles, quirts, shields and horse equipment are accurately rendered by the imaginative artist. This is both a cultural and historical 'document' par excellence, giving important insights into the complex culture that produced it.

Nowhere is rawhide more important than in the manufacture of the Plains saddle and stirrups. This Crow woman's saddle (right) dates from before 1870; it has a wooden frame with the high pommel and cantle so distinctive of Crow, Nez Perce and Shoshoni styles. The frame was covered with wet rawhide which when it dried, shrank to bind the various components into a tough, virtually indestructible, item. Stirrups, similarly made, are embellished with red cloth and seed beadwork – one of the earliest examples in this style.

cut-outs and even cradles, its commonest use was in the production of the parfleche[63] which was a flat rectangular and expandable case in which clothing, food and other materials were placed for storage and transportation.[64] Parfleches were generally made in pairs from a buffalo hide which had already been cleared of fat and tissue during the rawhide production process. The flesh side of the staked out hide was marked out using peeled willow sticks of different lengths defining the parfleche shape and the geometrical patterns which were to be painted on it. A bone 'brush' was used to draw the outlines of the patterns which were generally in a single color; the larger areas were then filled in with the desired colors. The surface was then covered with a thin coat of glue or size which gave a gloss to the paint and protected it from wear and tear when in use.[65] After the paint and glue had dried, the hide was turned over and the hair removed in the usual way: finally, the parfleche was cut out from the rawhide to the desired shape. Regardless of tribal

origin, most of the patterns on parfleches consisted of geometrical designs made up of rather massive rectangles, squares, triangles and hour-glass-type figures. There were, however, some definite tribal variations, thus the Blackfeet frequently used curved lines, the Crow put emphasis on using straight lines and the Sioux used a mixture of both. Some of the finest parfleches were made by the Cheyenne whose designs were

A fine example of a Plains parfleche (right) dating from about 1870. The parfleche was, in effect, the Plains Indians' suitcase, being used to transport dried meat and pemmican and also clothing. They were made of rawhide, cut and folded rather like a giant envelope, and then painted in tribally distinctive abstract designs. This one is Cheyenne, a tribe who were particularly famous for the elegance and beauty of parfleche designs.

unusually delicate and the combination of colors particularly distinctive.[66]

Moccasins

With the exception of the sandal-wearing tribes of the Southwest and Mexico, moccasins were universally worn throughout most of North America. The true moccasin – the term originating from eastern Algonquian dialects – was a type of footwear in which the 'soft sole and the upper, or part of the upper, are continuous, passing upwards from under the foot, forming a well-constructed foot covering which always has a back seam.'[67] There were considerable variations within this basic style but typical for the Plains Indians in the early-19th century, is Larocque's (1805) description of Crow moccasins, which he said were 'made in the manner of mittens having a seam round the outside of the foot only without [a] pleat'.[68] The Blackfeet referred to this earlier one-piece soft-soled moccasin style as the 'real moccasin'. Since soft-sole moccasins wear out

quickly in the harsh Plains environment, a modification in the form of an additional piece of leather was sometimes added to the sole but the basic pattern survived to at least the beginning of the reservation period (c. 1870), being preferred for winter wear when buffalo hide with hair inside was used.

Around the middle of the 19th century, another style progressively came into use. This was the two-piece moccasin which had a rawhide sole with a soft buckskin upper. Although this style came to have wide distribution on the Plains, even toward the end of the 19th century, some tribes – notably the Crow – were still using both types. As the army officer, Captain W. P. Clark observed in the 1880s, 'the Crows make their moccasins of one piece sewed at the heel, though some have separate soles'.[69]

On the southern Plains from around 1860 onwards, a high-topped style, particularly popular with the Kiowa and Comanche, was in use; a tube legging was attached to the moccasin, the seam being covered by a single lane of beadwork. The moccasins were always of the hard-sole variety and these, together with the attached legging, were painted yellow or green. Heavy German silver discs were usually attached to the leggings and the edging beadwork exhibited intricate patterns worked in small seed beads.

A floral design was invariably worked on the instep of Kiowa high-topped moccasins, a feature seldom used by their close allies, the Comanche.[70]

A pair of quilled and beaded moccasins (left) which were collected from the Hidatsa in the early years of this century by the anthropologist, Gilbert Wilson, who worked with the elders of the tribe recording their history and customs. The quilled discs on the instep are an early style of Hidatsa design, referred to as a warbonnet pattern and related to sun power. The beadwork around the lower edge of the moccasins underlines the transition from quillwork to beadwork – although the Hidatsa continued to do porcupine quillwork well into the 20th century.

A pair of men's beaded moccasins (left) which were collected from the Southern Cheyenne in 1891. These are hard-soled moccasins with an upper of soft-tanned buckskin which has been dyed with yellow earth paint. The moccasin design reflects a style typical of much Cheyenne beadwork where patterns are often in the form of colored stripes either in a parallel formation or as concentric rings, as shown here. The use of red beads combined with blue and white was also particularly popular with the Cheyenne in the last quarter of the 19th century.

PLATEAU AND BASIN

'The Cho-pun-nish or Pierced nose Indians are Stout likely men, handsom women, and verry dressey in their way. . . .
. . . as their Situation requires the utmost exertion to pr[o]cure food they are generally employed in that pursute, all the Summer & fall fishing for the Salmon, the winter hunting the deer on Snow Shoes in the plains and takeing care of ther emence numbers of horses, & in the Spring cross the mountains to the Missouri to get buffalow robes and meet . . .'

WILLIAM CLARK, 1805[1]

THE PLATEAU and Great Basin culture areas cover a vast and diverse area of the interior of western North America. The traditional Native cultures of the Plateau evolved in the upper Columbia River Basin in the present states of Washington, Oregon, Idaho, Montana and adjacent sections of the province of British Columbia between the Rocky Mountains on the east and the Cascade Mountains on the west. Numerous tribes, including the Wasco/Wishram, Cayuse, Umatilla, Yakima, Palouse, Spokane, Nez Perce, Coeur D'Alene, Kutenai, Kalispel, and Flathead all lived in the Plateau area. This location enabled them to draw artistic inspirations and materials from the Native people of the buffalo plains east of the Rockies as well as from the maritime cultures west of the Cascades. They did this both through extensive trade networks with other Native people and with Euro-Americans, as well as by extensive travel themselves. Central and eastern Plateau people, particularly the Nez Perce and Flathead, regularly made the difficult and dangerous journey east across the Rockies to the buffalo plains of Montana to hunt and trade. The people practiced a lifestyle that revolved around hunting, fishing, and gathering wild foodstuffs on a seasonal cycle, and they were consummate horse people after the mid-18th century. Trading and direct inter-tribal contacts with other culture areas resulted in

Plateau arts and crafts that are a unique synthesis of equestrian and maritime cultures. Native Plateau artisans worked with a wide range of materials and media to produce objects of utility and beauty.

The Great Basin is an even larger area between the Sierra Nevada Mountains on the west, and the Rocky Mountains on the east. It is centered geographically in the present states of Nevada, Utah, Oregon and Idaho. The traditional cultures of the Great Basin are diverse, varying from the desert-dwelling hunter-gatherers in the south and west to the big-game hunting, horse-mounted nomads in the north and east. Great Basin ethnography is sometimes confusing because groups of people with the same tribal name developed widely varying cultures. The Northern Shoshonis, Northern Paiutes (Bannocks) and the Utes of the semi-arid and mountainous areas of eastern Idaho, western Wyoming, eastern Utah and eastern Colorado developed a nomadic horse culture that was very similar to those of the Great Plains. They lived principally by big-game hunting and often ventured on to the plains after buffalo. By contrast, the Washoe, Paiute, Western Shoshoni, Goshute, Southern (Utah) Ute and other desert dwellers of southern Oregon, western Idaho, Nevada and western Utah never became horse nomads. Theirs was a naturally harsh and difficult arid environment which was one of the last areas of North America to be dominated by the Euro-Americans. The desert dwellers had the ingenuity to live and prosper

The Plateau and Basin regions, bordered as they were by five other cultural areas, tended to reflect their influences in their own tribal cultures to a greater degree than was the case in other regions where fewer interactions existed. Beadwork and quillwork (far left and right) were both predominant on the neighboring Great Plains but gained their own distinctive expression in the Plateau and Basin, as shown in the Umatilla floral design moccasins and Ute beaded and quilled hide robe (both in main picture).

Influences were ceremonial as well as artistic, the hide shield (above left) was collected from the Shoshoni among whom the Plains-originated Sun Dance was practiced. It is painted with visionary designs and hung with red cloth and eagle feathers to provide spiritual protection in battle.

Since the mid-19th century rectangular beaded bags with a beaded wrist strap (attached to the top corners of the bag) have been a popular accessory with Plateau and Crow men. They were used to store mirrors, paints and other toiletries.

This bag (right), attributed to the Nez Perce, is beaded in the classic Transmontaine style popular on the Plateau and with the Crow. Complex angular designs, a wide range of bead colors and pastel backgrounds, in this case pink, are all typical of the style. The other side is beaded in a different design.

there for generations, and through most of the 19th century continued to practice their ancient pattern of seasonal hunting and gathering, relying upon a wide variety of animal and plant foods. Their possessions tended to be few and light and this in turn had a significant impact upon their arts and crafts.

In both the Plateau and the Basin traditional arts and crafts were produced primarily by women. Basketry, porcupine quillwork, parfleche decoration, hide-tanning and clothing were all produced almost exclusively by women. Objects of stone, wood and horn, realistic hide painting and weapons were produced primarily by men.

Beadwork

The Plateau people already valued and used glass beads acquired in trade even before the time of their first recorded contacts with Euro-Americans in the early-19th century. The earliest surviving pieces of Plateau beadwork date from the 1830s and are heavily embroidered with predominantly black and white beads 3-4 mm in diameter. These beads, now called 'pony' beads, were manufactured largely in Venice and were acquired in trade from other tribes or from Euro-Americans.[2]

Plateau pony beadwork produced before 1850 was usually executed in only a few primary bead colors, including translucent sky blue, white, black, and rose (a translucent red with an opaque white center), although a variety of other colors such as shades of green, shades of blue, pink, translucent cranberry, and yellow were occasionally used. The beads were usually sewn onto a hide backing with animal sinew thread or sometimes with native fiber cordage. The geometric designs were simple and bold with strong color contrast. Womens' dress yokes, moccasins, shoulder and sleeve strips on men's shirts, men's legging strips, blanket or robe strips, cradle boards and a variety of horse gear were among the items commonly decorated with early pony beadwork. The visual impact of pony beadwork with its simple designs and strong color contrasts could be dramatic. About 1840 an observer noted that a

'young lady . . . in one of these dresses, upon a fiery horse well equipped with saddle & crouper, makes a fine appearance.'[3]

By the middle of the 19th century Plateau women began to use fewer of the larger pony beads and incorporated smaller (1-2 mm diameter) glass 'seed' beads. Seed beads were also manufactured primarily in Venice, and were used in a much wider range of colors than pony beads.[4] The small size and color variety of seed beads, used alone or in conjunction with the larger beads, allowed Plateau women to create more delicate and complex designs than was possible with pony beads alone. By at least the mid-1840s they were creating beadwork employing curvilinear designs, first in pony beads and later in seed beads. The earliest Plateau curvilinear beadwork in the 1840-60 period usually employed outlined, symmetrical designs based upon a double-curve motif on a hide or dark fabric background.[5]

There were several bead sewing techniques most commonly used. The lane stitch or 'lazy' stitch was used, for example, on the broad bands on women's dress yokes and on narrow bands outlining beaded panels. A stitch was taken in the foundation material, a sufficient number of beads was strung to cover the desired width, and a second stitch was taken to secure the row. These stitches were continued side by side to complete the band of beadwork. Curvilinear beadwork was done in a two-thread applique or spot stitch. Beads were strung on one thread, and a second thread was stitched between every second or third bead to secure the beadwork to the foundation. A third major technique was the 'Crow' stitch in which bands of lane stitch were completed and then secured to the foundation by a second thread that looped around the lane stitch at right angles between every four to six beads.

Lane stitch produces slightly humped or ridged rows of beadwork while the spot stitch and Crow stitch both produce smooth, flat beadwork. Lane stitch and Crow stitch were both used to produce geometric designs, while the spot stitch could be used for either geometric or curvilinear designs.

By about 1860 curvilinear beadwork was very popular on the Plateau. Bold, colorful symmetrical abstract floral designs were set against a light color background that was beaded in the same contours as the adjacent curved motifs. The texture of the background bead rows produced a subtle radiating or halo effect around the primary beaded designs. By the end of the century very realistic floral designs predominated, with out-

Plateau people in the 19th century made and used a variety of highly decorated horse equipment for festive occasions. This double beaded bag (left) – actually two complete bags joined at the top – could have been placed over the saddle horn so that one side hung on each side of the horse, similar to the rectangular bags in the photograph (above). It was collected from the Yakima and dates from about 1870. The beadwork is in the classic Plateau contour beaded style in which the background was beaded in rows that follow the outlines of the curvilinear designs.

lined, filled-in designs set against a fully beaded background in horizontal, not contour, rows. On many late-19th and early-20th century beaded pieces, particularly women's flat hand bags and men's vests, realistic often asymmetrical bead designs included not only floral but also animal figures.[6]

At the same time that Plateau women were perfecting the use of curvilinear, floral and animal designs, they were also perfecting what has come to be known as the Transmontaine style of beadwork. This term reflects the fact that this distinctive beadwork style was produced by women on both sides of the Rocky Mountains: principally by the Crow along the Yellowstone River, and by many of the Plateau tribes in the upper Columbia River, the foremost probably being the Nez Perce.[7]

One of the hallmarks of this style in its fullest development is the optical ambiguity created between what is a design element and what is 'background.' This is much like the line drawing which may first appear to be a vase and may then appear as the profiles of two faces. Transmontaine beadwork designs are closely related to painted parfleche designs, discussed below. The same design elements, design layout and to a certain extent the same colors were used in both painting and beading, at least in the 1860-1900 period. A wide variety of objects was beaded in

the Transmontaine style, including large bandoleer bags, otter bowcase and quiver sets, men's shirt and legging strips, cradle boards, horse equipment, gun cases, moccasins, and men's flat mirror bags.[8]

The beadwork traditions of most Great Basin people has never been thoroughly studied and is poorly understood. The available evidence indicates that little or no porcupine quillwork was produced in the area and that beadwork was not a major art form among the western, desert-dwelling tribes. The women of the eastern Great Basin tribes – the Shoshoni, Bannock and Ute – were active beadworkers, although only among the Ute was beadwork as prominent as it was in the Plains and Plateau. There are some surviving pieces of Ute pony beadwork which probably date from before 1850, and it is probable that the Great Basin beadworkers went through the same transition from pony to seed beadwork as did the women of the Plains and Plateau.

Late-19th century photographs of Shoshoni and Bannock people often show little or no beadwork, even though the people are wearing a variety of other types of ornamentation. The beadwork that appears is often executed in simple, blocky designs on light backgrounds. Historic photographs also show Shoshoni and Bannock people using curvilinear beadwork (usually on an open hide or cloth background), and occasionally with beadwork in the classic Transmontaine style common to Crow and Plateau beadworkers. It may be that Shoshoni and Bannock women produced beadwork in all three of these styles in the last half of the 19th century.

Ute women were prolific beaders who had regular contact with people from the Great Basin, the Plains and the northern Rio Grande Pueblo areas. The best known Ute style was characterized by bold, simple geometric designs in only a few colors on a light, usually white background. This style, which lasted from about the 1820s until the 1890s, is very reminiscent of early geometric design pony beadwork of the Plains and Plateau. Ute women worked first in pony beads

Ute people in the late-19th century (below) wore dress clothing that was similar to that worn by many Plains tribes. The men are wearing breechcloth and leggings, while the women are wearing cloth or hide dresses, two of them with heavily beaded capes. All have beaded moccasins, and the man and woman on the right are wearing early silver concha belts obtained from the Navajo. At left is an infant in a typical Ute cradle with an arched beaded border at the top and a twined willow hood.

and then in seed beads by the 1860s, and used both lane stitch and flat stitch techniques. Shoulder and arm strips on men's shirts, men's legging strips, women's dress yokes, women's leggings and men's tobacco bags all were commonly decorated in this style.[9]

Ute women were also fond of the Transmontaine style of beadwork, and Ute people sometimes used pieces 'imported' from the Crow or Plateau. However, Ute women also practiced this style of beading in small but significant numbers of pieces. Ute beadwork in this style usually incorporates a Transmontaine-style panel bordered by distinctly Ute panels in multi-row geometric lane stitch. Men's tobacco bags were often decorated in this fashion. Ute women also produced curvilinear beadwork, usually in symmetrical abstract floral motifs with cloth or hide for the background. This technique is most often seen on distinctive Ute cradles with wicker hoods, but also on other items such as horse gear and moccasins.

Porcupine Quillwork

Decoration with porcupine quill embroidery was a uniquely Native American art form. While early descriptions of Plateau decorative arts mention the use of quillwork, it is clear that Plateau women largely, but not completely, abandoned

This woman's hide dress (above) was collected from the Utes by the explorer Powell in the 1870s. The cape is beaded in typical Ute fashion in few colors and simple geometric designs. Ute cradles (left) had a board foundation covered with hide (yellow buckskin in this instance), and a twined wicker hood shielded the infant's head. The decorative beadwork is most attractive to look at.

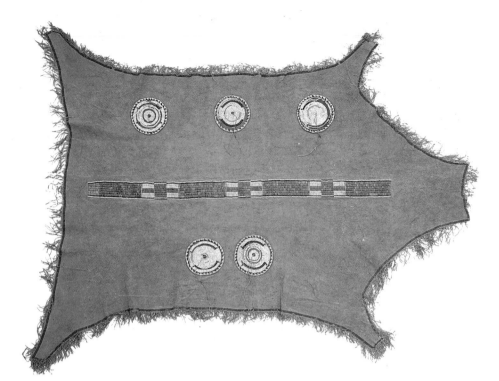

Powell collected this hide (above) from the Utes as a horse cover, but it was more likely worn as a robe. The 'pony' beaded rosettes wre probably recycled from a Plains or Plateau blanket strip. The presence of the central panel of porcupine quillwork is very unusual for a Ute piece. While Ute women produced quantities of beadwork in the late-19th century, they seem to have seldom done quillwork.

This painted Ute parfleche (right) is typical of the rawhide containers produced by the equestrian tribes of the Plains, Plateau and Basin.

quillwork by the mid-19th century. Therefore, little is known about early Plateau quillwork that would distinguish it from early quillwork from other areas.

One rare quillwork technique that persisted late into the 19th century in the Transmontaine (Plateau and Crow) art area was quill-wrapped horsehair. Quills were wrapped around parallel bundles of horsehair about one-eighth of an inch in diameter, and were sewn between the hair bundles as they were attached to the hide backing. These quill-wrapped bundles were sewn side by side to form decorative strips. Simple blocky designs were produced by altering the colors of the quills, or by wrapping with colored yarn instead. These strips, always edged with a single lane of beadwork, were used for the decorative strips on men's shirts and leggings, for blanket or robe strips and occasionally for moccasins.[10]

Plateau women may also have used other techniques of porcupine quill decoration, particularly multiple-quill plaiting. This technique involved weaving multiple flattened quills together to form decorative bands an inch or more wide. Usually two such bands of plaiting were worked parallel to

each other and were bordered with a single lane of beadwork on each edge, just like quill-wrapped horsehair. Some extant pieces of early quillwork, primarily blanket or robe strips and mens' legging strips, consist of quill-wrapped horsehair rosettes separated by rectangles of multiple-quill plaiting.

Hide Painting

The women from most Plateau tribes produced quantities of storage containers made from parfleche, which was cleaned, dehaired, but untanned hide, usually buffalo or elk.[11] The most common parfleche containers were envelopes folded from large rectangles of hide, but smaller flat envelopes and tubes with closed ends were also produced.[12] The outer surfaces of parfleche containers provided a smooth hard surface which was decorated in two different ways. In the first, designs were painted onto the wet, skin-side surface of the hide while it was stretched flat.[13]

A second, possibly older technique of parfleche decoration on the Plateau employed the dark brown epidermis on the hair side of buffalo hides. Designs were cut or scraped just through the surface of the wet hide, and when the hide dried the cut lines opened to show the lighter layer of the hide underneath. The design consisted entirely of light and dark areas of hide, and usually no paint was used. When buffalo hides were not available, the women used elk or other hides and darkened the epidermis with animal blood before incising the design. Traditionally the incised parfleche

was used for food storage, while the painted parfleche was used for storing clothing and food supplies. Surviving incised parfleches are now extremely rare.[14]

The horse-mounted nomads of the Great Basin – the Shoshoni, Bannock and Ute – shared the painted parfleche container tradition with the people of the Plains and Plateau.[15] The Northern Shoshoni parfleches were made of buffalo, elk and later, of cattle hides, and were very similar to those of the Crow and Nez Perce. Shoshoni women usually painted a three-panel or nine-block design layout using straight lines, blue outlining of the design elements, and a major central geometric design element. Ute parfleches were made of the same materials but the painting was different. Thin brown or black lines outlined the design elements; designs composed of blocks within blocks; rectangles filled with squares; and overall designs not enclosed by a border.[16]

Fiber Arts and Basketry

A variety of baskets and other fiber objects played an important part in the lives of the Plateau people.[17] The two Plateau basketry types most

well known today are the 'cornhusk' bag and the 'Klickitat' basket, both of which were produced by the women of several tribes in the area. The cornhusk bag was a flat basket originally woven from native hemp cordage by a simple twining technique. Decoration was applied by false embroidery using dyed grass as well as cornhusks and later, wool yarn. The earliest bags were large rectangles (up to two by three feet) with an opening at the top that closed with a drawstring, and were used primarily for food storage. Designs on these early bags were repeated simple geometric forms in soft natural browns and tans, typically arranged in horizontal bands across the bag. Decoration was almost always different on each side of the bag.

In the latter part of the 19th century as traditional food gathering and storage became less important, cornhusk bags were produced in smaller sizes that were more square than rectangular and which were used primarily for women's decorative hand bags. Brighter dyed natural materials and wool yarn were used for the false embroidery, and commercial twine began to replace native hemp cordage. By the end of the 19th century, designs became more complicated, employing symmetrical geometric forms and realistic figures such as humans, animals and plants. The earlier practice of asymmetrical designs on the two sides was retained, as was the uniqueness of virtually every bag design.[18]

Women from many Plateau tribes wove tall round baskets using the wrapped twining technique. The designs were usually rather simple colored bands, although more elaborate designs in false embroidery were used. The Wasco/Wishram round baskets were often decorated with distinctive stylized human and animal figures very similar to those used in woven beadwork. Plateau women also produced coiled spruce root basketry, usually decorated by imbrication.

PLATEAU AND BASIN

Wasco/Wishram women on the Columbia River were producing finely twined round containers like this (left) at the time of earliest contact with Euro-Americans. Similar distinctive human and animal designs are found on prehistoric bone and stone sculptures from the same area.

Plateau flat twined bags were originally woven from native hemp cordage and later from commercial twine. By the late-19th century, when this example (below) was probably made, the decoration was done primarily in dyed cornhusk and therefore bags such as this Nez Perce one are now commonly called 'cornhusk' bags.

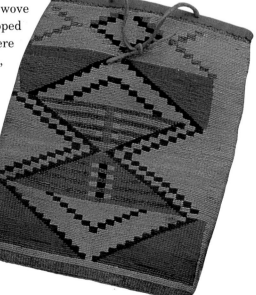

69

While these are usually referred to as 'Klickitat' baskets, they were produced by several other Plateau tribes including the Yakima and Nez Perce. The designs were usually executed in simple natural colors, but in elaborate geometric as well as stylized realistic designs. In the southern Plateau coiled baskets tended to be rounded oblongs with two small 'ears' or lifting loops on the top rim. In the northern Plateau the coiled baskets were similar, but tended to be more globular and rectangular in shape, sometimes with lids.

Basketry has been called one of the technological hallmarks of the Great Basin,[19] and the extremely arid conditions in much of the area have preserved samples of highly developed basketry from prehistoric periods. This aboriginal skill in basketry continued throughout the Basin in the Historic Period, although production and use tended to decline among the northern and eastern tribes that adopted the horse.[20]

Traditional Great Basin basketry was produced in several well-defined forms that reflected their utilitarian role in a hunter-gatherer society. Wild plant foods – especially seeds, berries and pinenuts – were important parts of the diet of the

Coiled cedar root baskets were made by many Plateau women. This Klickitat basket (above) has distinctly flared sides. Its designs were created by folding the decorative material and sewing it to the coils. On festive occasions most women wore rounded twined basketry hats, this Nez Perce one (right) is decorated with a zig-zag and a beaded tassle.

The finely coiled shallow basket produced by the Chemehuevi (below) has a distinctive style typical of the fine work of the late-19th century.

Great Basin people, and specialized basketry forms were developed to gather, process, store and consume them. The largest baskets were conical burden baskets, usually twined, which women carried on their backs using an attached tump-line or carrying strap across the shoulders or forehead. While gathering wild plant foods, women used a smaller conical or rounded gathering basket to do initial collecting, dumping it into the burden basket as it filled. Elongated, fan-shaped seed beaters were used to dislodge seeds and berries for gathering, while flattened trays were used for nut and seed gathering, sorting, winnowing, parching, cleaning and serving. Basket bowls were used for mush cooking (using hot rocks) and eating.

Tightly-woven water bottles waterproofed with evergreen pitch were widely used throughout the area. Great Basin women also wove and wore basketry hats much like those worn on the Plateau, but usually covering more of the head. Finally, most Great Basin cradles were made of twined willow rods, usually with a curved rod sunscreen and were often covered with buckskin.

extensive use of the horn of the bighorn sheep, carving and shaping it into bowls, ladles and hunting bows. Several varieties of local stone were carved into cooking vessels and pipe bowls used with wooden stems. The earliest pipe bowls were straight tubes, while the later ones were a curved elbow shape, sometimes embellished with lead inlay.

Most Great Basin people wove light, warm, twined rabbitskin blankets out of thin strips of hide with the hair left on, and also made robes of multiple small animal skins sewn together. Mountain sheep horns were used to make short, strong sinew-backed bows. Ladles and bowls were made from sheep and buffalo horns. Large vegetable fiber hunting nets and rush, feather-covered duck decoys have been found preserved in several caves, and were still in use into the 20th century. Small stone, wood and clay figurines have also been found. The Great Basin is also an area rich in representational and geometric rock art produced since prehistoric times by painting and by inscribing into the rock surface.

Powell collected this woman's two-hide dress (left), decorated with beadwork and elk teeth, in Utah in 1874. While labeled Southern Paiute, it is typical of Ute dresses of the period.

A Wasco/Wishram carver made this bowl (below) from the horn of a bighorn sheep. The zig-zag border and concentric square designs are typical. These durable vessels, as well as horn ladles, were treasured heirlooms and were widely traded throughout the Plateau.

Other Arts and Crafts

The Native people of the Plateau and Great Basin traditionally produced for themselves everything needed to sustain their life and economy. They continued to do so on a significant scale even after widespread trade allowed the substitution of Euro-American materials for many native materials. Tanning large animal hides for clothing and other uses, for example, was a constant chore at which most Plateau and Basin women were experts even after the general availability of cloth in the mid- to late-19th century. Even where cloth replaced hides for clothing, the garments were still largely handmade by the women.

The Plateau and horse-mounted Great Basin people produced a wide variety of horse equipment such as saddles, stirrups, ropes, halters, and cruppers. Canoes built on a bark-covered wooden frame were extensively used on the Plateau. These canoes were covered with cedar, birch, white pine and other barks, and had a unique long, pointed 'sturgeon nose' shape. Plateau people commonly made containers for temporary and more permanent use out of folded bark sewn with cedar root. Plateau people made

CALIFORNIA

THE AREA now known as California was one of the most linguistically and culturally diverse areas in the world prior to 1800; more than 60 'tribes,' all with their own languages and material culture, made their homes in the California region. For the sake of this discussion of arts and crafts, the California culture area can be divided into several major regions which share similarities in their arts and crafts: northwest (including Yurok, Karok, Hupa, Tolowa, Wiyot, and neighboring tribes), northeast (including Achomawi, Atsugewi and Shasta), central (including Pomo, Maidu, Yuki, Miwok, Yokuts, Patwin, Wappo and others) and southern (including Chumash, Cahuilla, Tipai-Ipai, Gabrielino, Juaneño, Luiseño, Cupeño, Serrano, and Tataviam).

In northwestern California, people shared a rich culture which relied on salmon, animals (such as deer), and a great variety of plants. Women made fine twined baskets of hazel or willow shoots and conifer root, overlaid with patterns in black maidenhair fern stem and shiny yellow bear grass. The men were skilled craftsmen, producing dugout canoes, split-plank houses, finely incised antler purses, and exquisite dance regalia.

In the northeastern part of the state, people had varied material cultures influenced by extreme variations in elevation, climate and vegetation in the region. From deserts, coniferous forests, swamps and meadows, the Achomawi, Atsugewi and their neighbors obtained a vast array of plant and animal resources to provide for their subsistence. They also produced a distinctive style of fine twined basketry, using some of the same, and some different, materials as people in northwest California. Their baskets were similar in appearance to those of the Klamath River, except that overlaid patterns were evident on both the inside and outside of the baskets. Men in this region made fine sinew-backed bows, which were an important trade item, and dance regalia, though it was not as highly developed an art as it was in the northwest. After the arrival of non-Indians, woven glass beadwork became firmly established in this area, and thousands of woven strips were made utilizing a limited repertory of patterns executed in hundreds of different interpretations.

People in the central portion of California relied on acorns as an important food source along with hundreds of other plant foods. Animals, including deer, elk, squirrels and various birds, were also important in their diets. The Pomo peoples made and used a great variety of twined basketry, primarily reserving coiled basketry for fancy baskets, often made as special gifts. Some of these baskets, fully covered with small, brilliantly colored feathers, have become the best known of Pomo arts. Coiled basketry for everyday use assumed more prominence among peoples to the east and south of the Pomo, including the Maidu, Patwin, Miwok, and Yokuts. Men among the Maidu, Patwin and Pomo produced exquisite dance regalia, including flicker-quill headbands,

The skill of native Californian artists is evident in this display of Hupa wealth (main picture). An 1870s woman's apron of woven bear grass, snail shells and pine nut beads, an incised elk antler purse used to store tusk-shaped dentalium shell money, and a dentalium and glass bead necklace owned by the Hupa Shoemaker Robinson during the early-20th century show the array of materials used to create objects of lasting beauty. Glass beads were used by many other peoples in California and woven glass beadwork reached its greatest development in the north. The detail (right and far left) is from a beaded bag made among the Wintu.

The basket (above left), collected in 1885 from the Yurok, has no utilitarian function. Woven of bear grass, maidenhair fern stem, conifer root and hazel sticks, it was carried by a male dancer in the Jump Dance.

73

This Karok woman, photographed in 1896, is probably Phoebe Maddux. Although the photograph is posed (as women do not wear ceremonial aprons and necklaces while weaving), it shows a diversity of baskets. Maddux's child is sleeping in a twined cradlebasket, which leans against a large, close twined storage basket. Maddux is working on a basket of this type, and another unfinished example is on the ground, next to the bundles of hazel sticks. The twined burden basket on the left is typical of the open twined basketry of the Karok and their neighbors. On her head she is wearing a basketry cap, an indispensable part of a well-dressed woman's wardrobe, and one of the finest products of northwestern California basketmakers.

belts woven of native hemp and ornamented with green and red feathers and white shell beads, and a myriad of feathered headpieces and cloaks.

In southern California, the Chumash on the coast utilized the wealth of the sea, while tribes living inland adapted to their more arid environments. Inland tribes used the various resources offered by the desert, including clay, which was formed into elegant and useful pottery vessels. In basketry, coiled baskets were made and used almost exclusively. Women from the Chumash, Cahuilla, Tipai-Ipai, Gabrielino, Juaneño, Luiseño, Cupeño, Serrano and Tataviam made elaborately coiled baskets which sometimes incorporated three colors. Men, apparently, executed the polychrome rock art characteristic of the Chumash region. A tradition of beautifully carved, steatite utilitarian ware and sculptures was centered in the Chumash-Gabrielino region.

Basketry

Basketry is perhaps the best-known art of California, and Native women have become well-known for it the world over. It is an ancient skill in California, and there are marked differences in baskets from different regions. Basket-making was primarily a woman's art; generally men made only a few coarse-twined baskets, like fish traps.

Women took great pains to produce their baskets according to traditionally dictated methods and ideals, although each basket was unique and identifiable as the product of a specific individual.[2] Weaving skills took many years to develop, and young girls were encouraged and expected to participate in gathering and preparing basket materials as well as weaving. By the age of 10 or 12, most girls were capable of good basketry.

Baskets were indispensable in the lives of California Indian people and they were woven in a multitude of shapes, each designed to function in a special niche of the Native lifestyle. Specific baskets were made for cooking and food preparation, storage, carrying loads, and cradling children.[3] Prized baskets, often made especially for the occasion, were given as gifts or burned or buried with the dead, and baskets were frequently burned during mourning ceremonies to honor the dead.

The study of basket form, manufacture and change over time does not extend far into the past, as baskets do not usually survive in archeological sites.[4] Different styles of basketry developed in distinct areas, and people often regarded their own style as the 'correct' one. The words of the Karok woman, 'Imakyanvan (Mrs. Phoebe Maddux), in about 1930 embody this principle:

'Each new year ceremony my deceased mother would go to Clear Creek to attend the new year ceremony. She would pack upriver two pack basket loads of bowl baskets and openwork plates, and dipper baskets; she would trade them for blankets, Indian blankets, and upriver hats, and juniper seeds, for all kinds of things, upriver things. They used to give us those upriver hats sometimes, but we did not wear them, it does not look right on us.'[5]

Mrs. Maddux's comments describe not only how desirable her mother's baskets were as trade items, but also how these Karok women viewed the women's basketry hats from upriver tribes such as the Achomawi as not quite 'right'.

Weavers of northwestern California produced baskets in plain twining with decoration overlaid on the baskets' exterior. Mush bowls, twined with conifer roots on a foundation of hazel sticks, were embellished with a horizontal band of design in shiny yellow bear grass. More elaborate baskets, such as the dress caps worn by women, were further ornamented with shiny black maidenhair fern stem and woodwardia fern stem dyed to a rust color with alder bark. Only the most highly prized women's caps were further ornamented with additional overlay in yellow-dyed porcupine quills. The quills surrounded by the shiny black of the maidenhair fern stem made a striking contrast to the lighter yellow bear grass background.[6]

A handful of Yurok baskets collected by members of the Vancouver voyage in 1793 are preserved in British museums, but otherwise few baskets exist from this region from before 1890. After that date, the tradition of destroying an individual's possessions (and, therefore, baskets) upon their death fell increasingly into disuse, so more baskets survived. Additionally, women started to make baskets specifically for sale to non-Indians. Many of the baskets produced after 1890 for non-Indians were made with patterns and shapes specifically designed to make the baskets more saleable, including motifs of realistic arrows and swastikas, and innovations such as pedestal bases and knobbed lids. In baskets made for their own use, as well as in most made for sale, women of this region still adhered to time-honored ideas of 'correct' patterns and basket forms. Some innovative weavers, such as Elizabeth Hickox (born in 1873), achieved a previously unrealized fineness and beauty by applying Karok patterns to a unique, lidded basket form. Her yellow-on-black baskets are among the finest from northwestern California.[7]

Baskets of northeastern California were produced in plain twining with a decorative overlay that shows on both the basket's interior and exterior. Like the Karok and Hupa to the west, women among the Wintu and Atsugewi wove their baskets on stiff warps of willow or other sticks. Some Achomawi women used twisted cordage (made from the sheath of the tule) for their warps, as did Klamath and Modoc people to the north, resulting in flexible baskets. By the early-1900s, some weavers were making changes in their baskets to make them more saleable to non-Indians. Many women wove large baskets with patterns that had previously only been evident in smaller baskets. Others experimented with new forms (such as oval baskets) and/or patterns (such as eight-pointed stars and serrated diamonds, patterns that reached the area with the arrival of woven beadwork). Some weavers covered their completed baskets with loose-warp-woven beadwork, producing striking objects that were a blending of ancient basketry with more recently learned glass beadwork technique and patterns.

Women in central California wove both twined and coiled baskets. Colored patterns were

California basketry is extremely diverse. The twined Wintu basket (left), collected in 1872, is typical of the baskets produced with patterns overlaid on split conifer root weft strands; the shiny yellow surface is from the dried leaves of bear grass. The Pomo feathered basket (above), made before 1890, is among the highest achievements of Pomo basket weavers. Woven of sedge grass roots over a foundation of willow rods, tiny feathers from acorn woodpecker scalps, orioles and mallard ducks are incorporated into the weaving. The basket is finished with a ring of valley quail topknots, a row of clamshell disc beads, and festooned with glass bead strands and abalone pendants.

A few coiled baskets use animal materials as part of their decoration. The Tubatulabal woman's cap (right), with patterns outlined in white porcupine quills, is a rare example of this type of basketry. The Chukchansi Yokuts basket (above) by Mrs. Graham uses split orange quills of the flicker, while the Pomo coiled basket from the late-19th century (below), is ornamented with the red scalp feathers of the acorn woodpecker, quail topknots and shell beads.

produced by substituting colored weaving strands for the background color strands. Pomo women excelled in both twined and coiled basketry, and they also produced feathered baskets. In these baskets, small feathers – such as scarlet woodpecker-scalp feathers, bright-blue bluebird feathers, brilliant-yellow oriole or meadowlark feathers, and iridescent-green mallard duck scalp feathers – were incorporated into the basket, held in with the basket's stitching. Thus, a completed basket's exterior was covered with a velvet-like coating of fine feathers. Such baskets were further embellished with abalone shell pendants and clamshell disc beads.

Many supreme Pomo artists created exquisite works of basketry art. While it was unusual for men to weave, both William Benson (1862-1937) and his wife Mary (c. 1878-1930) wove baskets of a quality rivaling the best produced anywhere; some of the coiled baskets had a stitch count of over 32 stitches per inch.

The Bensons, weaving for the non-Indian market, pushed basketry beyond the traditionally-accepted Pomoan style and made it into textile

sculpture.[8] Similarly, others weavers such as Joseppa Dick (c. 1860-1905), produced exquisitely designed basketry with fine stitching (sometimes as many as 41 stitches per inch).[9] Cache Creek Pomo-Patwin weaver Mabel McKay (1907-1993) was renowned for her feathered and beaded baskets, and she taught the art of basketry to both Indian and non-Indian weavers, helping to insure the art's survival.

Other central California peoples also produced excellent baskets; the Patwin and Maidu were renowned for their fine coiled baskets. The Patwin made baskets in both single-rod and three-rod coiling (like their Pomo neighbors to the east), but the Maidu produced only three-rod baskets. Farther south, the Yokuts and Western Mono made coiled baskets using a foundation of bunch grass stalks, and the Miwok made baskets using all of the above-mentioned coiling techniques.

Just after the turn of the century, Yosemite Valley, in Southern Miwok territory, became an important locale for the development of basketry into an art form produced solely for sale to non-Indians. Around 1910 weavers of mixed Southern Miwok and Mono Lake Paiute ancestry (Mono Lake Paiute people had come across the Sierra Nevada into Yosemite Valley) began to create a fancy style of three-rod coiled basketry with black and red patterns. The design style was encouraged by the Yosemite Indian Field Days, a rodeo-fair event held in Yosemite during summers of the 1920s; basketry contests at the Field Days spurred weavers to produce baskets with extremely fine stitching (sometimes exceeding 30

stitches per inch) and complex patterning. Individual women such as Lucy Telles, Carrie Bethel, Nellie and Tina Charlie and Leanna Tom were recognized as artists, and collectors eagerly sought to acquire their baskets.[10]

Women in southern California wove both coiled and twined baskets, though fewer twined baskets were made (they included winnowers, sieves, seed beaters and asphaltum-coated water bottles [made by the Chumash]). A wide variety of baskets, many very finely woven, were made with coiling. A highly developed design style evolved in certain Chumash groups; specific patterns and design placement were rigidly followed (for example, alternating colors of stitching on a basket's rim and the principal design band's placement on the upper part of the basket).

As early as the late-18th century, southern California Indian women began to make baskets for foreigners. Spanish officials stationed there often obtained Chumash baskets as gifts for visiting European dignitaries, thus excellent examples of Chumash basketry are contained in museum collections in Germany, Spain and England. By the end of the 19th century, when basket collecting became a fashionable hobby in the United States, southern California weavers again filled the demand by weaving thousands of baskets for non-Indian patrons.[11]

Ceremonial regalia

Ceremonial dances were an important part of Native people's existence throughout California. Dances often manifested supernatural power; they were extremely complex performances and were usually considered prayers in visible form. A great array of carefully crafted ceremonial regalia was indispensable to these dances.[12]

In central California, dance regalia differed among dances. Flicker-quill headbands were used in most of them, however. These bands were made with salmon-pink scraped-feather quills of the common flicker (a woodpecker-like bird) and each band required the feathers from 20 to 60 birds. Many of the dances also required dancers to wear feather capes (most often men wore them on their backs). The capes were made from large feathers obtained from hawks, eagles, vultures, condors or various waterfowl.

In addition to flicker-quill headbands, a wide variety of headgear was worn in different ceremonial dances, with many styles reserved for specific spirit impersonators. Pomo women sometimes wore fur-covered forehead bands decorated with short, projecting quills. Each quill was ornamented with a small mat made of sewn flicker quills and beads. Both men and women wore feather bunches on their heads. These were made of feathers tied and coiled into a bristling tuft.

The Patwin, Valley Maidu and Pomo made a headpiece known as the 'bighead' which was worn by spirit impersonators in the *Hesi* ceremony. The headpiece was over four feet in diameter and made up of about 100 stripped willow shoots. The shoots were usually painted red and tipped with white waterfowl feathers, then thrust into a bundle of tule tied on to the dancer's head. The headpiece looked like an immense pincushion.

Elaborately decorated, woven feather belts were perhaps the most remarkable achievement in ceremonial regalia of central California. The belts, produced primarily by the Valley Maidu (Konkow) and Patwin, averaged six feet (2m) in length and about five inches (12cm) in width. They were woven of native milkweed or hemp fiber in a weft-face weave; included in the weaving were small, scarlet scalp feathers of about 500 acorn woodpeckers, and iridescent-green scalp feathers of some 100 male mallard ducks. These feathers were arranged in alternating panels, and

This late-18th or early-19th century Chumash basket (top left), tightly woven of split juncus, was used to stone-boil acorn mush.

The Pomo artist William Benson (1862-1936) created this elegant man's hairpin (above) of incised deer bone and tiny woodpecker, bluebird, meadowlark and quail feathers bound with deer sinew.

Dance regalia differs greatly among California Indian groups. This Yurok man (right) wears the regalia for the Jump Dance, including a headband of brilliant red pileated woodpecker scalps. The trident-like hairpin (below) was popular with a variety of groups in central California. This example is most like those used by Pomo dancers.

the red panels were further ornamented with small olivella-shell disc beads which had been baked in ashes of a fire to turn them white. Such a belt was the most expensive item in the trade economy of central California, worth three large feathered baskets, several bearskins, or over 1000 clamshell disc beads.[13] The belts, which were worn by men in ceremonial dances such as the *Hesi*, testified to the group's wealth and dedication to using their best when dancing to ask for the spirits' protection.

In northwestern California, featherwork was also an important part of dance regalia. Woodpecker scalps (from pileated, or less commonly, acorn woodpeckers) were considered a visible manifestation of an individual's wealth and they were used in a myriad of ways: headbands worn by men in the Jump Dance required more than 30 pileated or 200 acorn woodpecker scalps; albino deerskins carried in the White Deerskin Dance and otter-fur quivers carried in the Brush Dance were trimmed with them; most hairpins worn by male dancers, and some women's basketry caps and braid ornaments were also ornamented with either entire scalps or individual tufts of scarlet feathers.

Women's dance regalia in northwestern California was elaborate, and produced its own music from the hundreds of shells and shell beads used in necklaces and as decoration on dance aprons. Women wore a front apron, which was often made of bear grass woven over buckskin cords and pine nuts or glass beads. This was worn with a back apron ornamented with beargrass and maidenhair fern stem with an upper fringe of beads and abalone shell pendants, and a lower fringe of fine buckskin thongs. The rustling of the shells against one another produced a pleasing sound that is inseparable from the music of the dances on the lower Klamath River region.

Dance regalia in southern California was more limited than that to the north. Perhaps the most elaborate regalia in the region was produced among the Chumash and their neighbors. Skirts were made of strings twisted from native fiber

incorporating eagle down, so that each string became a white, fluffy streamer; these were often tipped with sections of jet-black crow feathers or cinnamon-colored mature red-tailed hawk tail feathers. Men sometimes wore a high feather crown of magpie or roadrunner tail feathers surrounded with black crow feathers, and then with a band of white eagle-down tied across the brow. The headpieces also bore testimony to the owner's wealth and to the abundant bird life of the region, as only the center feathers from magpie tails were used in the headpieces, and more than 50 birds were needed to manufacture a single headpiece.[14]

Quill bands, similar to those of central California, were made by the Chumash and their southern neighbors. These bands differed, however, from the flicker headbands made farther north, as they were usually used as streamers and attached to poles at ceremonial sites, or worn

as bandoleers. They also differed in that the section of stripped quills was narrow (averaging about two inches/5cm) and were solidly bordered by the unstripped feather. The bands were made of feathers not only from flickers, but also from crows and jays, as well as small feathers of pelicans and condors.

Also worn by Chumash men, and by the Cahuilla, Tipai-Ipai, and neighboring groups, was a net skirt which had a lower edge fringed with eagle or condor feathers. The skirt, worn with a headband of owl fluffs and head plumes of stripped great horned owl feathers, comprised the costume for the Whirling Dance.

Beadwork

Beads were an important part of the economy of Native California long before the arrival of Europeans. Among the Yurok, Karok, Hupa and their neighbors, tusk-shaped dentalium shells (obtained in trade from the north) were a standard currency. Beads of bull pine nuts and juniper seeds were used by women to decorate ceremonial regalia.[15] The Pomo and Coast Miwok just north of San Francisco Bay were the primary suppliers of clamshell disc beads to northern and central California.[16] The Pomo also produced highly valued, pink stone beads made from magnesite. On the southern coast near Santa

Barbara, the Chumash produced olivella-shell disc beads as well as soapstone beads.

Glass beads were brought to California as early as 1542 with the explorer Juan Rodriguez Cabrillo, but they did not become common until they were distributed as a result of missionary activities between 1769 and 1800. By the first half of the 19th century, opaque, white glass beads and translucent green glass or white glass beads coated with a red exterior, along with less common green, blue and black beads were widely used in central California.

It was not until sometime in the later half of the 19th century, however, that woven beadwork bands were first produced in California. Woven beadwork technique, and many patterns, reached California from the Wasco and their neighbors in the Columbia River region through interior groups in Oregon. The method of making woven beadwork bands using a 'loose-warp' technique was quickly assimilated by the Klamath, Modoc, Achomawi, Wintu and their neighbors, probably sometime around or just before 1870.[17]

Along with the technique of making woven beadwork strips, certain patterns and forms came to California from the Columbia River Region. Eight-pointed stars, serrated diamonds and pairs of triangles linked together along a central dividing line were among the most enduring of motifs to be used in California. One form which was used in California with little change was the multi-tab, octopus bag of the Wasco. Produced entirely in woven beadwork, the Wasco bag was usually multi-colored with a variety of designs. The Wintu version of the bag was somewhat changed, incorporating a closing flap at the top

Clamshell disc beads were a valuable currency in California, and this necklace (left), further enhanced with woodpecker scalps, quail topknots and abalone pendants, was an extremely valuable possession of its Pomoan owner.

Woven glass beadwork, such as this Wintu shot bag collected in 1872, was popular in northern California. Bold designs and use of only a few colors characterize beadwork among the Wintu and their neighbors in the 1870s.

The Hupa and their neighbors, perhaps more than any other Californian group, made beautiful and functional objects from antler. These spoons (above), carved from the base of an elk's antler, were used by men for eating acorn soup. Highly valued, only one pair could be made from an adult bull-elk's antlers, since the bone at the top of the skull was needed to make the bowl of the spoon. The elk antler purse (below) is ornamented with fine incising and drilled dots. Its opening is covered with an incised bone slat, was hollowed out for holding valuable dentalium shell money.

(usually produced with red, black or blue designs on a white ground), and making use of only a few simple, but striking, geometric patterns.[18]

By the 1890s, Paiute people along the eastern flank of California were also producing woven beadwork bands, although they often made them using a bow loom. Their use of this style of beadwork facilitated the introduction of beadwork to groups such as the Southern Miwok and Maidu across the Sierra, although beadwork never gained a strong foothold with either.

Beadwork is still produced today by members of many groups in California some of it still relating to the earliest techniques, but much more of it is wholly new.

Sculpture

The archeological record in California provides ample proof of the antiquity of stone sculpture. While various types of plummet-shaped charms are known to have been produced since perhaps 2000 BC in central California, the most elaborate stone carvings were produced in the Chumash and Gabrielino areas.

A wide variety of effigies were produced by the Chumash, primarily from steatite (soapstone).

Some were small models of plank boats. The little boats were highly prized charms for boat builders, insuring good luck in fishing. The charms' owners sometimes kept several to be assured of fishing success. When the owner died, the small charms were buried with him.

Other sculptured effigies are representations of specific animals, but there is great variation in the degrees of realism with which they were made. Many of the charms represent whales: some clearly and accurately detail the mammal's anatomy, while others are more abstract representations, lacking fins, eyes and other details. Other effigies are phallic in nature, or represent fish, seals and birds.

In the northwest corner of California, the Yurok, Karok, Hupa and their neighbors produced a limited amount of utilitarian sculpture. Men carved sleek redwood canoes with elegant prows and sterns, each made from a single tree; the boats were the primary mode of conveyance on the Klamath River. Wooden trunks, carved from a solid block of redwood, were used to store ceremonial regalia and other valuables. Tubular pipes were made from dense yew wood, usually fitted with soapstone bowls. So exquisite was the workmanship on these pipes that early explorers marveled at their symmetry and thought they must have been turned on a lathe.

Antler provided another medium for sculpture among the peoples of the lower Klamath River. Sections of elk antler were scraped, carved, polished and incised to produce what the Native people called purses: small boxes with fitted lids used to store dentalium shell money. The section of the antler that attaches to the elk's skull was used to carve elaborate spoons that had intricately carved handles decorated with delicate cut-out patterns. These spoons were used by men to eat acorn mush and served as an elegant symbol of the people's wealth and prestige.[19]

Rock art

Although rock art is found throughout California, it appears to be concentrated in specific areas.

Both petroglyphs (patterns pecked, abraded or ground into stone) and pictographs (patterns applied to the stone with paint or pigment in one or more colors) are found, although there seems to be little overlap in the two techniques.

Rock art seems to be an ancient style of art in California, so old that in most areas Indian people ascribed the rock art to people who lived in the area before them, or to legendary beings. One of the few areas for which information exists about the ethnographic use and production of rock art is among the Chumash.[20] Chumash rock-paintings were probably produced by elite shaman-priests. They seem to incorporate astronomical data as it was associated with Chumash cosmology and mythology. The production of such paintings, at least among some of the Chumash, was tied to the time of the winter solstice. One Chumash story tells of a neighboring Gabrielino sorcerer who caused a famine and many deaths by producing a painting on rocks of many falling men and women who were bleeding from their mouths.

Indeed, some of the finest rock art in North America is found in the Chumash area. In the mountains north of Mount Piños, in the territory of the Emigdiano Chumash, is the most elaborate extant Chumash rock art site: it comprises four shallow caves, each of which has walls covered with finely executed paintings of large circular motifs with concentric rings, anthropomorphic and zoomorphic figures, dots, bifurcated and zig-zag patterns in black, white, yellow, cream, green, blue-green, red and orange. The green and orange are unique, among the Chumash, to this single site. It has been speculated that the colors were obtained from Mexican sources during the revolt of 1824, and that the use of these 'foreign' colors may have been an attempt to gain supernatural power over the Mexicans during the revolt.[21]

Today

Many of the arts discussed are no longer produced in California, while some skills, such as basketry, survive among some groups. On the lower Klamath River, weavers such as Susan Burdick

preserve and continue the fine weaving that characterizes the area, just as Konkow Maidu weaver Rella Allen and Maidu weaver Lily Baker make the traditional coiled basketry of their region.

Some skills, such as the manufacture of steatite carvings in southern California, had not been practiced for many years until they were revived in the past decade by William Pink (Cupeño) and L. Frank Manriquez (Tongva-Ajachme[22]); they produced pieces of high quality that rival the best of prehistoric examples. Similarly, Hupa-Yurok artist George Blake's fine sinew-backed bows, elk-horn spoons and purses, redwood trunks and canoes are among the finest extant examples of these objects.

Traditional artists demonstrate their skills to the public at special events and at recreated Native villages in many locations throughout California. Perhaps the best-known demonstrator today is Julia Parker, a Pomo woman who has demonstrated the traditional skills and basketry of her husband's Miwok-Paiute family to visitors to Yosemite National Park since 1960. An accomplished basket weaver, Mrs. Parker says:

'I always say I wouldn't be what I am and couldn't weave like I do without the women who came before me. I feel like a little bit of them comes out in me whenever I weave.'[23]

This painted panel was made by Chumash people near Pleito Creek. It is representative of the multi-colored rock art of the Chumash, which seems to have reached its most complex development in the Carrizo Plains, a barren region in the northeast corner of Chumash country. Pictographs such as this one were probably produced by elite shaman-priests of Chumash society. The exact significance of the bold geometric forms found in this panel are unknown. Many similar painted panels are found in remote areas and it is probable that these rock art sites are shrines or sacred spots. Other rock art panels are found near seasonal seed-gathering and hunting camps. Some of the finest pictographs in California were produced by the Chumash.

THE NORTHWEST COAST

'It is easy to become entranced by the soft curtain of age, seeing this instead of what it obscures. . . . This is not what their creators intended. These were objects of bright pride, to be admired in the newness of their crisply carved lines, the powerful flow of sure elegant curves and recesses – yes, and in the brightness of fresh paint. They told the people the completeness of their culture, the continuing lineages of the great families, their closeness to the magic world of universal myth and legend.

BILL REID (HAIDA)[1]

Sophisticated, vital and brilliant, the Northwest Coast visual arts have captivated the imagination and appreciation of foreign visitors for over 200 years. It is this time period Euro-Americans have designated as 'traditional' but which represents merely an epoch in an art tradition that has spanned hundreds, if not thousands of years. Contact with Euro-Americans resulted in a florescence in the art, and it is from about 1749 until the present, that our most impressive museum collections of Northwest Coast art derive. As with most non-western cultures, the Northwest Coast languages did not have a word for 'art', though by no means did their culture lack esthetic values, principles, or appreciation of the practice of the visual arts. Indeed, their culture had specialists in art production – both men and women – who enjoyed long careers and held intertribal reputations for excellence. Almost every aspect of their extensive material culture inventory was or could have been embellished by any number of the decorative arts. Art on the Northwest Coast was a fact of everyday life rather than simply reserved for the elite or in special locations.

The people and cultures of the Northwest Coast occupied the narrow strip of island-dotted land from Yukatat Bay in Alaska to the Columbia River in what is now the state of Washington. Facing the Pacific Ocean to the west and confined to the coastal waters by the towering and most impenetrable coastal range of mountains on the east, the people evolved a distinctive cultural response to their largely maritime environment. The northern groups were the Tlingit of the Alaskan coast, the Tsimshian of the inland coastal waterways of the Nass and Skeena Rivers, the Haida of the Queen Charlotte Islands, and their relatives, the Kaigani Haida of the Prince of Wales Archipelago. The Wakashan or central groups of the coast between the Tsimshian in the North and the Kwakiutl in the south were the Bella Bella (or Northern Wakashan), and the Salishan-speaking Bella Coola. On the north and eastern shores of Vancouver Island and adjoining mainland were the group of tribes known as the Kwakiutl. The west coast of Vancouver Island and the tip of the Olympic Peninsula were occupied by the Nuu-chah-nulth (formerly the Nootka or Westcoast) and their relatives the Makah. The southernmost tribe was the Coast Salish of the Puget Sound and lower mainland.

The Practice of Art

If we could take a journey back in time, travel by an elegant wooden canoe to our hosts' home, we would pull up on the pebble beach of the village's protected cove. The dense cedar forest rises dark, huge and formidable behind the row of houses glowing in the silver patina of their weathered cedar facades. Massive gabled houses lining the beaches and monumental crest poles creating a veritable curtain of images in front of the houses further diminish our human dimensions.

The Haida rattle (above left) is painted with classic northern formline designs. Subtle, precise carving places the painted lines of the spirit animal's face in low relief. The Tsimshian ceremonial *T'Kul* rattle (main picture), carved in fine grained wood, depicts supernatural frogs springing from the eyes of the Wind Spirit.

Robes or tunics were often worn for ceremonies. Here we have a Kaigani Haida painted robe (right and far left) and a woven Chilkat tunic (main picture) upon which the rattle rests. Using a painted 'pattern board' as the guide, formline designs, as seen on the tunic, were meticulously copied with all their intricate and subtle curves. The weavers were able to combine various sophisticated techniques with different weights of weft threads to render a technically exceptional tapestry.

This beautiful crest hat (below) was worn by a high-ranking member of the Chilkat tribe. A collaboration between a weaver and a carver, this hat is painted with a killer whale on its brim. The Raven's cry is almost audible from the animated carving on the crown. A tribute to the weaver's skill, some Tlingit carvers of solid wooden clan helmets (right) imitated the skip-stitched twined patterning of woven hat brims.

Experience of the monumental is precisely the theme underlying the production of the material culture of these coastal cultures.[2] Harnessing the invisible forces of society, nature and the supernatural by making them visible was a task particularly relished by Northwest Coast artists. Challenged by the task, these artists translated the idea of monumental not only in the size of their artistic productions, but by the degree of spiritual and material complexity in their arts. The same theme of monumentality may be found in a giant crest pole or in a tiny ivory charm; the conception guiding the artist's eye and hand is larger than a single human life; the art makes visible the contemplation of the invisible.

Who were the artists? As a general observation, women were the weavers of the Coast while men were the carvers and painters. There were exceptions, but generally women wove the garments, baskets and mats to furnish the comfort of daily life and enrich the spectacle of ceremonial life.[3] Men carved primarily in wood, though also in stone, bone and ivory, often combining their three-dimensional art with two-dimensional painted designs. Their arts formed the massive structures found in the material culture as well as the smaller embellished instruments of the hunt, food preparation, and ceremony. Not infrequently, the arts involved varying degrees of collaboration as the weaver's talents were combined with those of the carver.

There were distinct though shared artistic conventions on the Coast, each with their own principles of composition and esthetic rules. Northwest Coast artists' adherence to these rules over large geographic areas through the centuries is impressive – and forms a stunning chapter in world art history. Forging metals and making and firing pottery were virtually unknown in traditional times. Yet, with few and relatively simple tools, Northwest Coast artists employed a myriad of techniques to manipulate mostly wood and wood fibers into an astonishingly large inventory of cultural objects that served all the purposes of life.

Throughout the region, the visual images were almost entirely representations of animals or humans.[4] Though the exact meaning of an image might be restricted to those who know the artist's intent, learning the basic vocabulary of forms gives the viewer access to a visual syntax of tremendous depth. Conventionalized identifying features distinguish one animal from another: the long, slender straight beak of Raven differs from the heavy, sharply down-curved beak of Eagle; Killer-Whale's long, upright dorsal fin marked with a circle contrasts with the smaller, blunt dorsal of Gray Whale; Beaver's image is characterized by long incisor teeth and a cross-hatched tail (for the scales) whereas Grizzly Bear is known by a square snout and large-toothed mouth with prominent canines and a protruding tongue. The system of identification is relatively simple when the artist chooses a simple, naturalistic representation, but becomes more complex when these conventionalized features become hidden in the design or when the design itself is of a lesser known natural or supernatural creature. A sea-monster, for example may have a wolf or bear head, but dorsal fins on its back, and flippers or fins on the joints of limbs that end in claws. Subtle variations in the depiction of an

One of the most distinctive and sophisticated design elements known by northern artists was first academically analyzed by the art historian, Bill Holm in his definitive work on northern two-dimensional design. Holm described the calligraphic-like line found in northern design as the 'formline', a broad line with a single pulse that started and finished with a tapered point. Elements of two-dimensional designs were unified by seemingly continuous formlines. The primary forms of the design were defined first in black and called primary formlines. Secondary formlines, in red, further elaborated the form. The remaining spaces were either unpainted background spaces, or tertiary forms that were outlines with thin black or red lines, or were sometimes painted blue. Formline design

Carved and ornamented helmets worn by Tlingit warriors rested on a carved wooden visor that covered the face from the eyes down, thus rendering the armored man as a towering figure. Slat armor of hardwood slats wrapped in sinew cord, and an ornate dagger completed the impressive display. This scowling face (below) was made more fearsome by a bristling facial hair of inlaid bear fur; locks of human hair were pegged into place above the forehead.

anatomical part such as a beak may identify the specific species of bird.[5]

Esthetic considerations governed the arrangement of these conventional features of the subjects. Artists distorted, exaggerated and rearranged the anatomy of whatever was being portrayed to fit the design field. Artists composed designs through such conventions as: x-ray imaging where ribs, backbones, organs and joints are made visible; split-representation where the body image is split to show the frontal and back views or both sides of a figure simultaneously; and visual punning where one ambiguous feature may result in an image being read as two different subjects. Complexity of form was matched by complexity of iconography. Recorded information about what the art meant to owner and carver is surprisingly meager.[6] We cannot always know the full constellation of meanings surrounding a given object; some levels of meaning were personal and specific to a particular time and place. Yet understanding only some of the fundamental forms, techniques and principles of design opens lenses to a richness and complexity in the practice of Northwest art that allows stirring insight into some of those meanings and into the potential for innovation, invention, and excellence.

Elaborate serving spoons and ladles were made from mountain goat and mountain sheep horn. The most ornate and most complex of these were the two-piece horn spoons (above). The handle was made of intricately carved mountain goat horn that preserved the natural shape of the arched tapered horn. Brass or copper rivets attached the dark, luminous handle with its three-dimensional carvings of the family's crests to a delicate amber bowl of mountain sheep horn that had been steamed to a simple, yet elegant bowl. These horn spoons were made by master artists and reserved for formal feasts.

included distinctive elements given visually descriptive names by Holm: ovoids (and their elaboration, salmon-trout heads), to depict eyes and the joints of the body; U-forms (and the variation Split U-forms), to depict ears, flukes and fin shapes; and S-forms (and the variation Split S-forms), to depict ribs and feathers.[7]

Remarkably, this design system, given its economy of elements and conventions, permitted a limitless range of images and interpretive innovations. Though genres of objects – for example, spoons, boxes, dancing robes, frontlet headdresses – evolved specific design codes, individual artists varied their interpretation of the codes. Personal interpretation of the tradition resulted in the stylistic signatures of individual artists that can be identified from preliterate times.[8]

Less well-defined, but no less significant or impressive are the Nuu-chah-nulth and Makah two-dimensional design systems. Though clearly related to the northern design conventions, there are other design elements unique to the area: curlicues, thin crosses and rows of dots, and discontinuous, though sensuous, thin lines of solid color. Figures tended to be less abstract, more representational, and portrayed in dramatic profile with asymmetrical eyelid forms. Coast Salish

design was primarily expressed in three dimensions. Arguably, the Coast Salish were influenced by the pervasive northern design, for ovoids and U-forms with conventionalized cuneiform-like gouges in their centers were sometimes employed in low relief carvings, but their geometric compositions were freer in spatial organization than in the north. Usually, Salish three-dimensional design is characterized by bold geometric elements, broad flat planes intersecting one another, and generalized, though fluid, limbs and torsos.

Unfortunately we know much of this art from the objects that rest silently in museum and gallery collections; they serve as dramatic memories of voices, times and places in the not-too-distant past. We connect and reconnect the objects with the artists, the artists with the cultures, mindful that our attempts to contextualize and reconstruct usually fall short of a complete appreciation of that time of monumental achievements in making the social and the supernatural worlds visible. It will be useful to scan some of these high achievements, these 'objects of bright pride', to glimpse not only the tremendous power and elegance of their expression, but to gather perspective on an art that was a way of life.

Houses – Containers of the Cosmos

Virtually all of the early Euro-American explorers on the northern Pacific Coast were astonished and impressed by the huge dwellings of the Northwest Coast peoples. The massive structures towered against the forested stands, occupying the thin strips of beach on protected coves and bays. Planked and gabled, the houses were made of cedar and were large enough to hold several families. Usually arranged in a single row along the beach, or two rows if the frontage property was restricted, the rectangular structures imposed a built reality to the misty coast. Northwest Coast people lived in these permanent villages almost year-round, sometimes having a summer village location as well as a winter one.

Red cedar (*Thuja plicata*) was the material favored by Northwest Coast builders. The huge trees were selected, harvested, prepared and assembled by skilled craftsmen working under the directions of one or more specialists. In traditional Northwest Coast society, the building of these massive structures was a complicated and expensive undertaking requiring the commissioning of a coordinating architect who supervised the

selection, felling and transportation of large cedar logs to the building site, the splitting of planks and forming of posts and beams. The owner of the house fed, sheltered and compensated the workers at every stage of construction, from the assembling of materials to the raising of the posts and beams. Frequently artists were employed to embellish posts and beams with adzed flutes or carved crest images of animal spirits. Wealthier house owners commissioned massive paintings representing clan figures that covered entire house fronts. In postcontact times almost every northern-style house had a huge carved 'totem' pole gracing its facade.

The final expense was the ceremonial occasion or potlatch that marked the completion of the structure with feasting and the naming of the house.[9] Some families took years to build a house, and only the wealthy could begin such a commission after assembling and committing the resources of all the members of their extended family. The labor was intensive, traditionally undertaken with simple tools and without the benefit of tack or pulleys. Using levers, fulcrums, ropes and raw human strength, posts were set into the ground, beams hoisted to their lofty summits, and massive planks then attached to the

Raven rattles formed part of the chiefly costume of the north. One of the best known forms of rattles on the Northwest Coast, and iconographically one of the least understood, this rattle (above) depicts the supernatural Raven, neck and beak extended, wings close to the body, with the reclining figure of a human on its back. Usually the human has a protruding tongue that is shared or exchanged by another animal, frequently a frog or bird. *Skahemsen*, the Tsimshian name for the transformation image, is on the belly of the rattle and has a beaked nose curving into its mouth. Such ceremonial paraphernalia was abundant, as shown in this display of wealth (left) in the Tlingit Whale House at Klukwan.

between pairs of vertical poles placed along the outside of the house's frame posts.

The northern post and beam house built by the Tlingit, Haida, Tsimshian and Northern Wakashan people had gabled roofs formed by massive roof beams. In contrast to the southern type houses, northern houses for the most part had thick vertical planks up to 2ft (60cm) wide whose tapered ends slotted into grooves in the roof beams and ground level sills.[11] The interior of the house was similar in concept to southern houses, with raised platforms for seating and sleeping. At least one house in every village, usually that of the village chief and therefore the largest house, had an excavated interior. Entry into these houses was at ground level with one or two levels of concentric platforms surrounding the subterranean central fire. The chief's family occupied the rear of the house, their quarters often separated from the rest of the house by a large screen of painted planks. Families of lesser rank were to the left and right of the screen, with those of the least rank next to the front door. The roof planks of these houses were often secured with rock-weighted boards and there was a movable opening in the roof to provide optimum ventilation for the central fire. Doors were traditionally at the front of the house, often through a central or portal house post. Other doors at the rear of the house were provided for emergency exits, and a special door was made in the rear of a house to remove the body of a deceased family member after the period of lying in state.

The house remains one of the most impressive of Northwest Coast artifacts, splendid in design and execution of its form, and astonishingly monumental in its concept and function. The wonder of the early travelers to the coast is mirrored by all those who encounter Northwest Coast houses for the first time. The structures were massive, made from massive materials. Strangers, after suffusing their wonderment, ask why? Surely a people with such impressive technology for splitting and building shelters could have built smaller, single family dwellings. The answer is

This view of the eastern end of the Haida village of Cumshewa (above) illustrates some of the variety in forms of 'totem' or crest poles. Here house frontal poles were interspersed with single mortuary and memorial poles. The house on the right, named 'House That Makes a Great Noise' has a frontal pole with three *Skils* or watchmen at the top. House names, crest images, and the songs, stories and dances associated with them were the exclusive property of the owners and demonstrated the history and hereditary prerogatives of the lineage.

structures. If the labor to build a house was based on brute strength, the resulting architecture was simple yet elegant in thought and form. Northwest Coast houses were not only functionally durable, but they were also ingeniously suited to the environmental, spiritual and social needs of the occupants.

Fundamentally there were two kinds of architectural constructions for the post and beam framed houses of the coast; the northern type with house planking that was integral to the structure and the southern type with planked walls structurally separate from the main framework.[10] The southern type had two variations: the shed-roofed house, with rectangular posts, and the Wakashan house style with posts supporting two eave beams and one or two larger central ridge beams. Typically found in southern areas including the Coast Salish, Southern Kwakiutl, Nuu-chah-nulth and Bella Coola, both the shed-roofed house and the Wakashan house had walls of wide horizontal planks hung and lashed

cultural rather than technological. From a sociological viewpoint, a Northwest Coast individual was part of an extended family, a lineage. As such, the house sheltered more than one's parents and children; it sheltered the lineage. In contemporary terms, the Northwest Coast house was more of a small apartment building than a nuclear family home. The house was for part of the year a profane place, site of the mundane stuff of everyday life: fish and game hung drying in its smoky rafters; people slept, ate and worked in its roomy shelter, interior platforms provided hidden storage space for clothing, foodstuffs, tools, hunting and ceremonial paraphernalia. Attached porches and semi-attached decks provided warm-weather spaces for gambling, gossiping and otherwise enjoying the company of others.

From a ritual and ceremonial viewpoint, the house was transformed in the dark months of winter into a site of sacred events. Figuratively and literally the house became the center of the universe as the people gathered to witness the speeches, songs, dances, masked performances and rituals that enacted and validated their ancestral claims to the lineage's supernatural origins, property rights, wealth and traditions. Painted screens and interior houseposts carved with clan images heightened the sense of bringing together and making visible the social and the supernatural. New members of the lineage were thus socialized into the interrelationships of family and the supernatural; strangers and newcomers were educated to the valid claims of the lineage to supernatural ancestry and inherited social prerogatives that formed the exclusive property of the lineage. In this way lineages confirmed their relationship to every other lineage, to the larger clan units and ultimately to the cosmos. The names of some of the larger houses frequently referred to the vaunted position of the lineage's claims: The Monster House, House Split-in-Two-by-the-Sun, Thunder-Rolls-Upon-It, House-Chiefs-Peep-at-from-a-Distance, and Mountain House. The names are fitting to the sizes of the houses, but also to the monumentality

Representing the personal crests of Skidegate IV, owner of 'Raven's House', this interior house post (left) at the rear of the house faced the door. The figure of Raven on the top of the pole holds two frogs and a man in its beak. Below the man is Thunderbird with its large recurved beak. The Thunderbird lived on mountain tops and here holds its prey, a whale, in its talons. Deadly lightning is said to issue from this monster bird's eyes, and the flapping of its wings produced thunder.

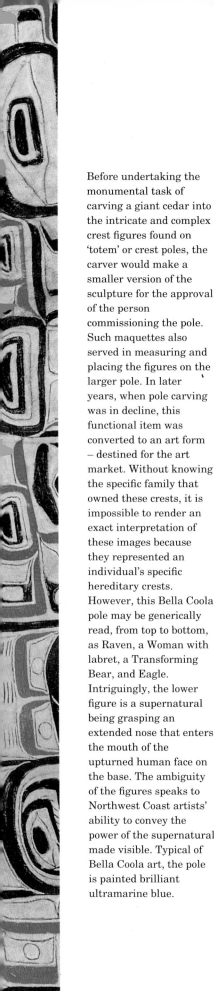

Before undertaking the monumental task of carving a giant cedar into the intricate and complex crest figures found on 'totem' or crest poles, the carver would make a smaller version of the sculpture for the approval of the person commissioning the pole. Such maquettes also served in measuring and placing the figures on the larger pole. In later years, when pole carving was in decline, this functional item was converted to an art form – destined for the art market. Without knowing the specific family that owned these crests, it is impossible to render an exact interpretation of these images because they represented an individual's specific hereditary crests. However, this Bella Coola pole may be generically read, from top to bottom, as Raven, a Woman with labret, a Transforming Bear, and Eagle. Intriguingly, the lower figure is a supernatural being grasping an extended nose that enters the mouth of the upturned human face on the base. The ambiguity of the figures speaks to Northwest Coast artists' ability to convey the power of the supernatural made visible. Typical of Bella Coola art, the pole is painted brilliant ultramarine blue.

of their social and symbolic function in Northwest Coast cultural life.

As quickly as Northwest Coast technology and culture changed with exposure to Euro-American culture, innovations to housing also appeared. Grander houses featured European-style doors and windows, gingerbread gables and even picket fences. With missionization and the dramatic decimation of the population through disease in the late-19th and early-20th century, the building of large communal houses eventually gave way to smaller, though often no less grand, two storey frame houses. Some of the villages, such as those of the Haida at Ninstints, Tanu and Skedans, suffered such extreme losses that the villages were abandoned before the houses could ever be built. Posts, beams, and planks have decayed – melted back into the forest that gave them life. In one site, fluted house beams that once supported the roof of the cosmos lie shrouded in the moss of the forest floor, giving new life to spruce. Skeletal is the wrong word to describe these fallen giants. For the Haida, they are fulfilling their destiny to complete the cycle of being first part of the natural world, then the cultural world, before returning – transformed and part of our memory – to nature.

Crest Poles – Heraldic Monuments in Cedar

The monumentality of the great planked houses of the Northwest Coast was complemented by the massive carved sculptures commonly but improperly called 'totem poles'.[12] The term 'crest poles' reflects what even the earliest Euro-American seamen knew: the images on the poles were never worshiped or part of religious ceremonies, but were a visual record of the owner's hereditary ancestors, a heraldic device that proclaimed for all to see the social positioning and antiquity of the family lineage.[13] Crest poles came in many forms and had various functions; generically however, a pole was made from a large vertical cedar shaft and covered with interlocking images of supernatural clan ancestors.

There are various types of crest poles. The most frequently depicted is the free-standing singular

crest pole. Depending on its function, the pole depicted the crests of a living family or commemorated the memory of a recently deceased person of high rank. Other memorial poles among the northern groups were sometimes simply tall cedar shafts, topped by a single massive crest animal, such as Thunder-bird, Raven, Bear or Eagle. Crest poles were also features of house architecture. Some were attached directly to the front of a house. When these house frontal poles had an entrance carved in the lower portion of the pole – usually through the belly or mouth of the lowest creature – the pole was a house portal or entrance pole. Usually these kinds of entrances were considered highly symbolic as orifices of the house and were thus used only on ceremonial occasions. Separate doors were placed beside the pole for every day use. Corner posts and interior house posts were also appropriate spaces to place crest carvings. Welcoming figures, such as those found among the Kwakiutl, were placed on the beach to welcome guests. These large human or animal forms were carved from a single log and had attached extended arms. Similar monumental sculptures have been recorded among the Haida as ridicule or shaming poles, where the purpose was not to welcome guests, but to humiliate them. Mortuary poles were most common among the Haida. The single mortuary pole had a cavity carved in the large end of the pole to receive a box containing the remains of the deceased. The tapered end of the pole was placed in the ground and a plank placed across the top of the pole to cover the opening. Double mortuary poles consisted of two poles with a platform between them to hold several burial boxes. As with the single pole, the covering plank was often carved in high relief and painted with the owner's crests.

Wealth was the key to demonstrating great social and supernatural power on the coast, and it was only the wealthy person who could afford the monumental sculptures adorning and surrounding the great houses. Crest poles were commissioned from recognized artists. Their reputations were well-known on the coast, and some traveled not only to other villages to fulfill commissions, but inter-tribally as well. As with house building, every aspect of making a crest pole, from selection, felling and transportation of the log to the carving and raising of the pole was paid for by the owner.[14] Compensation for this portion of the task was considerable.

Carving a crest pole was a lengthy process.[15] The prone log was stripped of bark and flattened on its back.[16] Large elbow adzes and chisels roughed out the preliminary shapes, and successively finer adzes and knives were used to refine the images. The artist used chisels to fashion mortise and tenon joints to attach appendages to the cylinder of emerging figures. Straight and curved knives completed the detail work: incised lines around the eyebrows and lids, cross-hatching on beaver tails, and undercuts for claws and wings. Small adzes gave some texture to large expanses; carvers preferred the precise, rhythmic, parallel adzing marks over smooth

Originally this Kwakiutl house pole (left) was the only entrance to a magnificent painted house front. The opened long bill of Raven served as a door to the communal house; outspread wings of the Raven were painted on the house front. Above the Raven are Bear, the Cannibal-bird *Hokhokw*, Wise One, Wolf, Killerwhale, and Thunderbird. The pole, erected in about 1899, belonged to Chief Wawkius of Alert Bay and was carved for the princely sum of 350 white blankets with black borders. In later years the pole was moved to Stanley Park in Vancouver, a reminder of its past glory.

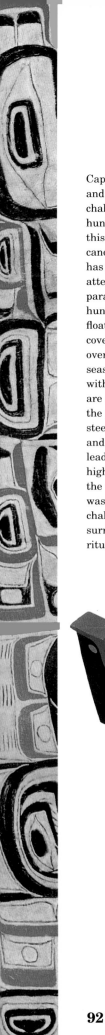

Capturing the excitement and intense focus of Nuu-chah-nulth whale hunters, the carver of this exquisite model canoe and figures (below) has paid meticulous attention to detailing the paraphernalia of the hunt: paddles, sealskin floats, harpoon, and mat-covered seats are carried over imaginary surging seas by this replica canoe with subtle grace. Eight are accurately depicted in the pursuit party: a steersman, six paddlers and the harpooner who is leader of the hunt. A highly spiritual event, the whale hunt, which was unique to the Nuu-chah-nulth, was surrounded by powerful ritual practices.

'unfinished' wood.[17] From early accounts, paint was used sparingly, if at all. Natural black, red, white and blue-green pigments were used to accent eyes, eye sockets, eyebrows, lips, tongues, and nostrils. After glossy commercial marine paints became available, southern artists added other colors to their palettes – greens, blues, yellows and whites – and painted most of the surfaces of their poles with gusto.[18]

When the pole was finished, the owner hosted a substantial potlatch. Invited guests assembled to admire the pole, to witness and validate the owner's claims to the crests depicted in the carvings, and the pole was carried to the site where it was to be erected by scores of men.[19] Drumbeats matched heartbeats as the pole inched up, dancing in the tension of ropes being pulled over the scaffolding and holding the unwieldly and precious column in balance. From a distance, the artist and his apprentices watched, their necks and waists circled with twisted cedar bark rings to which their carving tools have been attached. When the pole was up, the carvers danced at its base while those who hoisted on the ropes rested and celebrated the satisfaction of raising the pole and the triumph of its new owners.[20]

The florescence of crest pole carving probably lasted less than a century, for eventually the wealth diminished and the death rate increased. By 1920 the art had all but vanished, though almost every major museum in the Western world boasted a huge 'totem pole' in their grand entry halls. Crest poles are again being made, some for important art commissions, others to serve the age-old practices of commemorating one's claims to ancient heraldic crests and prerogatives. From lofty heights, Eagles and Ravens, Killer-Whales and Wolves, Thunderbirds and Grizzly Bears claim their places against the open skies and are cherished in the hearts of the people as emblems of a living culture.

Canoes – Monuments of the Seas

More than the principal means of transportation, the canoe was yet another feature of monumentality on the coast. Embellished with carving of prows and painted bows and sterns the canoe was more than a functional object. A floating artistic statement of rare grace and brilliant design, it is little wonder that the canoe was one of the principal measurements, along with the house and the crest pole, of a family's material wealth. The finished canoes ranged in size from large ocean-going vessels 50 to 70ft (up to 21m) in length with beams of 6 to 10ft (up to 3m). Family canoes were smaller, in the 18 to 35ft (up to 10m) range and holding 15 to 20 people, while smaller canoes

were constructed to be handled easily by as few as two people. From the Kwakiutl north, canoes were broad in the beam with both bow and stern ends swept upwards; a vertical fin under the bow cut the waves. Nuu-chah-nulth, Makah, and Quilleute hunting and fishing canoes were generally flatter on the bottom, with low rising vertical sterns and their concave prows rose dramatically into a distinctive 'snout' that abstractly resembled the head of a wolf.[21] Both of these styles of canoes had a groove in the prow to hold masts or harpoons.[22]

Carved from single massive cedar trees, the canoe required much the same expertise and expense of houses and crest poles.[23] Deep in the forest, master carvers would select sound trees with few knots, and then rough out the top and narrow the ends of the canoe. With hull, bow and stern adzed into perfect symmetry, the unfinished canoe was left over the winter to season. The following spring the canoe was righted, the interior hollowed with chisels and adzes, or on some parts of the coast, the interior was excavated using controlled burning with rocks heated red-hot in a fire.

Precision was the hallmark of the master canoe-builder. Symmetry of the exterior was matched by the even thickness of the hull.[24] The final step in making large vessels was to fill the canoe with water, drop red-hot stones into it to boil the water, and gently spread the softened wood at the gunwales. On larger canoes, prow and stern extensions were carved then pegged or sewn into place. The final embellishment of a canoe was done by a master artist who painted crest designs on the vessel. Some canoes were painted red or white in the interior; some had exteriors painted black. Others were fitted with elaborately carved crested figures that were lashed to both sides of the bow and/or stern.

Canoes were highly valued possessions, carefully protected from the elements so they would not split, lovingly and effectively patched when damaged, and handled cautiously so that they would last a decade or more. As with houses, canoes were often given hereditary names. At a potlatch, a canoe was an extravagant gift and similarly the destruction of a canoe during a potlatch was an ostentatious display of conspicuous consumption that enhanced the owner's status. Their value and grace inspired songs and their elegance inspired myth images for the mind's eye of great wealth and power.

Even functional items such as canoe paddles (top) provided a field for complicated and intricate crest designs. The formline images on these two Tlingit paddles likely came from the same hand. Beyond their obvious use, such paddles were often carried in potlatch ceremonies. Similar objects with ornate painted and inlaid surfaces were called 'song sticks' and were used to mark the words in singing.

The Haida village of Tanu (above) was still a thriving populated village at the time of this 1878 photograph. It helps to show the relative scale of monumental houses to enormous but graceful seagoing canoes. The small fishing canoe on the left is protected by a mat.

Bowls of animal horn (right) were made by cutting away the hollowed base of the horn and using moist heat to spread the sides of the bowl.

This beautiful Haida lidded container (below) is a product of superb joinery. A cedar plank was cut with three deep, grooved undercuts or kerfs that traversed its width in three precisely measured places, dividing it into four sections. The plank was then steamed and the softened wood bent 90 degrees at each kerf (see detail) to fold the groove into itself, resulting in four sides. The open corner was then pegged.

Bowls, Boxes and Baskets

Bowls of cedar, yew, alder, maple and other woods were sculpted into various geometric and anthropomorphic shapes using many of the same carving tools that were used to make canoes and crest poles. Wooden bowls could range in size from small personal feast dishes to enormous bowls used for potlatches that required several people to carry into the feast house. Animal-shaped bowls, bowls that imitated birch bark containers, bowls with supernatural human and monster figures as well as bowls with geometric contours reminiscent of canoe shapes were all part of the repertoire of Northwest Coast artists. Sometimes the rims of bowls were inlaid with opercula[25], sea otter teeth, or small pieces of abalone shell. Some wooden bowls were painted with crest designs, but most were not. Given the propensity of the wood to soak up the fish and sea mammal oils of foods served in the bowls, little more embellishment of the carved surfaces was needed. The glossy patina of well-used, oft-handled vessels was rich and mellow; the sensitive fit of the bowls'

surfaces to the embrace of human palms was timeless.[26]

So different from the bowls that were carved from single pieces of wood, the bent box or bowl with its kerfed corners and inlaid base was perhaps one of the most distinctive aspects of the Northwest Coast people's culture and technology. Using bent-wood construction, men created containers from cedar planks for everything a person would use from cradle to coffin. The cedar bent

box technology was used for obvious constructions such as storage and furniture and less obvious functions such as drumming and cooking. Bent bowls were made in the same manner as boxes, but begun with a plank that was pre-shaped with elegantly undulating rims and bulging contours with hollowed interiors. Boxes and chests were sometimes fitted with lids inlaid with opercula while bowls often had complex overhanging rims. Finishing touches to kerfed containers could include painted formline designs (flat or deeply incised), nearly three-dimensional carving in high relief, and/or abalone shell inlay.

Sometimes the weight and rigidity of a box was more than necessary for containing the stuff of life. Baskets were woven by women to function in almost all the same ways a box was used.[27] Lighter than wooden boxes, baskets were no less durable. Some baskets were designed to be flexible and even collapsible when not in use. Some baskets were of a generalized form, others were created for specific tasks; elegance of form frequently matched the ingenuity of function. There were baskets for holding babies, for collecting shellfish, for cooking, storing and serving food stuffs,[28] for carrying the tools and implements of the hunt or the harvest, for holding treasures, or for simply displaying the weaver's virtuosity. After contact with Euro-Americans and responding to a new market for their woven arts, women created basketry items that mimicked objects from the foreign culture: suitcases, dollies, lamp shades, bottles and lidded jars, plates and platters, and even tea cups and saucers.[29] Interestingly, though they were never intended for the indigenous use, these 'tourist' baskets nonetheless demonstrated some of the finest examples of the basket makers' art. Within Northwest Coast culture, well-made basketry items were valued trade items and prestigious potlatch gifts; many baskets on the coast were found far from their places of origin.

Besides the ubiquitous cedar bark, withe, and root, the Northwest Coast women harvested and used many natural materials for making their fine baskets. While no one fiber was specific to a given area of the coast, some groups had preferences. Spruce root was a favorite of northern weavers, especially the Tlingit and Haida. Nuu-chah-nulth women produced a very different kind of basketry from the many species of sedge grasses.[30] Cedar bark was an abundant and favorite construction material of the Coast Salish. Various grasses and reeds were employed by the weavers as foundation materials and for making the woven surface decoration on the baskets known as imbricating where tucks of light grasses and shiny bark strips were caught under the stitches on the basket's outer surface. Another decorative technique was known as false embroidery where bleached or dyed fibers were wrapped around the wefts at every stitch to form bands of geometric designs.[31]

The weavers used many techniques for basket making: coiling, plaiting, two- and three-strand twining, skip-stitch twining, twilled two-strand

Women were the weavers on the coast (below). Their consummate skills produced fine, decorated containers from a variety of barks and grasses for every aspect of life: from cradles to watertight cooking baskets, from lidded 'treasure baskets' (above) to potlatch hats.

Coast Salish women finger-wove ceremonial blankets on an upright fixed warp frame using reverse warping or tubular warping techniques. Some of the 'plain' blankets (top right) were of pure white mountain goat wool mixed with vegetal fibers, bird down or the hair of a small breed of now extinct dog. Decorated Salish blankets had sophisticated geometric designs – zig-zags, diamonds and triangles – rendered in natural dyes.

The photograph (bottom right) shows Tlingit dancers from Hoonah with their 'song staffs'. Many of them wear frontlet headdresses to represent their hereditary crests. The headdress was a stunning assembly of highly symbolic materials: a band of swan's down circled the head, supporting a cage of copper-colored sea-lion whiskers; red, black and copper shafted flicker feathers flanked the frontlet; a long train of white ermine skins flowed down the dancer's back. The frontlets were intricately carved and usually lavishly inlaid with abalone. Frontlet headdresses were worn by high-ranking Tlingit, Haida, Tsimshian (and, later, Kwakiutl) people as a display of their great wealth and spiritual enlightenment.

twining, warp twining, diagonal warp twining, and wrapped crossed warp, and flat weaving. While talented fingers did most of the work in creating the fine, regular surfaces of the baskets, the weaver's tool kit might also include a sharpened bone awl for piercing coiling strips, hard wood implements to press against smooth stones for flattening and smoothing the surface of twined strands, and bark splitting tools.[32]

Basketry designs were achieved with tremendous skill and dexterity. The catalogue of named designs seemed endless. Some representational designs included recognizable animal and human forms: 'wolf', 'merganser', 'man', 'dragonfly', 'butterfly'. The Nuu-chah-nulth weavers frequently depicted whaling scenes showing a harpooner standing in a canoe, his line firmly attached to a gray whale. Other design terms are more enigmatic, and seem to have a closer connection with the meanings given by the individual weaver rather than springing from a large, universal iconographic system. The names of the designs give some insight into the complex, precise woven arts that came from these consummate artists. The elegance of their artworks is matched by the poetry of the word images describing the design elements: Crow's shells, leaves of the fireweed, blanket border fancy picture, fern, porpoise, between-the-dice, double war club, mouth-rack of the woodworm, half the head of a salmonberry, and fish flesh.[33]

Woven Clothing

If boxes and baskets were containers of life, then blankets were the containers of people. Northwest Coast women wove botanical and animal fibers on upright looms to create blankets, tunics and robes that graced the human form. Labor intensive from the gathering and processing of raw materials to the manufacturing process, weaving was a specialist art that took years to master and perfect.

Everyday clothing appropriate to the raincoast had to be water-repellent, comfortable to work in, and warm. The ingenious response of all the

Northwest Coast people was to turn again to the cedar tree.[34] Shredded bundles of yellow cedar were hung on an upright loom and the weaver twined them at intervals with wefts of cedar bark, nettle or wool string. Soft yet durable clothing was produced; its multi-layers were worked with oil to shed the water easily, and wet surfaces could be dried quickly.[35] A versatile garment, the cedar bark robe could be fastened as a cape or skirt. Often adorned with fur or feathers, and some had designs worked in dyed fibers and a few had edgings worked in mountain goat wool. Some

struck by the elaboration and variety of the masking complex found all along the coast from the Salish in the south to the Tlingit in the north. Cognizant with every aspect of the art of mask making and masked performance, the artists of the Northwest Coast explored the concept of making transformation visible and credible through the construction of elaborate hinged, movable and mutable masks. Masks that metamorphosed, grew, shrank, spoke, danced in thin air, and were even destroyed and resurrected were due to the skills of consummate master carvers. Appropriate to the ritual at hand, masks were accompanied by intricately carved rattles, puppets, speakers staffs, headdresses, drums, whistles and other ceremonial paraphernalia to complete their presentation. Consummate in the art of suspending

Worn only by the high-ranking people of the Tlingit, Haida, Tsimshian and Kwakiutl these dancing robes (left) represented the hereditary crests of their owners. All Chilkat blankets have a border of black and yellow wool, a deep white fringe, and a large design field filled with the crest of the owner. Chilkat weaving probably originated with the Tsimshian, as did the entire chiefly costume with the raven rattle and frontlet headdress.

robes were painted with elaborate crest images and were probably for ceremonial use by high-ranking individuals.[36]

On the northern Coast, Tlingit, Tsimshian and Haida women created ceremonial robes known as Chilkat blankets for high-ranking people.[37] Myth records the Chilkat blanket as originating with the Tsimshian,[38] though it was developed by the Chilkat tribe of the Tlingit.[39] It took a master weaver a full year to complete the robe. Woven on an upright loom, on a warp of spun cedar bark and mountain goat wool with a weft of pure white, black, yellow and blue-green dyed mountain goat wool, the five-sided blankets resembled the shape of an upside down house front.[40] Part of the sumptuous chiefly costume of frontlet headdress with its six foot train of ermine, raven rattle, and dance apron, the Chilkat blanket had a deep double fringe that flared around the dancer's body.[41] As Bill Holm said of the blankets: 'No more royal robe ever draped a king. . . .'[42]

Masks and Ceremonial Paraphernalia

Without a doubt masks, headdresses and their associated ceremonial paraphernalia were and are one of the most distinctive cultural features of the Northwest Coast. The earliest explorers were

From the Koskimo tribe of the Kwakiutl, this mask (left) represents the supernatural Grizzly Bear. In elaborate Kwakiutl winter ceremonials, Bear Dancers appear with Fool Dancers. Both are frequently associated with the *Hamatsa* or Cannibal Society members. When a singer makes a mistake in a song, Bear Dancers become excited and chase the culprit out of the dance house, beating and scratching him. The person redeems himself by paying compensation for the error.

The Haida-carved Raven headdress (right) is a masterpiece of design united with function. The tail and wings would have covered the side and back of the dancer's head. The Raven head appeared to emerge from the dancer's forehead in a dramatic union of the social and the supernatural.

These Kaigani Haida potlatch dancers at Klinkwan (below) are displaying visual symbols of their prestigious clan emblems and hereditary rights. The costumes reflect the diversity of clan affiliation, high rank, great wealth and supernatural power.

disbelief, the artists restored and reinforced belief in the social, natural and supernatural.

The panoply of mask types was massive for each group along the Northwest Coast, except for the Nuu-chah-nulth and the Coast Salish. Cataloging that impressive array would be a monumental task. For every crest, for every lineage, for every ancestor, for every personal hereditary property or heraldic event, for each member of the culture there could be and probably was at least one if not several artistic interpretations commissioned by that lineage. The inventory was staggering if not infinite, bound only by our imagination – and that much can be concluded from museum collections alone. Museum collections, made mostly from the decades surrounding the turn of the century contain mere samplings of what must have existed.[43]

From the Tlingit, powerful shaman's masks seem to freeze the human face in a moment of the healing trance.[44] The Haida were renowned for a kind of mask Euro-Americans have called the 'portrait' mask that depicted in wood with sensuous accuracy the skin stretched or wrinkled over the bones of the skull.[45] The *naxno'x* ceremony required masks of the Tsimshian carvers known as the *Git'sontk* or 'the People secluded' who created all the paraphernalia for the most sacred part of their potlatches.[46] From their hands, humanoid masks with movable eyes and mouths,

were exceptional and in the dim light of the fire, terrifying realistic. The Northern Wakashan and Bella Coola artists championed in the creation of bold bird masks with sloped foreheads, large overhanging brows and piercing eyes: a stunning blend of stylized abstraction and naturalism.

The Kwakiutl's propensity for the theatrical and for flamboyance has been characterized by Holm as fundamental to their 'distinct and aggressive' culture.[47] The masks created for the *Hamatsa* or Cannibal Society dances fit the drama and prestige of portraying human encounters with the monumental supernatural birds at the edge of the universe.[48] The narrow elongated beaks of the *Hokhokw* were said to crush men's skulls; the beaks of some of these masks ranged in length from a modest two or three feet to up to ten (3m). These masks required the aid of a body harness and rigging, concealed by heavy fringes of shredded cedar bark, for the skillful dancer to carry the weight of the mask while snapping the movable mandibles of the supernatural birds. The neighboring Nuu-chah-nulth used a unique blend of smooth, spare sculptural form and decisive, abstract painted forms to create the subtle images of wolves with large nostrils, raptor-beaked thunderbirds, and slender-nosed lightning snakes for the *Klookwana* ceremony.[49] The Coast Salish had but one mask, the *Sxwayxwey* that appeared always with three

others of its kind. Huge and spectacular, the *Sxwayxwey* had large peg eyes that projected from the facial plane, with no lower mandible and a vertical flange below the nose.[50]

Frontlets were not masks. They were the individualized, exquisitely carved wooden portion attached to the front of headdress worn by high-ranking Tlingit, Tsimshian and Haida chiefs.[51] The headdress was almost always worn with the other prestigious items fitting the owner's high rank: a Chilkat blanket, dancing aprons and leggings, and the enigmatic, complex Raven rattle. This impressive raiment, reportedly used in 'welcoming dances', representing the synthesis of the supernatural and social power of the chief. It was, in effect, the crown jewels and a bishop's miter all in one. In the ritual occasion for displaying the headdress, the chief acted as head of state and like a shaman: the roles were merging into a spectacular display of social and spiritual power.[52]

Increasingly, non-Native and Native people have discovered and rediscovered a fascination for these traditional arts and it is a fascination built not only on an appreciation of form. The images are timeless. They speak through the culture and across cultures, and hold our imagination. As anthropologist Wilson Duff observed, Northwest Coast art has this power because '[These] images seem to speak to the eye, but they are really addressed to the mind. They are ways of thinking, in the guise of ways of seeing. The eye can sometimes be satisfied with form alone, but the mind can only be satisfied with meaning, which can be contemplated, more consciously or less, after the eye is closed . . . The meaning is in the relationships being expressed . . . Images hold ideas apart so that they can be seen together.'[53]

The Tradition Continues

Living traditions change and develop and the visual art tradition of the Northwest Coast is no exception. The Euro-American trade brought new materials, new technologies and new wealth. The result was nothing short of a cultural revolution as social, economic, linguistic, religious, material,

This Kaigani Haida ceremonial skin robe (above) dates from before 1875. It is edged with fur and painted with crest designs representing semi-human beings with bear-like claws. The central figures are identical except that the uppermost image depicts a female, her gender defined by a prominent lip plug or labret.

This early Tlingit frontlet (left) was collected in about 1870 and depicts Bear and Frog, important crests of the Wolf and Raven clans. Frogs were associated with shamanism and witchcraft, while bears figure in many mythical events.

This small but monumental argillite sculpture is called 'Bear Mother Nursing her Cub' and was made by Skaows-ke'ay or Tsagay of Skidegate. It represents the mythical story of Bear Mother, a high-ranking woman who unwittingly married a foreign prince who revealed himself to be the personification of a supernatural bear. She gave birth to half-human, half-bear children. Metaphorically the story may warn of the danger of marrying outside of one's tribe or of marrying a non-Native. This story was told by many peoples of the Northwest Coast, particularly in the north, and themes from this narrative featured strongly in the repertoire of Haida argillite carvers.

and artistic ideas felt the impact of the foreigners. There were subtle changes in the art resulting in the decline of some forms and the rise of others.

The Northwest Coast people had skilfully hammered copper nuggets into items of personal adornment in precontact times, and after contact with Euro-Americans, they purchased commercial copper wire to make some of the same items: bracelets, anklets, earrings, nose-ornaments and beads. Engraving techniques were well-known to the early Haida and Tlingit artists, and when gold and silver coin was introduced to the Northwest Coast, these techniques were used on the new materials to create expertly crafted silver bracelets and other jewelry.[54] With a revival in the 1950s, the tradition continues to the present, with bold, finely carved formline designs sweeping across mirror-bright surfaces.

Unique to the Haida, a new art form emerged in the early-19th century: the carving of a slate-like, soft stone known as argillite. In the early years of contact, argillite was much sought after by Euro-American seamen and commanded high prices, only to be scorned in later years as an art of acculturation. As Holm noted, 'In fact, some of the great masterpieces of Haida art as well as some of the most trite souvenirs' were produced by canny Haida artists who created and developed an

exclusive market for this rare stone.[55] Carved with woodworking tools, argillite takes on a high luster. The earliest carvings were 'pipes' (though most could not be smoked) with clusters of Haida images and/or Euro-American ship motifs. Later new forms emerged as images of the people and materials from foreign visitors were faithfully, if not mockingly, carved in free-standing sculpture. A third period in the art, which occurred after 1865 when the Haida population was decimated by disease in less than a generation, marked a dramatic return to bold sculptural images of Haida life and mythology. The art failed to develop for a while, then was revived in the 1960s by Haida artists reestablishing connections to the past. Today, argillite sculpture is a flourishing art form, still created primarily for sale to non-Natives and still making dynamic artistic statements about all that it means to be Haida.

After contact, commercial blankets replaced cedar bark clothing and the art all but disappeared. While plain commercial blankets were worn over Euro-American clothing, a new style of ceremonial blanket was developed with goods introduced shortly after the time of contact.[56] The spectacular robe was known as a 'button blanket' and it took the place of painted cedar bark, hide, or sail canvas robes, replacing their use all over the coast by the turn of the century. Adapted to an older concept of a dancing robe with elaborate borders and a central crest figure rendered with an outline of abalone shell, the button blanket was constructed of dark blue or black Hudson's Bay Company blankets and a broad border of red melton cloth. Red cloth was used to create an appliqued crest image in the center of the blanket. Mother-of-pearl buttons were sewn along the edge of the red border and along the outlines of the appliqued formline design: sometimes buttons alone were used to render the crest figure. Great care was given to selecting buttons of regular size, color and shape. These elegant ceremonial robes, worn with the design at the back flashed with the brilliance of a matador's 'coat of lights' in the fire light of the winter house.[57]

The renaissance of Northwest Coast art is wonderfully exemplified in the thriving serigraph studios in the Pacific Northwest[58] This is an example of a new art form – the silk screen print – being adapted to the tradition of two-dimensional formline design. Begun in the latter half of this century, this new tradition draws directly on earlier forms. With a vast visual library of published images Northwest Coast serigraph artists have been able to draw inspiration from their prolific ancestors to create a body of work that reflects a continuity between past motifs and styles, and exciting innovations of contemporary minds.[59]

Of course all the other traditions of carving and now even weaving are alive and well – thanks to their resurrection by dedicated and innovative Northwest Coast artists and art schools such as the school of art at 'Ksan, Hazelton. In the dedication to their first art catalogue, the artists have written:

'Walk on, walk on, walk on, on the breath of our grandfathers. These words follow the *wsinaax*, the songs we sing beside our dead. The words proclaim our strong sense of continuity, our belief in the constant reincarnation of thought, deed, and man; our knowledge of the presence of yesterday in today, of today in tomorrow.'[60]

After the devastating smallpox epidemics of the late 1860s, that literally decimated the Haida population in less than a generation, powerful images of Haida culture and history were represented in argillite sculpture, an art form unique to the Haida. Primarily destined for the non-Native art market, the visual message sent to the encroaching world of foreigners through this brilliant art was one of assertion and pride in being Haida. The box (top left) has a Killer-Whale design in low relief on the lid. The Sea-Lion heads on the ends and the Bear face on the front are separately carved and attached. The abalone-inlaid platter (bottom left) depicts the voracious Raven and his favorite food, halibut.

Northwest Coast art has endured to the present. Flourishing in contemporary art markets, the art also flourishes in traditional ceremonial events such as the potlatch. Here, female members of his lineage perform the Shark Dance at Robert Davidson's 1981 potlatch in Masset. The occasion was the adoption of Nuu-chah-nulth artist Joe David into the Haida Eagle moiety.

THE SUBARCTIC

THE SUBARCTIC region of North America, as the name implies, lies directly south of the Arctic. A vast area of approximately 2,000,000 sq miles (3,219,000 sq km), it includes interior Alaska and most of interior Canada. The predominant features of the landscape are barren tundra to the north and dense forest to the south, but there are also areas of open woodland and swamps, mountains, river valleys and lakes. The winters are long and bitterly cold, with limited daylight, heavy snowfalls and piercing winds. The short summer is warm and humid, but plagued by swarms of biting insects. A harsh and inhospitable land, it has, nevertheless, supported small bands of nomadic hunters and fishermen for thousands of years.

These bands were composed of two linguistic groups, the Athapaskans or Dene in the basins of the Yukon and Mackenzie Rivers, and the Algonquians in the regions south of Hudson Bay and the highlands of Labrador. Their lives were regulated by the abundance and seasonal migration patterns of the animals they hunted. Caribou, for example, were hunted in summer on open ground and in winter in the forests where both humans and animals could find shelter. Yet food resources were unpredictable and starvation and death were not uncommon, particularly in the winter months. Mobility was essential to survival. In providing mobility, even in deep snow, snowshoes were perhaps the most important Subarctic invention. Indeed, it might be claimed that it was only the use of snowshoes which enabled people to survive the bleak, often bitter, Subarctic winters.[2]

Besides food, animals also supplied raw materials in the form of hides for tents and clothing, bone and horn for tools, sinew for thread and bowstrings. Nearly all remaining materials – wood, bark and plant fibers – came from the forests. It was a lifestyle which encouraged self-reliance and children were instructed at an early age in the skills required for later life. Boys, for example, were taught to hunt and fish, to build houses and canoes and to make tools and weapons. Girls learned to tan hides and make sinew thread, to sew and decorate clothing and to make baskets and bark containers. Naturally, some became more proficient than others and were recognized as being so. However, such a meager subsistence economy did not permit the luxury of full-time specialists in particular arts and crafts.

Women were the main craftworkers and were thus best able to demonstrate artistic skills. Such skills, however, were expected to operate within established traditions. Esthetic values were based on respect for technical competence and good craftsmanship and there was little room for imagination or innovation for its own sake. It is this basic conservatism which helps to make regional preferences identifiable. Nevertheless, within these traditional confines artistic expression flourished, and the decorative art of the

The skill and ingenuity with which Indian women utilized both traditional materials and those introduced by traders is illustrated by this Kutchin shirt and Tahltan knife sheath (main picture). The shirt, of caribou skin stitched with sinew, is decorated with a band of dyed porcupine quills, red ochre and quill-wrapped fringes. The knife sheath is also of caribou skin, but covered with blue and red trade cloth and embroidered with glass beads. The geometric design imposed by the quills contrasts with the more fluid effect of the beadwork. Other materials came from the forests. Throughout the area, birch bark was folded into baskets and etched with intricate patterns (right and far left), while in Alaska ceremonial masks were carved from wood (above left). Although this mask has elements of Eskimo iconography, the shape and the ear ornaments identify it as Ingalik.

Subarctic is at its richest and most sophisticated in the painted designs, quillwork and embroidery in moosehair, beads and silks created on clothing and other utilitarian objects.

The Prehistoric Period

Although documentary sources for precontact life are meager, limited to the relatively few accounts by early travelers, fur traders and missionaries, there can be little doubt that the artistic traditions which, in many cases, only began to be recorded in the 18th century, had been an integral part of Subarctic life for centuries.

Unfortunately, at many sites, any organic matter has been destroyed by the acidity of the soil so that, while stone tools for working skin, bone, antler and wood have survived, the materials for which they were intended have not. There are a few exceptions where unusual conditions have led to a greater degree of preservation. For example, bone tools engraved with plain or ticked parallel lines have been excavated from prehistoric sites in northern Yukon. One of the most attractive objects recovered is a carved fish effigy – probably a fishing lure. Whether the engraved lines were intended simply as ownership marks or whether they should be regarded as symbolic – perhaps as stylized representations of animals or natural phenomena – remains a matter for conjecture.[3]

Sites around copper deposits such as those on Lake Superior and in the Copper River area have produced a range of objects hammered from copper nuggets in the form of arrowheads, knives, fishhooks, awls, chisels, beads and other ornaments. Evidence from sites elsewhere shows that such items were widely traded throughout the Subarctic.[4]

The shards of decorated pottery which also appear in prehistoric sites point to the development of a distinctive pottery-making tradition in Manitoba and Ontario.[5] In western Alaska the pottery made around the time of historic contact by the ancestors of the Ingalik and Koyukon reflects the influence of their Eskimo neighbours.[6]

Changes to traditional Algonquian culture began early in the 16th century when British, French and Portuguese fishermen came ashore to process the fish they had caught on the Newfoundland Banks. Trading metal knives, hatchets and kettles for meat and furs, they soon attracted hundreds of Indians to the north shore of the Gulf of the St. Lawrence every summer. As a result, tools and utensils of iron and brass came to replace stone and bone over much of northeastern America during the 16th and 17th centuries.

European contact began for the Athapaskans in the late-17th century with the establishment of trading forts on the southwestern shores of Hudson Bay. During the 18th century trapping and trading activities extended westwards, with the Cree, Chipewyan, Yellowknife and Dogrib acting as intermediaries between the traders and the northwestern groups. By the early-19th century the fur trade had reached the Tanaina, Tanana and western and northern Kutchin, although some Alaskan Dene on the uppermost reaches of the major rivers did not actually set eyes on a white man until about 1900.[7]

While the disruption caused to traditional society by imported diseases and missionary activity contributed to the discarding of old ideas and activities, practical considerations should not be underestimated. There can be little doubt that the advent of European technology greatly eased

Regular trading links existed between the Ingalik and their Eskimo neighbors, with the Ingalik exchanging their wooden dishes and ladles for seal skins and oil. The Ingalik food tray (far right), painted with the face of a stylized animal, was collected from an Eskimo village in the 1870s. The painting was done with red ochre and charcoal mixed with seal blood, which helped to fix the colors. Birch bark containers do not appear to have been items of trade, although, intriguingly, an Ingalik bone knife (below) used for stripping birch bark from the tree, is etched with typical Eskimo designs, including the raven's footprint motif.

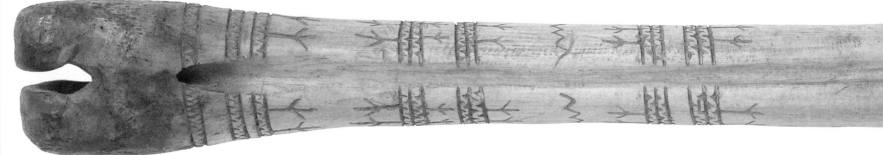

the workload of Indian women. The merchandise offered by traders – metal tools and cooking pots, woven textiles and ready-made clothing, decorative materials like beads, silk thread and ribbons – was both attractive and labor-saving. Moreover, the possession of trade goods and the wearing of fur-trade fashions conferred considerable social status and prestige. It is hardly surprising that by the end of the 18th century Sir Alexander Mackenzie was able to report of the Cree: 'They are fond of European articles and prefer them to their own native commodities.'[8]

Wood and Bark

It was from the forests that people, quite literally, built their lives. The forests supplied the materials for building shelters, whether substantial log houses or simple pole frameworks covered with skin or bark. They supplied materials for transport – for sleds, toboggans and snowshoe frames, and for canoes made of sheets of bark fitted over a wooden frame, the seams stitched with spruce root and caulked with spruce gum.

Bark and roots, as well as wood, were used for hunting and fishing equipment. Fishing lines and nets, for example, were made from willow bast, cut while green and torn into strips, then rolled on the naked thigh to produce a strong and durable twine. A fishing net made from willow twine could last a year or more.

Dishes, ladles and cups were carved from solid pieces of wood and decorated with notching or with incised or painted designs. In some areas, water buckets or cups were made from thin wooden slats (usually of spruce or larch) steamed and bent into circular or oval shapes. The overlapping edges were stitched with split spruce root

and pieces of wood were cut and fitted in order to form the bases.

Not all woodwork was so utilitarian. For their winter ceremonials, the Ingalik of Alaska carved elaborate wooden masks, often painted and decorated with feathers and beads. Some had moveable appendages with which the wearer could imitate the movements of the being represented. Both the style of the masks and the ceremonies in

Carved and painted wooden masks (below) were worn during the Ingalik Mask Dance, held to honor the game animals and to ensure their continued availability.

Baskets took various forms, ranging from the open-twined storage bag used by this Ahtna family (above) to the closely-woven and watertight Chilcotin cooking vessel (below), to this Cree birch bark container with its tightly-fitting lid. (above right).

which they were worn were greatly influenced by those of the neighboring Eskimo.

Baskets, both for cooking and storage, were made from sheets of birch bark and from twined spruce root (*watape*). Sir Alexander Mackenzie spoke approvingly of the spruce root baskets made by the Sekani in the late-18th century: 'Their kettles are also made of *watape*, which is so closely woven that they never leak, and they heat water in them by putting red hot coals into it.'[9]

Bark was cut from the tree in spring, while it was still flexible enough to be folded into the desired shape. The sides of the basket were stitched with strips of spruce root, which was also used to bind the rim. Baskets for cooking or for storing liquids were made watertight by applying spruce gum to the seams. Those intended to hold trinkets and other small objects sometimes had a buckskin top, closed with a drawstring.

Regional differences are apparent in both the shape and the decoration of bark containers. Those made in the Yukon and interior Alaska took the form of a bucket with a curved rim. Decoration consisted of horizontal or diagonal bands of lines and triangles, formed by scraping away the dark outer layer of bark to expose the paler bark underneath.[10]

Elsewhere in the Subarctic, bark baskets (referred to as 'mococks') had rectangular bases, sloping sides and oval rims. The sides (and lid, if one was attached) were often decorated with stylized plant or naturalistic animal motifs. In this case, decoration was achieved by scraping away the background, leaving the design in dark relief.[11]

Skindressing

According to the 18th century explorer Samuel Hearne, the making of a complete set of Chipewyan winter clothing could take as many as

eleven caribou hides.[12] A hunter required a new set of clothing at least once a year and a new pair of moccasins every two to three weeks. It is small wonder then that for Indian women dressing skins was a constant occupation.

It was also a laborious occupation, involving de-hairing (if the skin was to be used for summer clothing), along with repeated scraping, soaking, stretching and rubbing with animal fat and brains. Finally, the skin was often smoked over a smoldering fire to give it a golden brown color. This last process also helped to make the skin waterproof and items like tent covers and moccasins were always produced out of smoke-tanned skin.

A whole range of items, including gun cases, quivers, tump-lines, baby carriers, dog packs and bags of various forms, were made from skins. Babiche, thin-cut lines of rawhide, was (and still is) one of the most versatile of traditional resources. It was used for snares, for snowshoe lacings and for infilling ice-scoops, for making strong, yet light, netted bags and for fastenings and lashings of all kinds. When modern technology fails, it has been used to make running repairs to chainsaws and outboard motors.[13]

The most important use of skins, however, was in the manufacture of clothing. Everyday clothing was similar for both sexes – a shirt or parka (generally longer for women), leggings or trousers and moccasins. Some western groups like the Kutchin wore trousers with footwear attached. A cap or hood, mittens and a fur-lined robe or coat were added in cold weather.

The skins were cut up with a sharp flint or obsidian (later metal) knife and the pieces stitched together with sinew threaded through small holes punched along the seam lines with an awl.[14] Different types or parts of skin were preferred for different items of clothing – leg skins for mittens and moccasin uppers, for example, and calfskin for undergarments. When large game was scarce, shirts and robes might be made from rabbit skins, cut into strips and woven to make a warm fur fabric.[15] Fish skin was used in some parts of Alaska, where the Kolchan, for example, wore rain capes made of salmon skin.

With the establishment of trading posts, people increasingly came into contact with European manufactures, including ready-made clothing of wool and cotton. As early as 1809, David Harmon, a trader among the Beaver, noted that 'the greater part of them are now clothed with European goods.'[16] By the beginning of the 20th century traditional everyday skin clothing, apart

The French term 'babiche' refers both to finely cut strips of rawhide and to the webbing made from it. Throughout the Subarctic area, babiche was used in the making of snowshoes. Here (left) a Naskapi maker is infilling the shaped wooden frame of the snowshoe with inter-woven strips of babiche. Netted babiche bags were made in different sizes for a variety of purposes. This Tahltan example (below) has loops for attaching a carrying strap. Even such a utilitarian object is decorated with horizontal stripes of red pigment.

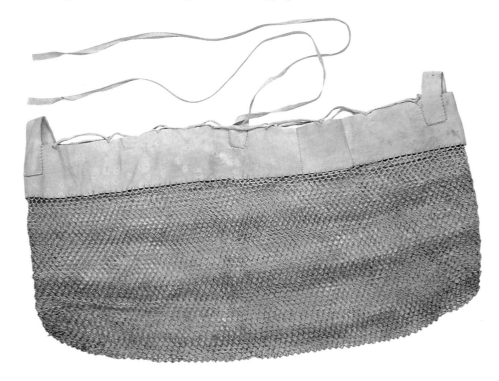

from a few items like mittens and moccasins, had more or less disappeared, replaced by garments of European style and fabric.[17]

Painting

Paint, most commonly red and black, was used to decorate a variety of objects, including snowshoes, sleds, canoe gunwales, drums, dishes and garments, particularly along the seams. Red, the most popular color, was originally obtained from local earth pigments, but vermilion, brighter and clearer, was supplied by traders from the earliest period of contact. Black was probably derived from burnt bones or charcoal.

Designs tended to be highly symbolic. In the early 1770s Samuel Hearne watched Chipewyan warriors painting their shields with red and black designs in preparation for battle –

'. . . some with the figure of the sun, others with that of the moon, several with different kinds of birds and beasts of prey and many with the images of imaginary beings . . . I learned that each man painted his shield with the image of that being on which he relied most for success in the intended engagement.'[18]

Perhaps the best-known examples of Subarctic painted decoration are to be found on the caribou-skin coats which were worn by Montagnais-Naskapi hunters at least from the 18th century until the 1930s.[19] Part of their interest lies in the way in which they reflect the changing styles of European fashion during this period. In fact they illustrate a trend found all over the Subarctic (although generally not until the 19th century) whereby garments, while continuing to be made from traditional materials, began to borrow European stylistic features such as centre front openings, collars and cuffs.

The main significance of the Montagnais-Naskapi coats, however, lies with the designs, for these coats were made and worn in order to enlist supernatural aid in hunting the all-important caribou. A hunter received instructions in dreams concerning the symbols which would give him the special power he needed. He passed the dream instructions to his wife, who translated them into visual form by painting the skin.[20]

The designs themselves – intricate combinations of double curves, crosses, dots, lozenges, triangles, leaf- and heart-shaped motifs, among others – were applied to the coats with tools made of caribou antler or bone. The pigments used were yellow (derived from sucker fish roe), red (locally obtained hematite or vermilion), black (possibly burnt bone) and blue (indigo supplied by traders and, from the mid-19th century, laundry blue).[21]

The layout of the painted designs is remarkably standard and clearly subscribes to established tradition, the main pattern areas being the hem, the center back and fronts and the collar. The most important constant feature of the coats is the back gusset, a narrow triangle of skin inserted where another triangle of skin has been cut out. As Dorothy Burnham has suggested, this painted area is almost certainly the symbolic centre of the coat's power, representing 'the Magical Mountain where the Lord of The Caribou lived and from the fastness of which the caribou were released to give themselves to the hunter.'[22]

Quill and Hair Embroidery

Although very few precontact examples survive, quillwork was among the very earliest artifacts collected by European explorers, and from their comments it is evident that quill weaving and embroidery were already well-developed and sophisticated crafts by the time of contact.

Mackenzie, at the end of the 18th century, expressed admiration for the work done by Slavey and Dogrib women:

'They make their Clothing of the Rein or Moos Deer well dressed . . . some of which they embroider very neatly with Porcupine Quills & the Hair of the Moos Deer painted Red, Black, Yellow & White . . . The cinctures of garters are of Porcupine Quills wove with Sinews & are the neatest thing of the kind that ever I saw . . .'[23]

Quills included both porcupine and split bird quills, usually goose, and hair included moose and caribou, although where both were available the former was preferred. All these materials could be colored with dyes derived from plant or mineral sources, but the natural colors were used as required. Quills were sometimes dyed black or dark brown by being tied up and boiled with lichen. A later variant of this technique was to boil quills with blue or red trade cloth so that they absorbed the color. In modern times crepe paper has been used in the same way to produce red, green and yellow quills.

There were various ways of using quills, the most straightforward being to lay them in parallel rows, each being held by a stitch in the middle and at either end. This was the method applied to the stiffer, less malleable bird quills, and was used for items like belts and tump-lines.

The simplest method of decorating clothing was by wrapping flattened porcupine quills around

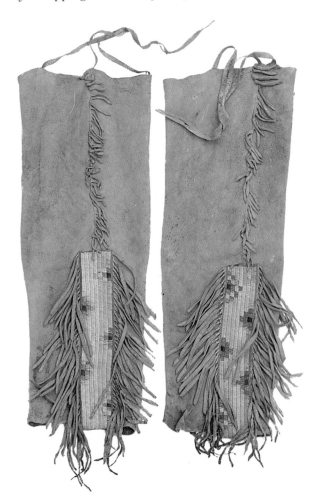

The supreme importance of the caribou hunt to the Naskapi, Montagnais and Cree of the Quebec-Labrador Peninsula is reflected in their painted caribou-skin coats (far left). By wearing such coats, decorated with powerful symbols, hunters hoped to enlist supernatural aid to bring them success in the hunt. Caribou-bone tools were used to apply the red, blue and brown painted designs on this Naskapi hunter's summer coat.

Porcupine quill weaving was highly developed in central Canada and Alaska. Designs created by the Athapaskans of the Yukon and North West Territories were of particular fineness and complexity, in contrast to the bolder patterns produced by Algonquian groups such as the Cree. Besides woven quillwork, various forms of braided and sewn work were also done, producing strong geometric bands of color. Quilled panels like those decorating these Cree leggings (left), were often so highly valued by their owners that they were transferred to new garments when the old ones wore out.

As the 19th century progressed, European designs, as well as materials, became increasingly incorporated into Indian art. At the same time, traditional materials were adapted for the souvenir market. The unusual form of this Montagnais birch bark box (below), together with its floral quillwork decoration, reflects European influence and it may in fact have been made for sale rather than for use. The quills were applied to the bark by being pushed through tiny holes in the surface and then covered with an inner lining to keep them from working loose.

thong fringes. More complex techniques involved folding the quills over and under one or two sinew threads to produce lines or bands of color which could be combined to make patterns of rectangular blocks, stepped triangles and crosses. However, undoubtedly the finest porcupine quillwork was that which was woven either on a bow loom or directly on to the skin ground on a sinew cross-weft. Almost certainly, it was woven quillwork which so impressed Mackenzie.

Traditional woven and applied quillwork produced intricate geometric patterns, but during the 19th century curvilinear and floral patterns, first produced in eastern Canada via the European embroidery tradition, moved rapidly westwards.[24] By1850 Dr. John Rae had acquired, probably from the Cree, a guncase decorated with double-curve moosehair scrolls.[25] Ten years later Andrew Flett of the Hudson's Bay Company collected for the Industrial Museum of Scotland a pair of Kutchin mooseskin moccasins embroidered with a floral motif in red and blue porcupine quills edged with moosehair.[26]

By that time too Indian women had acquired steel needles and silk thread and, influenced by fort life and mission schools, were producing skin

moccasins, mittens, gloves, bags and other items decorated with silk floral embroidery entirely in the European tradition.[27] When both silks and quills are used to decorate the same object, the stiffness and formality of the quillwork is in striking contrast to the exuberance of the embroidery. Although quillwork continued to be used to decorate clothing, it is clear that Indian craftswomen had come to recognize its limitations and that, as European materials became more freely available, it would increasingly be relegated to a secondary position.

Beadwork

Beads made of bone, shell, copper, seeds and dried berries were used as jewelry and to decorate clothing in precontact times and into the historic period. After European contact, imported glass beads and metal ornaments began to be found alongside native materials.

'All the natives of the interior,' wrote Lieutenant Zagoskin, visiting the mouth of the Yukon River in the 1840s, 'are passionately fond of finery and bright colors. They have contrived to adorn their simple clothing by sewing on porcupine quills, deer hair, borders of threaded beads, shells, pendants cut out of copper, little bells and so on . . .'[28]

Glass beads came in a range of colors and sizes. The large beads supplied by Russian traders on the North Pacific coast from the end of the 18th century varied from 'necklace' beads (7mm or more in diameter), to 'pony' beads (3-4mm). Further east 'seed' beads (2mm or less) were in use by the mid-18th century, becoming widespread by the second half of the 19th century.[29] Faceted metal beads became popular towards the end of the 19th century, the 'silver' beads being polished iron and the 'gold' ones brass or copper.

As beads became more readily available in the 19th century, they were incorporated into the established geometric design tradition and it is possible to trace the continuity from quilled designs to very similar ones produced with beads or by combinations of beads and dentalia shells.[30]

Kutchin garments and accessories collected in the 1860s show dentalia and glass beads being used in equal proportion to produce chequered bands of color on the yoke seams and cuffs of dresses and shirts and down the seams of leggings.

Beads were attached to skin and cloth using a two-thread couching technique, whereby the beads, strung on one thread, are stitched to the surface at intervals by a second thread passing between every two or three beads. This technique allowed the beadworker greater flexibility of design since the strung beads could be turned in any direction desired and this, together with the introduction of steel needles and cotton thread, led to the great development of floral beadwork throughout most of the Subarctic region in the latter half of the 19th century.

Some of the far western groups like the Tahltan did retain more geometric patterns adapted from quillwork and basketry and their bold, rectilinear beadwork designs are in strong contrast to the conventionalized floral and curvilinear designs being produced elsewhere. The woven beadwork in some areas also retained the rectilinear designs necessitated by the weaving technique.

Present-day beadworkers continue to practice and develop floral beadwork, although always within the established design tradition, because 'that is how it is done'. The respect for technical quality remains, with emphasis on matching beads for size and color, even stitching and symmetry of design. It is these qualities which Indian craftswomen find esthetically pleasing – in the words of a modern beadworker, Minnie Peter of Fort Yukon, – 'I like to make something bright. If I want to sew, I like to make something pretty.'[31]

At the onset of puberty girls underwent a period of ritual seclusion, during which they were subject to a number of rules governing their food, clothing and general behavior. When they emerged from seclusion, they were regarded as ready for marriage. This skin-covered collar (above) was worn by a Tahltan girl during the period between puberty seclusion and marriage. The collar is decorated with dentalium shells, red and blue glass beads, and tassels of colored wool or worsted.

'In the evening, the lights were turned off in the qasgi
*and slow songs were made in the dark. Also, they bent
wood to make bowls. They also made water pails.
Women made new clothes. Before they made all these
new things they danced.'*

KAY HENDRICKSON (NUNIVAK ISLAND)[1]

The North American Arctic features a surprisingly varied land mass with distinct ecological and cultural zones. The extensive coastline and tundra interior encourages mixed maritime and inland hunting economies. Major river systems penetrate the interior; their fertile deltas provide rich feeding grounds for fish, seals, and small mammals. In Alaska and on Baffin Island, ranges of snow-capped mountains rise majestically from low-lying coastal plains. The treeline marks a meandering route staying within 250 miles (402 km) of coastal Alaska but sloping sharply south beyond the Mackenzie Delta. Marked with patches of dwarf willow, the central Canadian Arctic features a seemingly boundless expanse of tundra. Rich in vegetation, the tundra provides summer grazing land for herds of caribou and musk oxen, as well as migratory wildfowl.

For over 2,000 years, Aleutian, Yup'ik, and Inupiat-Inuit peoples, descendants of the Eskimo-Aleut linguistic family, have skillfully exploited local resources, sustaining a remarkably productive life in a wide range of environmental conditions.[2] At the time of contact with Russian explorers in 1741, the Unangan (Aleuts) occupied the Aleutian archipelago, clusters of islands which extend from the Alaskan peninsula 1,300 miles (2092km) towards Asia. With scarce land resources, Aleutian hunters pursued whales, sea lions, fur seals, and sea otters by baidarka (kayak) in coastal waters. Fish, nesting birds, and marine life collected on beaches, provided additional food and raw material.

The Yup'ik speaking cultures of southwestern Alaska constructed villages of semi-subterranean houses on the Bering Sea coast and off-shore islands, and along the Yukon and Kuskokwim Rivers. The Yukon-Kuskokwim Delta, a crescent-shaped area extending from Norton Sound to Kuskokwim Bay (and 200 miles inland), is the heartland of Central Yup'ik country.[3] The river deltas provide rich sealing areas while the rivers and their tributaries offer access to fish and wildlife resources in the interior.

The Inupiat-Inuit peoples of northern Alaska, Arctic Canada, and Greenland share a common language with a continuum of regional dialects. Scattered in camps and villages across an extensive territorial range, they too developed distinctly regional hunting economies. During the spring migration of bowhead whales, Inupiat in northwestern Alaska, for example, conducted a highly ceremonialized form of whalehunting under the direction of *umialit*, whaling captains.[4] Across the Canadian Arctic Inuit families lived in camps of extended kin, shifting location in response to the seasonal movement of game. From coastal communities on Baffin Island and along the west coast of Hudson Bay, kayak hunters pursued whales, walrus, and narwhal. They seal-hunted at breathing holes in winter and hunted caribou inland in spring and fall. Fish (fresh, frozen or dried) provided an important food source throughout the year.

Both skilled and decorative craftwork of the Arctic region are represented by the Aleutian and Inupiat parkas (main picture, right and far left), together with the Greenland Eskimo boot of sealskin embellished with thin strips of red, yellow and black painted skin applique. The magico-religious art so characteristic of the culture is illustrated by the pierced hand from a wooden *tunghak* mask.

Of extreme importance for survival in a hostile environment was the production of the waterproof outer parka which vividly underlines the remarkable employment of natural materials to best effect. Made of strips of walrus or seal intestine, they were joined by an ingenious waterproof sinew-sewn seam. Exceptional basketry skills were also evident. This Aleutian basket (above) is made from wild grasses, its figures worked in tiny stitches.

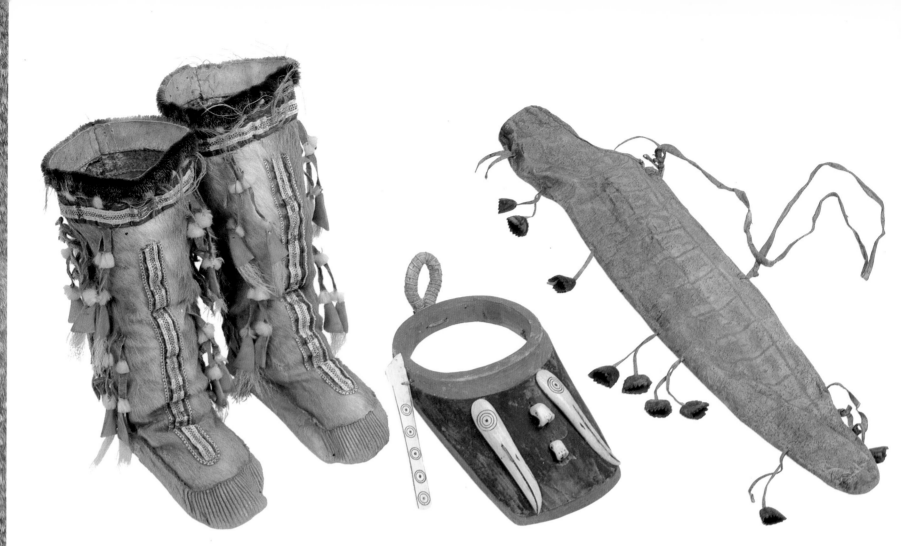

Great effort went into producing children's clothing, especially for ritual and social occasions. This pair of child's boots (above left) was collected from the Yup'ik prior to 1866. They exhibit the highly technical and decorative craftwork in leather and fur so characteristic of the region. The Aleutian child's shade (left center) has a talisman of diving waterbirds of carved ivory. The combined bow-case and quiver (right) contains a bow and eight arrows for hunting small game. The symbolic decoration alluded to the child's role as a prospective hunter.

In tandem with extreme winter temperatures, the Arctic experiences a dramatic seasonal change in light and animal resources. As the sun disappears in early fall, caribou, whales, geese and ducks abandon the north. They return each spring to give birth and nurture their young. This annual cycle of light and dark, scarcity and abundance, makes the Arctic a land of sharp contrasts. In winter families relied on available game and reserves of stored food. Through social gatherings and ritual ceremonies, they appeased spirit forces which controlled the supply of animals. The sun's reappearance in spring, accompanied by the return of the whales, migratory birds, and thundering herds of caribou, heralded a period of regeneration and renewal.

Historical Art Forms

Flawlessly designed implements, produced from wood, bone, antler, ivory, and stone, comprised the remarkably efficient toolkit that enabled hunters to procure game on land or sea. With ingenuity and technical expertise, women used

sewing skills to fashion objects necessary for everyday use. Animal hides and furs furnished women with raw material for clothing, tents, umiak and kayak covers, quivers, storage bags, and various hunting and domestic equipment.

Despite clear regional differences in language, dialect, hunting pursuits, and social practices, Arctic cultures shared broadly similar ideological concerns which imbued the production of traditional art forms. These are an intimate physical and metaphysical relationship between humans and animals; a profound awareness of the tenuous nature of human existence; a firm respect for craftsmanship with social prestige vested in skill and productivity; a deep love of children and desire to impart the knowledge and skills necessary for them to achieve a productive life in an exacting, and often unforgiving environment.

Arctic peoples believed that well-crafted objects pleased spirit forces and secured good will towards the maker and his/her family.[5] Impeccably tailored clothing, and finely carved hunting tools, provide evidence of the value placed on the artistic combination of form and function. Today, well-made, skillfully decorated clothing remains a treasured gift from a seamstress to her husband, daughter-in-law, or grandchild.

Clothing as Art

'A parka is a beautiful art form. It is our cultural heirloom, which we call paitaq. *The parka is pieced together from the animals of our area. . . . It's all the life forms coming together through the hands and skills of a seamstress.'* MARIE MEADE (YUP'IK) 1990[6]

Throughout the Arctic extraordinary time, skill, and talent were invested in clothing production. Women possessed expert knowledge in treating animal skins to maximize warmth or waterproof garments. Rendered from animal products, clothing underscored human dependence on the animal. Clothing design was functional as well as symbolic. Since clothing styles were regional, they served as an important sign of social identity and collective cohesion.[7]

Waterproof garments made from sea mammal intestine were used for maritime hunting throughout the Aleutians, coastal Alaska, St. Lawrence Island, and the eastern Canadian Arctic.[8] Yards of tubular intestines were scraped, inflated, and dried. Treated as such, the gutskin appears as translucent parchment, seemingly fragile but surprisingly resilient when oiled. On St. Lawrence Island gutskins were bleached in freezing temperatures to achieve their creamy color and soft texture. To fashion the parka, bands of gutskin were laid in horizontal tiers or vertical columns. The seams were folded over and stitched without fully penetrating the skin. Whale or walrus sinew was often used for thread; it swelled when wet, helping to seal the hole.

Gutskin garments were frequently decorated with alder-dyed hair of unborn seals, cormorant feather tufts or tiny auklet crowns, inserted at regular intervals in the seams. Such decoration was both visually pleasing and profoundly symbolic. Cormorant feathers alluded to the bird's diving and fishing ability; the hair of unborn seals

A Bering Strait Eskimo carver (left) uses a traditional style of bow and drill on a walrus tusk, the end product almost certainly being to satisfy the demand of early white traders. Such work was produced by the Nome Eskimo where this man was photographed in 1912. The mouthpiece technique demonstrated here goes back centuries though. Large objects are not representative of early Eskimo sculpture, much of which was done in the miniature with a fine eye for detail. The parka has the sinew-sewn seam attractively decorated with small feathers and tassels.

symbolized the propagation of the species. Women, as well as men, wore exquisitely decorated gutskin parkas. These served a utilitarian function as rain cover, but were also featured in ceremonial contexts.[9] In the wake of European contact and trade, bits of red, blue, and green yarn replaced traditional forms of decoration.

Although apparently regarded as a poor man's clothing choice, bird skins provided an important source of parka material, particularly in areas of limited resources. Eider duck, emperor goose, murre, puffin, squaw duck, loon, and cormorant skins made lightweight and water-repellent parkas. Certainly, the doll of a Yup'ik hunter, dressed in a cormorant parka with elaborate personal adornment, presents an image of affluence and prestige.

In general, Yup'ik seamstresses preferred ground squirrel (marmot), mink, otter, and muskrat furs for parka material. Flensed, dried, and scraped to soften, the small pelts were laid in horizontal rows, sometimes with tails intact. Traditionally, Yup'ik parks were long, dress-like garments, often hoodless with a high standing collar. Today, women's parkas (*atkupiaq*) are hooded with a 'sunburst' trim of wolverine and wolf similar to hood styles in northern Alaska.[10] Plates of white calfskin (formerly *pukiq*, white caribou fur) are fixed with wolverine, otter, or mink tassles and attached in horizontal tiers across the parka front and back. They are highlighted with decorative stitching (*kelurqut*) on thin strips of black or red painted skin. 'The red earth paint is called *uiteraq* or *kavirun*. It is the representation of the blood of our ancestral mother *An'gaqtar*. *An'gaqtar*, who some people say is the daughter of Raven, the Creator, left pockets of her menstrual blood in various [sacred] places in southwest Alaska.'[11]

Caribou fur and ground squirrel were preferred by the Inupiat of northern Alaska. Men's parkas were thigh-length with slightly rounded hems in front and back. Trousers and boots completed the outfit. The creamy white mottled fur of domesticated Siberian reindeer, obtained from itinerant Chuckchi traders or St. Lawrence Island middlemen, was considered extremely valuable.[12]. Wolverine or wolf tails, an eagle feather or loon's head were often attached to the parka back, evoking respect for the subject's predatory skill and serving as a talisman for the wearer.[13]

Throughout the Arctic women were trained as expert seamstresses. They used animal pelts and skins, even those of birds and fish. Clothing styles identified gender and region. Men's parkas had references to the role of hunter, women's that of the procreative, maternal role. These parkas (right) are both women's. The Inupiat one (left) is made of squirrel and sealskin and was collected by E. W. Nelson prior to 1897. In contrast is the Inuit one (right) of caribou skin collected by Lucien Turner in the early 1880s and heavily embellished with trade goods including pewter spoons, lead drops and seed beads. Both garments, however, underline the first necessity of efficient clothing to cope with the harsh Arctic environment.

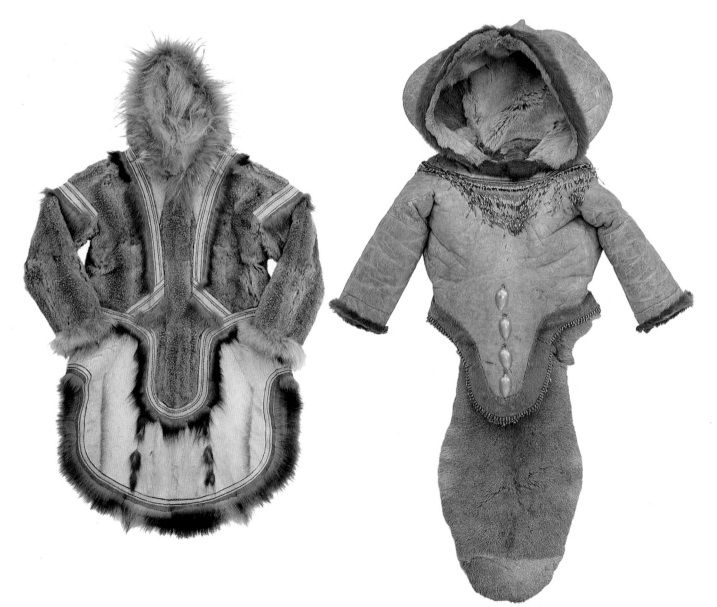

Caribou fur provides exceptional hypothermal protection and was favored by Inuit throughout Arctic Canada.[14] While traveling or hunting in winter, the parka was worn in two layers. The uniform design of the outer parka signified one's regional and gender identity while the inner parka was decorated with amulets which alluded to the wearer's personal relationship with spirit forces.[15]

Sealskin parkas were prevalent in Greenland, Baffin Island, and Labrador. Lightweight and water-repellent, they were worn especially during the wet spring and warm summer months. The sealskin was scraped on the inside, stretched and laced to a drying rack to air dry. For parkas and trousers, the hair was left intact. Women took great pride in contrasting the skin's silver tone with dark decorative inserts. As Lucien Turner notes, 'The woman may be several years in getting the right kind [of sealskin] and may have effected many exchanges before being suited with the quality and color'.[16]

Clothing styles contained specific design elements which identified the wearer as male or female. Inuit women's parkas, for example, were identified by a back pouch (*amaut*) used to carry a baby. The *amaut* emphasized the woman's maternal role on both a functional and symbolic level.[17]

Trade played a prominent role in the design of clothing and personal adornment. Blue trade beads from China, purchased from itinerant Siberian traders, decorated labrets, clothing, needlecases, and hunting implements.[18] Russian and European explorers, whalers, and traders, introduced manufactured cloth and beads. Tartan shawls, wool berets, and calico covers became the height of fashion in different areas. In Greenland, women devised an elaborately netted collar of colored beads in bold geometric patterns. Strands of beads formed variegated color bands that were draped from shoulder to shoulder on women's parkas on Baffin Island and in northern Quebec. In the central Arctic, seamstresses created narrative and abstract designs by sewing seed beads to a stroud backing attached over the chest, shoulders, wrists, and hood. The woman adhered to regional design norms, but the pictorial images were the creation of each seamstress.[19]

Carving and Graphic Arts

While women's art was primarily demonstrated through sewing,[20] men were proficient in producing hunting equipment and household implements. As noted earlier, superior craftsmanship was believed to please the souls of prey and enhance the efficacy of an object. Moreover, Arctic cultures believed that animals possessed a soul (Yup'ik: *yua*; Inupiat: *inua*). In response to the respect paid to the animal and its spirit, animals allowed themselves to be captured. A hunter demonstrated his respect for the animal by virtue of his moral character, personal appearance, and the care taken in producing and maintaining hunting equipment.

Hunting equipment was often designed to attract prey. Ivory fishinghooks were carved as fish with precious blue trade beads for eyes. Arrow straighteners took the form of complacent caribou. Passing repeatedly through the device, the arrow became used

A group of Bering Strait Eskimo (left) photographed at St. Michaels, Alaska, in 1902, shows the traditional clothing worn at the time in the region. Dependent largely upon sea mammals and caribou for food, clothing, and shelter, they made maximum use of what was available.

In western Alaska women carried sewing implements in decorated bags known as 'housewives'. This bag (below right) exhibits beadwork in large blue beads. The needle-case (below center) consists of an ivory tube through which runs a thong of rawhide in the folds of which the needles were kept. The comb (below left) is of bone. All carry symbolic references to animals, signifying the seamstresses' dependence on animal resources.

Meat trays with painted pictographs also combined pragmatic and spiritual functions. The wood was carved, steamed, bent and fitted. Seams were stitched with spruce root. Trays and ladles were painted with mythological images in the early fall and accompanied men in the ritual sweatbath in order to fix the pigment.[23] Food contained in these trays fed spirits, deceased ancestors, and other guests. The painted images alluded to spirit forces and animal procreation. For example, a bentwood tray shows two figures, a male caribou and its *inua*, energized by a mystical power line. The exposed penis sexually charges the image, emphasizing the fecundity of the species. A delicately carved snuff box takes the form of a mother sea otter, playfully carrying her offspring on her belly. The pair are incised with skeletal markings studded with white trade beads, a design recalling the practice of marking joints, the site of souls, with nucleated circles.[24] Its function as a snuff box also demonstrates the hunter's generosity in sharing his valuables, and serves as a form of spirit propitiation.

In the central Arctic, Inuit were reluctant to accumulate unnecessary personal possessions. Moving seasonally from camp to camp, families used caches, marked by stone formations known as *inukshuit*, to store food and unneeded seasonal goods. Wood, a scarce commodity, was reserved for kayak and umiak frames, sleds, tent poles and

Wood could be worked as skillfully as ivory. This oval dish (above left) from the region of Nulok Tokok, Alaska, is made of a bottom piece and separate wooden rim, the outer and inner sides of the rim being painted red. Mythical reindeers, linked by a symbolic power line and painted in black, embellish the slightly concave bottom. The superbly carved and inlaid snuff box (above right), is a sea otter at play with her cub.

to the caribou's body while the animal learned to accept the hunter's weapon.[21]

In Alaska, hunting gear was stored in covered wooden boxes. The interior was often painted with hunting trophies, mythological beings, and explicit sexual images. The sexual energy conveyed in these pictographs also empowered the hunter. In fact, the hunt itself was frequently perceived in sexual terms. Sexual abstinence was encouraged, for a woman's smell was believed to be abhorrent to the animal. Young men were discouraged from looking at women in order to preserve and intensify their hunting vision.[22]

A unique style of kayak (right) was developed by the Aleutian Eskimo to transport non-Native travelers. This ivory model of a three-hole baidarka shows the split prow kayak with three figures, the man in the middle is lighting his pipe whilst the two Aleuts prepare to throw harpoons.

essential hunting equipment. In its place, Inuit relied heavily on stone, bone, antler, ivory, and animal skins. Among the Copper Inuit, musk ox horn was boiled, carved and shaped into ladles; bone marrow picks were handsomely rendered with decorative finials; seal hide, bird skins and ducks' feet were sewn into exquisitely designed containers. Families traveled widely to trade and to obtain raw materials. Indigenous names for places and social groups often derived from the most prominent resource available in a region.

Dolls and Models

Throughout the Arctic, parents fashioned ivory, wood, and skin figures, as well as model umiaks, kayaks, hunting and domestic equipment for the entertainment and instruction of children. Ivory storyknives, carved by male relatives in the *qasgi* (men's house), were used by Yup'ik girls to depict mythological and historical epics, and to relate personal narratives.[25] More than an entertaining pastime, these stories served a key educational function. Similarly, girls learned the pattern designs (and decorative codes) of adult clothing by sewing miniature replicas for their dolls. Model-building allowed an older generation to convey details of large-scale construction to children and grandchildren.[26]

Thus, child-scale equipment was produced with exceptional care. The future hunter's quiver and visor replicated their full-scale counterpart, even in details of magico-religious decoration.[27] As well, time was reserved in social gatherings for children to demonstrate their novice skills. This practice continues today and serves as an important occasion of social pride in the physical and cultural development of a new generation.

Magico-Religious Art

Arctic cultures acknowledged their dependence on spirit forces through an annual cycle of ritual ceremonies. Their complex cosmology demanded that respect be paid to celestial beings, the spirit of animals, and deceased ancestors. Festival gatherings, ritual or secular in nature, consisted of appropriate combinations of songs, dance, social play, comic scenes, and dramatically staged masked performances.

The extensive resources and large settled populations in the Yup'ik area supported an impressive ceremonial cycle. Ceremonies included food offerings made to children (*Qaariitaaq*), gift exchanges between men and women (*Petugtaq*), formal thanks for the annual harvest of seals (*Nakaciuq*), memorial celebrations dedicated to the spirits of the deceased (*Elriq*), elaborate gift

This pair of Alaskan Eskimo dolls (above left) show elaborate Arctic costume in the miniature. Such dolls were not mere playthings but were used to instruct girls in the techniques of patterning and sewing to enable them to produce practical and esthetically pleasing costume demanded by the Arctic environment and culture. The male doll (left) is from Tuniakput and the female doll (right) from Bristol Bay.

Finger masks were small wooden masks carved with human, bird or *tunghat* features. Danced as pairs by women, the images were either identical or complementary. These (above) are from the region of the mouth of the Togiak River, Alaska. The embellishment of fur, feathers or caribou hair accentuated the movements of the hands.

A carved model (right) depicting an episode in the ancient Bladder Festival. The model was collected from the Eskimo of Nushagak and is made of walrus ivory, wood, sinew, gut, nails, and trade cloth. The winter festival lasted several days and was held to propitiate seals whose skin, meat, blubber and other parts were essential to survival.

This Eskimo mask (below) was probably carved at the request of a shaman who during a trance or journey into the unknown, encountered supernatural beings and spirits. This particular mask, a *tunghak*, was believed to impersonate the spirit forces which had control over the supply of animals (note the carvings of species above his face).

distributions in honor of a child's first catch (*Kevgiq*), and ritual feasts (*Keleq*) directed by shamans for ensuring a 'time of plenty'.[28] The *qasgi* (men's house) served as the ritual center in which ancestor and animal spirits were hosted by those present. New clothing, bentwood trays, and ladles were made in early fall at the start of the ceremonial calendar.[29]

Nakaciuq, the Bladder Festival, took place over a five-day period in December, known as *cauyarvik*: 'time for drumming'.[30] Hunters reserved the bladders of seals they had caught throughout the year. Bladders lost or destroyed by dogs were replaced by the stomach or other organ. Participants washed in urine, rinsing their bodies in the snow. During *Nakaciuq* the inflated bladders were displayed in the men's house; their souls (*yua*) were feted with food, song, oratory, and dance. At dawn following the full moon, the hunters returned the bladders to the sea through a hole chipped in the ice. Confident of being well-treated, the seal's spirit, contained in the bladder, returned to the hunter the following season.

During *Elriq* namesakes received gifts of food and clothing presented to honor the deceased. Bits of food were dropped through the floorboards to ancestor spirits gathered beneath. For *Keleq*, the Inviting-In Feast, one village hosted another

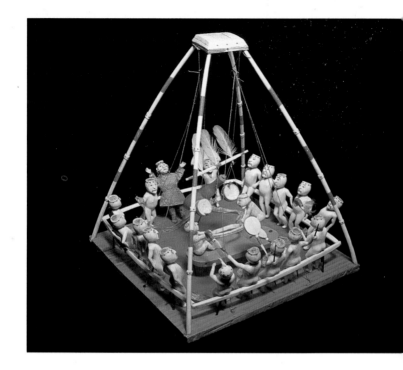

with several days of masked performances staged to please animal spirits and thus ensure a plentiful hunt. Masks, commissioned from carvers, were often made under the direction of shamans. The masks illustrated supernatural visions, personal narratives, or symbolized the relationship between a participant and an animal *yua*.[31] Bird feathers often surrounded the mask. In ritual contexts birds served as messengers between the natural and supernatural worlds. Large-scale *tunghak* masks were grotesque impersonations of the spirit force which controlled the supply of animals. Frequently depicted with a leering grin, the *tunghak*'s hands were characteristically pierced with an unopposable thumb, signaling its benign authority in releasing animals to the hunter.[32] Wooden carvings of select species were placed tauntingly about the *tunghak*'s face.

An assembly of seated male drummers accompanied the dancers. The drum covering was struck with a long narrow baton. When women danced, they performed with downcast eyes, holding a pair of finger masks which served as their surrogate eyes.[33]

Dance styles between the south and north differed radically. In the early-20th century, Hawkes contrasted the 'raw vigor' of northern dance with the graceful, fluid motions used in the south.[34] Moreover, the material richness of festivals in the western Arctic contrasted sharply with the more austere gatherings of Inuit in Arctic Canada.

In the eastern Canadian Arctic, early ethnographic accounts provide some evidence of communal ceremonies with skin masks, transsexual costuming, and the formal propitiation of animal spirits.[35] However, few references fully describe annual ritual cycles. Social gatherings provided a context for shamanistic performances in which the shaman (*angakuq*) was called upon to heal the sick, locate game, predict or change the weather, and ascertain metaphysical causes for any disaster confronting the community. Dances were held to greet visitors and to establish relationships between hosts and guests. Accompanied by the resounding pulse of the large skin-covered drum (almost a meter in diameter), a male or female dancer performed stylized movements of birds and animals, sang songs of hunting exploits and personal experiences, or lampooned themselves or a joking-partner.

Transformations in Artistic Expression

From the early-20th century, and particularly following the Second World War, Arctic peoples have faced an increasingly cash-dependent economy with few employment opportunities for unilingual individuals. In this context, one cannot underestimate the economic importance of independent artmaking or community-based, often government-supported, art and craft programs. Yet it is only now that we are beginning to appreciate their cultural and historical importance. For example, small ivory carvings once produced for whalers, missionaries, and traders are often dismissed as 'souvenir art'. The ivory model of a bidarka (page 118), however, embodies significant historical and cultural information. The center hole carries a European-dressed figure

lighting his pipe while two Aleuts paddle. There is humor and irony in this depiction, particularly in a cultural setting that places a high value on self-sufficiency and deplores indolence and pretentious authority.

The work of contemporary sculptors, printmakers, textile and graphic artists throughout Alaska, Arctic Canada, and Greenland comprises a valuable source of personal and collective history. Stone and wood carvings, works on paper, and textile art offer perceptive, first-hand insights into the social, spiritual, economic, and intellectual life of northern peoples.[36] Research among elders by native and non-native ethnographers affirms that the rich mythological and cosmological traditions of Arctic societies remain a vital cultural force.[37] Furthermore, scholars point out that despite centuries of trade and culture contact, imported materials were often syncretically adopted, bringing about superficial rather than substantive changes in material culture.[38] Thus, as Aleutian, Yup'ik and Inupiat-Inuit peoples seek to rediscover and reclaim cultural traditions as a vital source of knowledge, the testimony of elders, the witness of museum artifacts, and the creative work of contemporary artists, all serve as essential resources in ensuring the continuing strength of indigenous Arctic cultures.

This modern fabric art from the Baker Lake region in the Canadian Arctic is called One Man's Dream and was made by Inuit Marion Tuu'Luuq. Made of felt, stroud and cotton thread, the image illustrates a myth widely known in the Arctic region. It refers to a girl who takes a lover in a darkened igloo. To find out who he is she marks his face with soot, only to discover it is her brother. In shame, she takes up a blazing torch and is carried up to the sky where she becomes the sun. Her brother pursues her but his torch grows faint and he becomes the moon. In myth and art, the Inuit associate the female with procreative power. Here, from the tattooed face of a woman, emanate ever-expanding circles of land and sea animals, birds, transformed beings, plant forms, and human life.

THE NORTHEAST

WITH THESE words, this Mesquakie (Fox) artist establishes the essential significance that the arts and crafts of the Northeast Woodlands and Great Lakes region hold for these people. Not only do the words exemplify the Native understanding of the complementary halves of reality and spirituality, of the visible and the invisible, of the past and the present, but they also reflect the reality of two separate, yet strongly interactive worlds of Indians and Europeans. While we, as non-Natives, may see the visible part presented in the tangible forms of Native arts and crafts, much still remains hidden from view, evoking a desire to learn more. Wanatee's final words also attest to the role that tribal women held, and continue to hold, in the transference of cultural knowledge through material expression. These words also imply women's adaptability and innovative skills which incorporated trade goods and non-Native features into these works of art endowing them – whether for tribal use or as trade items – with a distinctively Native voice.

The Northeast Woodlands and Great Lakes area, extending from the shores of the Atlantic Ocean in the east to the western shores of the Great Lakes, was the first region to be exposed to continuous European contact. Beginning in the early 1500s, Basque fishermen were soon followed by traders, missionaries, French and British officials and adventure-seekers. With them came trade goods to be exchanged, first for furs and then for exotic items. An historical overview of indigenous arts and crafts reflects the impact of this early interaction. The ability of the various groups to adapt Native materials and techniques to provide satisfactorily the exotic and the practical to fulfill European perceptions of esthetics and requirements, attests to the flexibility and fluidity of native culture and establishes an innate entrepreneurial spirit. At the same time, Native Americans continued to create material objects to fulfill their own needs, esthetic values and religious expression. It was through this transformation of intangibles into dynamic and symbolic aspects of material culture that both individual tribes and broader culture areas established and maintained their identity.

Despite overlaps of art forms, techniques and materials, there is often a distinctive art tradition that has become associated with a specific group and/or area. Differences can be attributed to divergent subsistence economies, access to materials restricted by environmental features, encroachment of Europeans onto Indian lands, and any number of social, economic and political circumstances. Examples presented here underscore several of these elements. Certainly economic necessity and a local non-Native market stimulated the expansion of the traditional woodsplint basketry craft among the Algonquian-speaking New England tribes on the southeastern Atlantic Coast. Farther up the Atlantic Coast, the Micmac (also Algonquian) shifted their porcupine

Combining indigenous materials with those acquired through trade to create items for their own use and for the tourist market, echoes Native responses and interactions with the non-Native newcomers to the Northeast. The heavily beaded Chippewa (Ojibwa in Canada) bandoleer bag (background, main picture) colorfully illustrates the incorporation of European trade beads into a traditional Native art. The late-19th century Micmac moccasins (top, main picture), made expressly for the tourist trade, demonstrate the skilful amalgamation of local deerskin and porcupine quill decoration on a cloth-covered birch bark vamp with imported beads, silk ribbon and silk lining. Other products remained unaffected, woven items like a twined Winnebago bag (right and far left) and a carved miniature Delaware mask (above left) inspired by a dream.

quillwork techniques from decorating native birch bark objects to decorating forms more acceptable to European tastes. In the St. Lawrence Lowlands, Iroquois, Huron, and Abenaki, having been taught the fundamentals of true embroidery using indigenous materials by the French Ursuline nuns, refined this skill into the production of a made-for-trade commodity. To the south of the Great Lakes, the horticultural Iroquois carved wooden masks for performance in public and private tribal rituals. As the Chippewa moved westward into the northern Great Lakes area, they adapted quillwork techniques to create elaborate beadwork items. The tribes of the Great Lakes region, comprising both Algonquian and Siouan speakers, continued to twine fiber bags according to prehistoric traditions. Concurrently, these same groups adeptly transformed European trade textiles into a distinctly Native art form.

Thus each and every art and craft form voiced the Native esthetics, innovations, creativity and complementary roles of men and women that constitute the essence of dynamic artistic expression.

Birch Bark Biting

Creating pictures on folded sheets of very thin layers of birch bark with the teeth was a ubiquitous art form throughout the entire region wherever the white birch tree (*Betula papyrifera*) grew. Historical accounts from the 17th, 18th and 19th centuries establish the antiquity of this unusual craft and ethnographic accounts of the early-20th century continue to record the practice.[2] More recently, recognition of birch bark dental pictographs as both an entirely Native and an endangered art form has prompted collectors and museum curators to acquire the work of the very few contemporary artists who possess the ability to create these bitten bark transparencies.

According to current knowledge, bark is collected in the spring when the sap first starts to run. Criteria for the selection of the perfect tree entail the color (which should be pure white), the correct age and size, freedom from imperfections and knots. From this living source the bark (the

best is ten layers thick) is removed and is then painstakingly peeled into fine paper-like pieces, of which only half may be suitable. The sharpest pictures result by biting the prepared bark while it is still fresh. However, written accounts of frozen birch logs releasing tissue-thin layers of bark as they thawed by the fire and of warming pieces of bark from dried logs would have ensured a winter supply as well.[3]

Various folding procedures determine the configuration of the designs. Most of the bark is folded in half to make an oblong and in half again to form a square, and finally folded from corner to corner to form a triangle. Holding the folded bark with the fingers, the point is inserted into the mouth. Using the incisor and canine teeth to make impressions in the folded bark, the piece is moved about in the mouth with the help of fingers and tongue. After the biting is completed, the bark is unfolded to reveal an intricate symmetrical design formed in the translucent medium. A second method of folding begins with a rectangular piece folded in half lengthwise, the upper third folded down and then diagonally to form a triangle. Teeth impressions are made along the hypotenuse thus formed. The bottom third of the oblong is folded only once on an oblique angle. The result resembles similar patterns of flowers with

Using readily available products of their forest environment, Algonquians such as the Chippewa bit thin sheets of folded birch bark to create symmetrical designs (right). It became a magical moment bringing awe and delight to young and old as the bark was unfolded and held up so that the light would suffuse it with a golden glow and shine through the tiny perforations.

leaves and stems worked on moccasin vamps. By leaving the bark unfolded and biting it according to the position of the artist's fingers, single realistic and/or asymmetrical figures can be produced. Those with expertise can, by regulating the force of the bite, produce a shaded effect. In a matter of minutes a pattern emerges that may be geometric, abstract, or representative of particular life forms, handsomely revealed when the pieces of bark are held up to sunlight or campfire light.

Several recorded accounts suggest that dental pictographs were made purely for pleasure.[4] Certainly as a diversion around the camp fire or stove, women and children (and occasionally men) derived great pleasure from this creative activity. By imitating their mothers, aunts and grandmothers, children learned new skills and absorbed new ideas and cultural values. Although results varied in artistic quality depending on expertise, most if not all efforts were consumed by the fire. If, as some researchers have suggested, these bitten patterns were used as guides for making beadwork designs and scraped patterns on birch bark, a few would have been kept.[5]

Bitten bark designs constitute a truly ephemeral art, providing pleasure only for the moment. However, the implications that arise are significant. It has been considered by some to be the only example of 'art for art's sake' among

Native North Americans.[6] As an art form, it demonstrates the multiplicity of designs possible, and lends itself to design experimentation. More importantly, it affords insights into the cognitive skills that utilize mental templates in the designing of an artifact. 'A woman never copied one pattern from another – it was original work, and a peculiarity was that **the pattern was clear in the mind of the worker before she made her first fold.** She said that she knew how the finished work would look before she began to work . . .'[7] The 'portability' of such a capacity was of supreme value to earlier hunting and foraging groups who, out of necessity, carried their worldly goods with them. The capability to recreate objects using 'the mind's eye' diminished the burden of excess material culture.

In its own small way, this art form establishes Native creativity and innovation to set the stage for other forms of arts and crafts utilizing either indigenous or foreign materials for personal use or for exchange purposes.

Woodsplint Basketry

Prevalent throughout the Northeast Woodlands it was among the New England tribes of the eastern Maritime regions that woodsplint basketry attained its greatest expression. First developed through an intimate knowledge of the woodland environment, basketry became an integral aspect of maize horticulture and the related preparation of maize foods. Baskets also served traditional needs as eel and fish traps, containers for berry picking and for a multitude of uses as storage containers. Later, basketry skills provided necessary products for early European settlers and as such, continued as a source of subsistence income for the Indians. Within the Native community basketry, as a means of communication, became a source for regional, ethnic, family and individual identity.

The processes involved in creating a basket begin with the initial steps of preparing the flat sturdy strips of wood splints, usually undertaken by a man. Selection of the preferred black ash

Carefully fashioned from birch bark with seams stitched together and covered with spruce gum, this small, watertight *mokuk* (left) was commonly used by the Chippewa for collecting and storing maple syrup, wild rice or berries. Only the bark stripped from the tree in the spring has the soft cambium inner layer which can be scraped away to reveal the whiter bark. Containers intended to be decorated have this brown layer on the outside. Although a bark template is often used to trace a pattern onto this soft surface, the geometric design seen here was created freehand. Once the design has been traced, either the background area or the design itself is scraped away to create a negative or positive design. As the cambium darkens over time the contrast increases.

Pictured in 1900, Abenaki basket maker Caroline Masta is shown (right) weaving fancy baskets with splints and sweetgrass sent to her by relatives in the Canadian province of Quebec. The products of her efforts were sold to tourists.

The uniformity of the narrower wefts of this Passamaquoddy covered 'work basket' (below) suggest that it was made after the introduction of the metal basket gauge. The form and the fine quality of the weaving furnish an esthetic subtlety that requires no further decoration.

(*Fraximus nigra* Marsh.), or 'basket' tree growing in bogs and along streams is done in the spring when the sap is running. Tobacco offerings propitiate the spirit of this slow-growing hardwood as it stands straight, its trunk marred by few knots, before it is cut down. Once felled and the bark removed, the entire circumference of the log is pounded with overlapping strokes using a wooden maul. This releases anywhere from one to six annual growth layers, called grains, six to ten inches in width at one time.[8] This process is continued until the heartwood is reached. As black ash is a ring-porous hardwood, the cells laid down during the rapid growth period in the spring are coarser and less dense than those laid down during the summer. When the log is pounded, these coarser cells collapse allowing the grains to separate easily.[9] The rough, grainy remains of the soft cellular tissue between each ring are scraped off to reveal smooth, light wood. These splints can be separated further into finer splints, and then divided into widths appropriate for the type and size of basket desired. Specialty but non-essential tools in the form of splitters, scrapers, basket gauges and forms introduced during the mid-19th century, continued to ease the preparation process and establish uniformity in materials.

Prepared splints are then transformed into baskets of innumerable shapes, sizes and purposes, decorated and plain. Primarily three weaving techniques were used: 'checker' in which the warp and weft have the same thickness and pliability and are woven one over, one under; 'twill' in which the warp and weft alternate at a ratio other than one to one, creating a diagonal pattern; and 'wicker' in which flexible, narrow splints are woven onto a wide and inflexible warp in a basic one over, one under pattern. Occasionally 'twining' is used in which two or more flexible wefts are twisted around individual warps.

The addition of color in various ways comprised early decorative applications. Splints could be completely permeated by dyes, swabbed on one side with color before weaving, block stamped with designs cut from potatoes, turnips or wood and dipped into pigment, or hand-painted with a brush or chewed twig on the finished basket. Textural patterns, generated by alternating scraped and unscraped splints, or those created by using narrow and wide wefts, were also intentional decorative devices. Greater texture and shadow were added when basket weavers began to incorporate secondary twisted or 'curlicue' wefts into their baskets. In this latter technique the outermost of a pair of wefts is twisted to form patterns of loops or curls commonly referred to as 'porcupine', 'shell' and 'diamond'.

Regional, cultural, individual and blended styles can be distinguished through materials, techniques, form, decoration and function during specific time periods. Regional styles are composites of ideas and techniques used by two or more contiguous groups living in an area. Cultural styles reveal the ethnic identity of specific groups. Imbedded within these styles are individual or family expressions recognized through certain features or innovations. An overlapping or combining of traits from two styles is called blended.

By way of illustration, baskets made by the Schaghticoke, Mahican and Paugusett peoples of the southwestern New England region during the 18th and 19th centuries were woven with both wide and narrow wefts of black ash and decorated by swabbing and/or stamping. In contrast, during the same period, the baskets of the southeastern New England Mohegan, Pequot, Niantic, Nipmuck and Wampanoag were constructed with wide wefts of white oak enhanced with elaborate painted designs. From the late-19th century onwards, both regions began to produce virtually identical undecorated narrow-weft splint baskets.

Cultural styles such as those evident in the painted designs of the Mohegan, also reveal temporal changes reflecting native reactions to changing political and social environments. During the period of forced removal from their lands, basket decoration acknowledged their resistance by enclosing a traditional four-domed medallion or rosette symbolizing the Mohegan people inside a boundary or enclosure. Outside the ancestral lands, Mohegans were often represented as a strawberry or a flower. Thus, through continued use of symbols on their basketry, Mohegans maintained their sense of ethnic identity and documented their grief.

Individuals and families of basket makers gained recognition with the intensification of their skills in response to an increasing tourist

market. As specialty tools (gauges, splitters and blocks) became commonplace, weavers transformed the exceedingly fine narrow splints into elaborate Victorian-inspired styles eagerly purchased as souvenirs. With the development of summer tourist resorts certain individuals or families retained rights to these areas to sell their winter's production.[10] Elaboration was expressed in both the form of the baskets, encompassing everything from novelty items to fancy household items to serviceable shopping bags and in the decorative elements of ingeniously twisted and curled splint. Children learned the craft through observation, producing small rimless baskets and developed their marketing skills by selling these for five cents during the early-20th century.

Micmac Quillwork

Unique to the Micmac of the Atlantic Provinces is the decorative insertion of dyed porcupine quills into birch bark found primarily on covered boxes. The fairly complete chronological sequence for this quillwork affords insights into the development of forms, styles, decorative techniques,

Fanciful shapes and new decorative techniques illustrated by this Central Algonquian splint basket (left) were developed to meet the increasing Victorian tourist market. By way of contrast, the tiny covered trinket basket (below) with its narrow weft and simple decorative elements remained a favorite tourist item long after the more elaborate styles lost favor. This piece is probably Abenaki made.

The oversized ring handles on this undecorated Penobscot basket (left) woven with narrow splints suggest that its intended purpose was more ornamental than practical.

motifs, and functions. While early historic documentation establishes that the Micmac used five different techniques of quillwork, by the beginning of the 17th century all but insertion appears to have fallen from use.[11] It was this fast and easy technique that became the basis for the Native entrepreneurial spirit. The Micmac response to the 18th century European desire for souvenirs and curiosities was to continue to use Native materials in the production and decoration of European forms. By 1750 a distinctive Micmac style was already evident in the round and rectangular lidded containers completely covered with dyed quills. As the Victorian mania for tourist items took hold over the following century, the repertoire of forms expanded to include such novelty items as tea cosies, lamp shades, fire screens, fans, cigar cases, purses and chair seats.

Materials were birch bark, porcupine quills, spruce roots, and the occasional use of thin wooden box liners. The bark of *B. papyrifera* or white birch was harvested by the men from the living tree during the latter days of July when the bark is pliable.[12] Porcupine quills, actually modified hairs with tiny barbs on the points, are plucked from the dead animal's back by the women, separated from the other hair and sorted according to size.[13] Coarser tail quills were also used for specific finishing details. Prior to the 1860s quills were dyed predominantly red, yellow, black or white (the natural quill color) from

vegetal sources. Additional sources provided blue and violet. After that time, inorganic aniline dyes from trade sources expanded the color palette but increased the susceptibility to color fading. From the black spruce (*Picea mariana*) came long slender roots split lengthwise into fibers for sewing birch bark and for decorative applications. The colors of dyed spruce roots faded rapidly, producing a more or less uniform soft brown tone. In the production of quilled boxes and purses, the softwood of pine, spruce or cedar was used for bases, pegs, linings, handles and hoops. The addition of sweetgrass (*Hierochloe odorata*) as a finishing edging imparted a sweet, long-lasting fragrance.

Round and oval lidded boxes, the most frequently encountered forms, are also the simplest to construct. A piece of birch bark cut to shape is rolled into a cylinder, the ends held together with quills. Once quilled this cylinder is stitched with spruce root to a bark base or pegged to a wooden base. Into this is inserted a bark liner (or for rectangular boxes, a thin wooden liner) extending above the box height equal to the depth of the box lid. The sides of the lid were then flush with those of the box. The lid itself was composed of a top of quilled bark sewn to a root-wrapped or quillworked bark ring side. For some boxes the bark liner served as the foundation over which rootwrapped rings were built up to form the exterior.

The insertion of the dyed quills into the birch bark to produce the typically vibrant mosaic patterns entailed a number of steps. Both bark and

quills were worked while slightly damp, the bark being dipped into warm water before beginning and the quills moistened as needed. A tiny insertion hole was made from the outer side of the bark with a beaver incisor or bone awl (and more recently with a darning needle). Once the quill was inserted into the hole, the bark contracted as it dried holding the quill tightly in place. The process was repeated for either end of each quill until the desired area was covered with closely inserted parallel rows. On the underside the barbed ends of the quills were burnt and all remaining ends were cut flush with the surface.[14]

Further steps in the design process built upon the basic principles of running quills all one way within a single color area and by contrasting colors or design areas by placing quills at angles to other sections. The break created by these placements was filled in first with a single quill-width, then two, and eventually this 'fill' developed into a complete design element such as that used to divide a pattern into four quarters. Also possibly introduced during the 19th century are designs of flattened quills overlaid on solidly quilled areas. Readily recognizable is the lattice-like design first used as an overlay but which evolved into being used alone on bare bark. Checkered patterns on root-wrapped rings were obtained by weaving natural colored quills into the vertical warp of the roots. Border edges were often finished with lengths of flattened tail quills or bundles of sweetgrass with fine spruce root.

Similar to other groups, early Micmac dream-inspired designs rendered tangibly on material items provided protection, healing and power. The symbolic meaning of these designs has become lost over the years and all of the traditional names forgotten, except for an eight-pointed star called *gogwit* or *kagwet* (Eight-Legged Starfish) and a fan-shaped motif called *waegardisk* (Northern Lights). The earliest dated design of 1760 has a double two-dimensional arch or rainbow which by the 20th century had degenerated into a token arched line incorporated into a central design element. Often found

in combination with this double rainbow is a stepped design. The most common motif is the chevron (and the variant, half chevron) traditionally found on the sides of lids and boxes.[15] Over time the visual dominance of the chevron pattern gave way to zig-zag lines created visually through the use of color. The chevron also occurs in a half form as well as integrated with diamonds and triangles. Circles, crosses, stars, double curves, squares, 'fylfot', and several realistic forms comprise the majority of the design elements.[16] With the introduction of aniline dyes, the intricacy of

Collected during the 1830s by artist-traveler George Catlin, this marvelous hide garment (below) exhibits period Indian iconography and decorative techniques. In addition to the painted border motifs and the woven quillwork on the top of the sleeve, a band of pony beads on front and back utilizes trade goods.

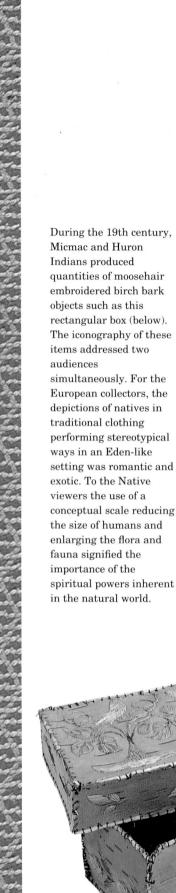

During the 19th century, Micmac and Huron Indians produced quantities of moosehair embroidered birch bark objects such as this rectangular box (below). The iconography of these items addressed two audiences simultaneously. For the European collectors, the depictions of natives in traditional clothing performing stereotypical ways in an Eden-like setting was romantic and exotic. To the Native viewers the use of a conceptual scale reducing the size of humans and enlarging the flora and fauna signified the importance of the spiritual powers inherent in the natural world.

earlier designs was replaced with stronger ones placed on a white background to accentuate the brilliant colors.

Although virtually all the quillwork produced over the centuries was for trade, this art form is so strongly identified with the Micmac nation that they themselves have come to regard it as a traditional form.[17]

Moosehair Embroidery

The use of animal hair – moose, caribou and reindeer – as a widespread medium of artistic expression among northern aboriginal groups became the medium of instruction used by the Ursuline nuns to demonstrate French embroidery techniques to young Native girls. By the early 1700s in the St. Lawrence River Lowlands, Iroquoian (most notably the Huron) and Algonquian artists had become adept at creating exquisite floral designs and pictorial depictions of Native life. These moosehair masterpieces, embroidered on to black tanned hide,[18] trade cloth and birch bark, formed the basis of a strong commercial venture.[19]

Moosehair, the primary decorative material, was procured from the winter pelage of the moose (*Alces alces*). Fine white hairs, four to five inches in length with long tapering black tips, removed

from the dead animal's cheeks, mane, rump and 'bell' were washed and then dyed. Initially, the dyeing process involved steeping the hair in hot vegetal infusions to acquire various shades of red, blue and yellow to be used in combination with the natural white ones. These indigenous organic ones were quickly replaced when the introduction of aniline dyes offered an easier process and a wider selection of colors. Tied into bundles for storing, dyed hairs merely required moistening in the mouth to be ready for use.

Three precontact techniques of line-work (spot stitching or appliqueing bundles of the moosehair into straight, curved or zig-zag lines on to a background), loom weaving and false embroidery were supplemented by the European introduction of true embroidery which relied upon steel needles threaded with a filament (in this case, moosehair). The continued use of line-work can be recognized by the distinctive bead-like effect created by the slight twisting of the hair bundle just before the couching thread is pulled tight. However, with the new technique of needle embroidery, depth, shading and further three-dimensional texture were achieved through color variation and various embroidery stitches. Simple patterns soon became elaborated into complex designs and earlier non-representational motifs became dominated by floral ones.

By the beginning of the 19th century, Huron floral-decorated items epitomized the height of this expression. Rich colors and intricate designs accentuated by their background of black tanned hide were rendered on mittens, moccasins, pouches and leggings. Cloth panels enhanced with floral designs were sewn to collars, cuffs, epaulettes, lapels and borders of hide and cloth coats. Similar decorations appeared on 'pockets' formed from the lower legs of moose and caribou, knife sheaths, belts, garters and bandoleers. Although long considered as items made solely for the tourist market, their native forms suggest probable indigenous functions as well.

A second genre, well-developed by the first half of the 19th century, was moosehair embroidery on

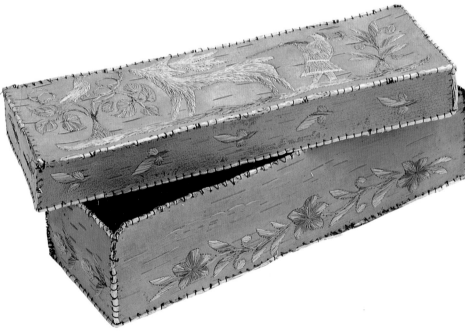

130

birch bark items. This souvenir work was either entirely floral in design or depicted narrative vignettes of native life enhanced with flowers and trees. Traditionally-garbed Indians were embroidered in romanticized settings in canoes, in front of wigwams, smoking peace pipes, hunting in the forest, juxtaposed with larger-than-life flowers and berries, all designed to appeal to the then current European notion of the Noble Savage. Imbedded within these images, however, are invaluable iconographic details of Native ideals concerning the environment, establishing individual and group identity through clothing, and such symbolic referents as strawberries with their association of an idyllic afterworld. Decorated with either flowers or pictorials, the forms of this second genre are non-traditional containers, boxes, whimsies, cigar cases, bases for women's reticules and so on, designed specifically for trade and as gifts for foreign dignitaries.

Iroquoian Masks

Two types of Iroquoian masks, classified according to materials used are carved wooden ones associated with the False Face Society, and those-woven of cornhusks for the Husk Face or Bushy-heads' Society. Individually each form reflects one half of the complementary features that comprise the synergistic whole of Iroquoian culture. False Faces are carved by men from the material of the forest domain while Husk Faces are woven by women from products of their horticultural endeavors. Together, the False Face and Husk Face Societies, men and women, hunting and horticultural, function to ensure the health and well-being of the society.

Origins of the False Face masks arose as a result of a mythic contest between the Great Creator and the First *Hodo'win*, the most powerful of the forest faces.[20] To test the strength of their powers they each attempted to summon a mountain to them; success would acknowledge supremacy. The first to try, *Hodo'win* achieved only partial success. So anxious was he to see what the Creator was achieving, *Hodo'win* turned

The carved Seneca False Face mask with white horsetail hair (left) represents *Hodo'win* after his encounter with a mountain. As the Great Doctor, 'Crooked Nose' played an important role in the healing rituals of the Iroquois people. The wearer of the mask became transformed into the spiritual being. To ensure the continuing strengths of masks, they are rubbed with sunflower oil and fed tobacco, and carefully wrapped until needed.

sharply, striking his face on the mountain which had appeared directly behind him. The impact broke his nose; his mouth twisted from the pain. The successful Creator, recognizing the strength of the loser, entrusted him to assist humans to combat illness and other evil influences. Henceforth, as the Great Doctor, it became *Hodo'win*'s responsibility to instruct men in the art of carving masks and in the ceremonies in which they were to be used.

As a mask was carved from a living tree to acquire the earth power and sky power imbued within this cosmic axis, this necessitated ritual preparation of both carver and tree. In order to retain the potency and spirit of the basswood or other softwood tree, three days were spent

The photograph (right) of a False Face in the process of being carved from the living basswood tree was a posed picture arranged by Arthur Parker in 1910 at the Cattaraugus Reservation of the Seneca. It serves, however, to show the technique.

This Upper Cayuga version of *Hadu'i* (below) was carved in 1943. Worn by shamans and dancers in ways that were revealed to them in dreams, it personified the essence of the spiritual being.

ceremonially feeding tobacco (*Nicotiana rustica*) and tobacco smoke to the Tree Spirit and entreating forgiveness for the impending injury. Appeased, the Tree Spirit requested that its life spirit be continued in the mask to be carved and hewn from its trunk.

Before the introduction of steel tools, woodworking was accomplished by burning the area and scraping away the charred wood. With steel tools, carving was performed directly on the wood. Once the bark was removed, the face was roughed out, and only when the carving was nearly completed was the mask released from the tree. The finished mask was smoothed inside and out, metal eye rings were attached, the face was painted and long hair inserted into holes. If the carving of the mask was begun in the morning, it was painted red; black was indicative of an afternoon start. These colors represented the belief that the daily journey of the first False Face followed the sun; therefore his face appeared red in the morning as he came from the east, and black in the evening as he looked back from the west. A mask painted half-red and half-black represented a divided being – half-human, half-supernatural

– whose body was split in two and who stood facing south, his red cheek to the east, black one to the west.

The features of masks vary according to their intended function, dream visions experienced by the carvers, and local styles. Generally, the masks possess deep-set eyes accentuated with metal 'whites,' large noses bent in imitation of the Great Doctor's, and often a deeply creased forehead. The mouth is the most variable feature, leading to contemporary classifications based solely on this feature.[21] The twisted mouth of the Great Doctor is replaced alternatively with a smile, a grimace with teeth showing, a pucker as if whistling, a pucker with spoon-like lips, or with lips distended to blow ashes. A number display protruding tongues.[22]

Sanctification of completed masks consisted of a number of steps. A tiny bag filled with tobacco was attached to the forehead of the mask; its face rubbed with sunflower oil to feed it; and then it was placed near the fire and tobacco was thrown into the fire. As the mask became suffused by wood and tobacco smoke, the carver told the mask what it was supposed to do.[23] The mask was then ready to perform in curing rituals. Periodic feeding of sunflower oil and tobacco continued to maintain the strength of the mask as long as it was used. Boys learned to carve by first making small masks.

Visually and tactilely pleasing, the significance of the masks rests, however, in their power which is especially efficacious in healing rites. The best-known, although not the most important, curing rituals were performed by the False Face Society. When a person fell ill, the members of the Society would don their masks and creep towards the sick person's home. There they scraped their snapping turtle rattles against the wooden door frame before entering the house, shaking the rattles all the while.[24] Using sacred ashes and tobacco in specific rites, the masked healers effected a cure. Once cured, the patient became a member of the Society along with anyone who had an appropriate visionary dream. Although most curing

Given the strong emphasis placed on agriculture by the Iroquois, it was natural that cornhusk masks such as this Cayuga plaited one (far left) were intimately involved with the agricultural spirits, Three Sisters.

This Menominee couple (left) pose proudly with their artistic endeavours. The woman is wearing a loom-woven beaded bag similar to this colorful Chippewa version (below). Of particular interest are the two distinct patterns used for each half of the strap.

sessions were held privately, the False Faces also performed curing rituals during the public Midwinter Festival.

The Society of Husk Faces or Bushy-heads are earthbound spirits, who in their capacity as messengers of the Three Sisters – corn, beans and squash – taught agricultural practices to humans. Although not as integrated or prominent as their counterparts, the False Faces, they shared certain functions. Under a condition of remaining mute, members of this group, nevertheless, possessed their own tobacco invocation, a medicine song, and the power to cure by blowing ashes. Wearing cornhusk masks, they appeared at the Midwinter Festival to dance with the people and beg for food.

The fabrication of these masks by the women is based on an ancient craft technique wherein cornhusks are shredded and braided. Two different methods are used to give them the desired shape: sewing of coiled husk braids, and twining. In the first, long strips of cornhusk braid are sewn into three coils to form the eyes and mouth, and the nose, which is often a sheathed corncob is attached, and then the fringe is added. Twined

masks were begun at the nose with eight warps which were later extended by twisting on new elements. A pair of wefts was twisted around each warp until the rim was reached. At first sight there appears to be little variety in these faces, which are always surrounded by husk streamers, but closer inspection reveals much individuality. Paint was only occasionally applied to these masks.[25]

Beadwork

A kaleidoscope of colors and patterns dominates Chippewa (Ojibwa) beadwork. With the introduction of glass trade beads early in the 17th century, techniques already in use for porcupine quillwork were easily adapted to accommodate this exciting new medium of artistic expression. First 'pony' beads and later tiny 'seed' beads, pinpoints of light and color, readily lent themselves to the complex forms of woven and appliqued beadwork. Through the subtle blending of vividly-colored transparent, translucent and opaque, round or faceted seed beads, artistic masterpieces emerged. For more than two centuries beadwork was a major artistic focus for the Chippewa, and

The Fox (Mesquakie) bead loom illustrated here (right) is an artwork in itself. Carved in the late-1800s from hardwood and incised with designs on both faces, its technology is more sophisticated than the smaller looms normally used for beading straps. In this example, half the warp threads passing through perforations in the middle of the heddle are held firm while the other half passing between the heddles are free to move up and down. The sheds thus created allow the warp to be interwoven so that the pattern appears the same on both sides.

Floral beaded moccasins with silk ribbon appliqued ankle flaps are most often associated with the tribes of the Great Lakes region. This pair (below) was collected at Niagara Falls in the mid-19th century. Note the different colored pattern of silk on either flap.

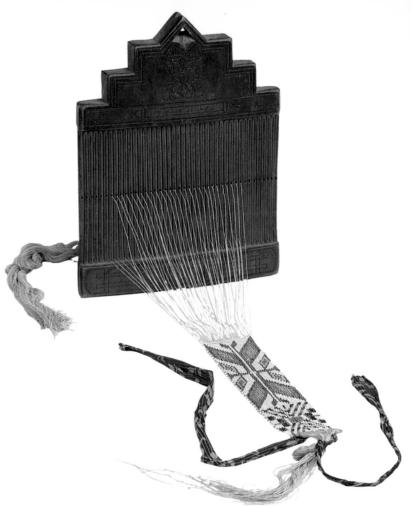

continues to gain them as much recognition from within their own culture area as it does from non-Native audiences.

Loom-weaving produced beadwork in which the fibers carrying the beads are also the sole foundation of the finished item. The earliest loom was the bow loom, a flexible stick with birch bark or hide heddles to hold and separate the sinew warps fastened at each end. Exchanging beads for porcupine quill, women wove beaded bands suitable for garters, belts, headbands and decorative strips to be sewn on to articles of clothing. Limitations in length and width of finished pieces led to the development of the simple rectangular box loom devised of four pieces of wood fastened together at the corners. On this loom one continuous warp thread is strung evenly-spaced around the frame, including one warp row more than the number of beads required for the width of the pattern. To weave the beads on either loom requires a long, fine beading needle, threaded and with one end tied to an outside warp. The appropriate number of beads for one width are strung onto this weft thread. First the threaded and bead-strung needle is passed under the warp to the opposite side. Holding the thread tight, each of the beads is pushed up between a pair of the warp threads all the way across so that the holes in them are above the level of the warp threads. The threaded needle is then passed back through all the beads while they are in this position, thus

weaving the first row. All subsequent rows follow this procedure. Loose ends are woven back into the beadwork to produce a stronger foundation. Sometimes the warp threads are braided or woven into fringes. The introduction of the box loom expanded the earlier repertoire of beadwork with longer and wider forms. Wider pieces were sewn whole on to bandoleer bags and smaller pouches. Understandably, this technique of square weaving dominates design, creating motifs and patterns which are basically geometric. Even floral motifs are reduced to the artificial 'curves' of tiny square steps.[26]

Appliqued beadwork involves the stitching of beads to another material such as hide or cloth which serves as the foundation. Basically, a line of sinew-threaded beads is sewn to the foundation by means of a second thread tacking (spot stitching or couching) the first one after every two or three beads. In contrast to woven beadwork, this beadwork application permits the design to dominate the technique. As a result, a wide range of decorative possibilities abound: curves pose no problem; both outline patterns and solid areas are

beaded with equal ease; and colors can be changed at will. Great examples appear on clothing, ceremonial items, cradle boards, and bags.

Both types of beadwork appear together on bandoleer bags, 'the apex of the beadworker's art.'[27] A shoulder strap or 'baldric' of woven or appliqued beadwork was attached to a rectangular pouch of heavy floral applique work and to the bottom of this was stitched either a fringe or a wide loom-woven panel. Asymmetrical patterns on the strap with motifs and configurations changing at mid-point in the length, serve as an identifying feature. These ornate bags, worn cross-wise over each shoulder in ceremonies and dances, once served as fire bags carrying smoking pipes and tobacco. As their significance and popularity increased, esthetic properties supplanted practical ones and the bags were made without true pouches. Ultimately they became a symbol of wealth with an individual wearing anywhere from the usual one or two to as many as 12 or more. Sometimes referred to as 'Friendship Bags,' bandoleer bags were presentation gifts at tribal and inter-tribal gatherings, enhancing the prestige of artist, donor and recipient alike.

Twined Fiber Bags

All the Great Lakes and Northeast Woodlands tribes were proficient at twining fiber bags for their own use. Regional evidence dating from at least AD 300 establishes this craft's relationship to widespread ancient finger-weaving techniques which no machine can duplicate.[28] It is the people of the Great Lakes area – Fox, Sauk, Menominee, Winnebago, Potawatomi, Ottawa – whose inventory of materials and finger-weaving techniques showed the greatest variety. Decoration, somewhat limited by the twining technique, was restricted to patterns formed through the use of contrasting color fibers and complex methods of twining. Stripes, geometric shapes and stylized birds, felines, deers and humans constituted the basis of the imagery. While coarser utilitarian bags that functioned as harvesting and storage containers were sometimes decorated with

colored patterns, it is the smaller, softer bags that have received greater attention.[29]

These softer bags were made of fine *Apocynum* fibers.[30] The stalks of this plant were first soaked in stagnant water until the fleshy parts could be beaten off, leaving fibers three or four feet in length. Rolling these fibers into an S twist on the knee yielded strands that were then twisted together to produce the two-ply cords preferred for weaving. Dark brown buffalo wool was sometimes used for natural color contrast. As trade with the Europeans, increased, these native fibers were replaced with colored yarns.

To twine the bags, prepared warp elements are hung over a stick suspended horizontally. Beginning closest to the stick, two weft cords are passed one in front of a warp element and one behind it and then twined (twisted) at each crossing. This procedure is continued from left to right in a continuous spiral around the loose-hanging warps. Weaving is discontinued four or five inches from the ends of the warp elements. These ends are braided horizontally to form the opening of the bag. By removing the stick from between the warps, a seamless bag results.

This flat bag (left) is an early example of a twined bag utilizing fine strips of lindenwood (basswood) bast and was acquired from the Fox (Mesquakie) Indians in Iowa. The body of the bag, decorated with simple stripes of natural and black, is finished with false braid on the margin of the opening. The attached strap and tassel are also made from bast.

Collected from the Menominee of Wisconsin in 1908, this small bag (below) is twined from yarns dyed with bloodroot and other plants. Once used by a medicine woman to hold herbs gathered for healing, the alternating colored stripes and the herringbone pattern of the bag itself create a dynamic sense of an inherent energy that complements the potential medicinal power of its herbal contents.

Made for native use rather than as a trade item, twined bags such as this large Winnebago one (above) reflect both the natural and social environments of many generations. Of the cotton, wool and buffalo hair used to finger-weave this bag, the latter two may have been acquired through trade. The imagery, although constrained by technique, incorporated the cosmological views of the makers. The designs on the side of this bag are abstract representations of the Upper World Thunderbirds bounded by vertically repeated diamonds (mirror images of zig-zag lightning). Balanced with the Underwater Panther, these opposing forces are mediated by the Earth materials of the bag.

Decorative elements are created by setting up double warps of light and dark contrasting colors. Whichever of these two warp colors is pulled forward during the weaving process is the one that appears at that point on the surface of the bag. Due to the limitations of the twining technique, motifs tend to be angular, with representational figures rendered in a stylized manner.

The imagery on a number of bags reflects the cosmology of the Great Lakes area. Birds and felines appearing on opposite sides of these bags are interpreted, respectively, as depictions of the mythical Thunderbird and the Underwater Panther. The Thunderbird is most often depicted as two triangles joined to form a stylized hourglass shape to which down-thrust wings are attached. In some versions the hourglass is filled with concentric triangles, chevrons or diamonds. A central diamond on the torso indicates the heart. Often associated with a large central Thunderbird figure are smaller thunderbirds and recurrent geometric patterns in the form of parallel zig-zag lines representing lightning or thunderbolts. On the other side of the bag the Underwater Panther (or group of Panthers), as the key figure, is depicted with horns, ribs, dorsal

scales and an exceedingly long tail coiled around the cat-like body. Associated with this figure are elongated hexagonal forms identified as representing sacrifices of food in bark dishes as well as zig-zag, wavy or castellated lines interpreted as wavy or roiled water.[31] These associated geometric designs become significant in the absence of life figures on some bags; for wherever these non-representational geometric designs are present, they can be construed as symbolic of manitous.

Both the Thunderbird and the Underwater Panther were extremely powerful manitous who, respectively, controlled the Sky World and the Under World. The power of each was manifested in both beneficent and malevolent aspects with the Thunderbird responsible for rain and victory in war but who also caused devastating storms. Balancing the Underwater Panther's malevolent forces that roiled the waters and drowned the unwary were its curative powers that could heal and prolong life. Mythic accounts place them as opponents in a continuing battle. Conflicts of power and strength between these two opposing manitous are mediated by elements of the Earth zone represented by the vegetal and animal fibers of the bag. By this means a balanced tri-partite cosmos is rendered tangible in these fiber bags.

Twined bags functioned within the societies as containers for individual personal medicines or as components of larger medicine bundles. Intriguing are those bags that were 'rigged with internal mechanical devices and used by medicine men to perform spectacular tricks in public performances, such as the appearance or disappearance of seemingly live but actually wooden snakes or puppets.'[32] Only after their power was no longer efficacious were these personally significant Native-made bags of indigenous materials acquired by non-Natives.

Ribbonwork

Ribbonwork is the art of cutting and sewing brightly colored silk ribbon to trade cloth for decorative purposes on clothing and other paraphernalia. The technique, first developed in the early-18th century, initially had a wide distribution throughout the entire cultural region. However, it is among the Great Lakes tribes that it reached its apogee and continues there today as an important art form. While the development of this art form was entirely dependent upon the introduction of trade goods – cloth, ribbon, thread, scissors or knives, and needles – the origins, forms, motifs, color selection, and intended use, are totally Indian.

Silk ribbons, first presented as gifts to the Indians, continued to be available through trade. Early ribbons were narrow, often only one-half to one-and one-half inches in width. Later ones reached widths of three and four inches (up to 10cms). Woolen trade cloth, providing backgrounds of black, dark blue or red, was fashioned into women's blankets (shawls) and skirts, men's shirts, leggings, moccasins and other miscellaneous items.

In its simplest form, the ribbonwork technique consists of cutting a design into a silk ribbon of one color and hand sewing it on to a background panel of another color and then stitching the panel to the fabric of the garment. Mirror images, repetition and asymmetrical designs are typical. Positive and negative styles are identified by

pairs of ribbons sewn to produce a bilaterally symmetrical four-ribbon strip. The distinguishing feature is determined by the layer in which the figure is created. Positive style is identified by the cut and sewn top layer which is perceived to be the design. Negative style is created when the top parts of the ribbon are cut away to reveal the bilaterally symmetrical figure on the bottom layer of ribbons.[33] Around 1850 these basic styles became elaborated with design units larger, more varied and more complicated in shape and incorporating several layers of various colored ribbons. Simple geometric designs in earlier work were later augmented with intricate curvilinear ones. Patterns to create these designs were cut from birch bark or paper, and a collection of these became a woman's most treasured personal possession.[34]

Preference in ribbon colors was given to those with symbolic meaning in addition to their esthetic value. For the Menominee, colors from the realm of Sky Woman were associated with the cardinal points: red for east; white and yellow for south; blue for west; and black for north.[35] For Mesquakie Ada Old Bear, red signified the Fox clan and black was associated with spiritual enlightenment and prayer.[36] Color selection performs as an integral aspect of the interplay between foreground and background, between dark and light, and between pattern form and color. This interplay and the tensions of mirror images and pattern reversals creates a dynamic vitality, the carefully balanced designs changing as the perspectives of the viewer shift. Creativity, innovation, and a common regional esthetic of these Native artists is superbly demonstrated through this manipulation of non-Native textiles.

It is fitting that many contemporary examples of ribbonwork shirts and skirts are made especially to accompany the dead,[37] for in this way the metaphor of duality, of a whole being split – half in this world, half in the spirit world – is brought to life as the corporeal body transforms into the spiritual one, as the past world becomes the new world.

The richness of color captured in silk became the artistic palette of the Great Lakes Indians. Cutting and stitching this trade material into geometric and curvilinear designs to create vibrant mirror image or appliqued work is illustrated here by the Menominee legging (above) and the woman's shawl from Minnesota (left). This combination of Native artistry and European materials reflects reconciliation of the Native's split social world.

BIBLIOGRAPHY

INTRODUCTION

Books

Boas, F. *Primitive Art*, 1927.
Bourke, Capt. J. G. *Mackenzie's Last Fight With The Cheyenne*, reprinted Bellevue, Nebraska, 1890.
Coe, R. T. *Sacred Circles*, London 1976.
Coe, R. T. *Lost and Found Traditions*, New York, 1986.
Culin, S. *Games of the North American Indians*, 24th Annual Report of the Bureau of American Ethnology 1902-03, Smithsonian Institution Washington D. C., 1907.
Farge, O., et al, *Introduction to American Indian Art*, Glorieta, New Mexico, 1931.
Feder, N. *American Indian Art*, New York, 1965.
Kroeber, T. *Ishi In Two Worlds*, London 1987.
Seton, J. M. *American Indian Arts: A Way of Life*, New York, 1962.

Other

Taylor, C. F. 'Costume with Quill-wrapped Hair: Nez Perce or Crow?' in *American Indian Art Magazine*, Vol. 6, No. 3, Scottsdale, Arizona, 1981.
Taylor, C. F. '*Wakanyan*: Symbols of Power and Ritual of the Teton Sioux'. Edited by D. McCaskill in *Amerindian Cosmology, Cosmos 4,* Brandon, Manitoba, 1989.
Whiteford, A. H. 'Southwestern Indian Baskets', Santa Fe, New Mexico, 1988.

THE SOUTHEAST

Books

Brose, D. S. and Brown, J. A. *Ancient Art of the American Woodland Indians*, New York, 1985.
Dockstader, F. J. *Weaving Arts of the North American Indians*, New York, 1978.
Fundaburk, E. L. and Foreman, M. D. F. *Sun Circles and Human Hands: The Southeastern Indians Art and Industries*, Luverne, Alabama, 1957.
Gilliland, M. S. *The Material Culture of Key Marco Florida*, Gainesville, Florida, 1975.
Haberland, W. *The Art of North America*, 1964.
Hudson, C. *The Southeastern Indians*, Knoxville, Tennessee, 1976.
Leftwich, R. L. *Arts and Crafts of the Cherokee*, Cullowee, North Carolina, 1970.
Speck, F. G. and Bloom, L. *Cherokee Dance and Drama*, Berkeley, California, 1951.
Turnbaugh, S. P. and Turnbaugh W. A. *Indian Baskets*, Westchester, Pennsylvania, 1986.
Wood, M. *Native American Fashion*, New York, 1981.

Other

Carr, L. 'Dress and Ornamentation of Certain American Indians', in *Proceedings of the American Antiquarian Society*, Vol. 11, Worcester, Massachusetts, 1897.
Cushing, F. H. 'Primitive Copper Working: An Experimental Study' in *American Anthropologist*, Vol. 7, Arlington, Virginia, 1894.
Dixon, D. and Domjanovich, S. 'Native American Cane Basketry', in *Shuttle, Spindle, and Dye*, Vol. 13, No. 4, West Hartford, Connecticut, 1992.
Downs, D. 'Patchwork Clothing of the Florida Indians', *American Indian Art Magazine*, Vol. 4, No. 3, Scottsdale, Arizona, 1979.
Fewkes, V. J. 'Catawba Pottery Making, With Notes of Pamunkey Pottery Making, Cherokee Pottery Making, and Coiling' in *Proceedings of the American Philosophical Society*, Vol. 88, No. 2, Philadelphia, Pennsylvania, 1944.
Goggin, J. M. 'Style Areas in Historic Southeastern Art', in *Indian Tribes of Aboriginal America: Selected Papers of the XXIX International Congress of Americanists*, New York, 1967.
Hally, D. J., Smith, M. T., Langford, J. B. 'The Archaeological Reality of de Soto's Coosa', in *Columbian Consequences, Vol. II, Archaeological and Historical Perspectives of the Spanish Borderlands East*, Washington D. C., 1990.
Hamilton, H. W., Hamilton, J. T., Chapman, E. F. 'Spiro Mound Copper' in *Memoir of the Missouri Archaeological Society*, No. 11, Stillwater, Oklahoma, 1974.
Harrington, M. R. 'Catawba Potters and Their Work' in *American Anthropologist*, Vol. 10, No. 3, Fairfax, Virginia, 1908.
Howard, J. H. 'The Southeastern Ceremonial Complex and Its Interpretations', in *Memoir of the Missouri Archaeological Society*, No. 6, Stillwater, Oklahoma, 1968.
Larson, L. 'A Mississippian Headdress from Etowah, Georgia', in *American Antiquity*, Vol. 25, No. 1, Menasha, Wisconsin, 1959.
Mason, O. T. 'Aboriginal American Basketry: Studies in a Textile Art Without Machinery', in *Annual Report of the Board of Regents of the Smithsonian Institution*, Washington D. C., 1904.
Medford, C. 'Native Clothing of the Southeastern Indian People', in *Indian America*, Vol. 9, No. 1, Tulsa, Oklahoma, 1975.
Porter, F. W. 'Basketry of the Middle Atlantic and Southeast', in *The Art of Native American Basketry: A Living Legacy*, New York, 1990.
Speck, F. G. 'Decorative Art and Basketry of the Cherokee', in *Bulletin of the Public Museum of the City of Milwaukee*, Vol. 2, No. 2, Milwaukee, Wisconsin, 1920.
Sturtevant, W. C. 'Seminole Men's Clothing', in *Essays on the Verbal and Visual Arts, Proceedings of the 1966 Annual Spring Meeting of the American Ethnological Society*, Seattle, Washington, 1967.
West, G. A. 'Tobacco, Pipes, and Smoking Customs of the American Indians' in *Bulletin of the Public Museum of the City of Milwaukee*, Vol. XVII, Milwaukee, Wisconsin, 1934.
Witthoft, J. 'Stone Pipes of the Historic Cherokee', in *Southern Indian Studies*, Vol. 1, No. 2, Chapel Hill, North Carolina, 1949.

THE SOUTHWEST

Books

Adair, J. *The Navajo and Pueblo Silversmiths*, Norman, Oklahoma, 1962.
Bedinger, M. *Indian Silver, Navajo and Pueblo Jewelers*, Albuquerque, 1974.
Berlant, A. and Kahlenberg, M. H. *Walk in Beauty*, Salt Lake City, 1991.
Brody, J. J. *Beauty From the Earth, Pueblo Indian Pottery from the University Museum of Archeology and Anthropology*, Philadelphia, 1990.
Bunzel, R. *The Pueblo Potter, A Study of Creative Imagination in Primitive Art*, New York, 1972.
Coe, R. T. *Lost and Found Traditions*, 1986.
Dillingham, R. *Seven Families in Pueblo Pottery*, Albuquerque, 1974.
Dillingham, R. *Acoma and Laguna Pottery*, Santa Fe, New Mexico, 1992.
Fox, N. *Pueblo Weaving and Textile Arts*, Santa Fe, New Mexico, 1978.
Frank, L. and Harlow, F. *Historic Pottery of the Pueblo Indians 1600-1880*, Boston, 1974.
Harlow, F. *Historic Pueblo Indian Pottery*, Santa Fe, New Mexico, 1970.
James, G. W. *Indian Basketry*, New York, 1972.
Kent, K. P. *Prehistoric Textiles of the Southwest*, Santa Fe, New Mexico, 1983.
LeFree, B. *Santa Clara Pottery Today*, Albuquerque, 1975.
Marriott, A. *Maria: The Potter of San Ildefonso*, Norman, Oklahoma, 1986.
O'Bryon. *The Dine Myths of the Navajo Indians*, Washington D.C., 1956.
Reichard, G. A. *Spider Woman: A Story of Navajo Weavers and Chanters*, reprinted Glorieta, New Mexico, 1968.
Rozaire, C. *Indian Basketry of Western North America*, Santa Ana, California, 1977.
Schaafsma, P. *Kachinas*, Albuquerque, 1994.
Sturtevant, W. and Ortiz, A. *Handbook of North American Indians, Vol. 9, Southwest*, Washington D. C., 1979.
Trimble, S. *Talking With the Clay: The Art of Pueblo Pottery*, Santa Fe, New Mexico, 1987.

Other

Bloom. 'Bourke on the Southwest', in *New Mexico Historical Review*, XI, 1936.
Cushing, F. 'Zuni Breadstuff' in *Indian Notes and Monographs: 8*, Museum of the American Indian, New York, 1886.

THE PLAINS

Books

Bebbington, J. M. *Quillwork of the Plains*, Calgary, Alberta, 1982.
Best, A. and McClelland, A. *Quillwork by Native Peoples in Canada*, Toronto, Ontario, 1977.
Brownstone, A. *War Paint: Blackfoot and Sarcee Painted Buffalo Robes in the Royal Ontario Museum*, Toronto, Ontario, 1993.
Catlin, G. *Letters and Notes on the Manners, Customs, and Condition of the North American Indians*: Vols I-II, London, 1841.
Catlin, G. *Indian Art in Pipestone: George Catlin's Portfolio in the British Museum*, Edited by John C. Ewers, Washington D. C., 1979.
Clark, W. P. *The Indian Sign Language*, Philadelphia, 1885.
Denig, E. T. *Indian Tribes of the Upper Missouri* Edited by J. N. B. Hewitt, Washington D. C., 1930.
Ewers, J. C. *Plains Indian Painting*, Stanford, California, 1939.
Ewers J. C. *Blackfeet Crafts*, Lawrence, Kansas, 1945.
Ewers J. C. *Blackfoot Indian Pipes and Pipemaking*, Bureau of American Ethnology Bulletin 186 (64), Washington D. C., 1963.
Ewers J. C. *Plains Indian Sculpture*, Washington D. C., 1986.
Fardoulis, A. *Le cabinet du Roi, et les anciens Cabinets de Curiosités dans les collections du Musee de l'Homme,* Paris, 1979.
Fletcher, A. and La Flesche, F. *The Omaha Tribe, 27th Annual Report of the Bureau of American Ethnology, 1905-06*, Washington D. C., 1911.
Grinnell, G. B. *The Cheyenne Indians: Their History and Ways of Life*: Vols. I-II, New Haven, 1923.
Hail, B. A. *Hau kola!* Bristol, Rhode Island, 1983.
King, J. C. H. *Thunderbird and Lightning*, London, 1982.
Kroeber, A. L. *The Arapaho*, Bulletin of the American Museum of Natural History, New York, 1902.
Larocque, F. *Journal of Larocque from the Assiniboine to the Yellowstone, 1805*. Edited by Lawrence J. Burpee, Ottawa, 1910.
Lewis, M. *History of the Expedition under the command of Capts. Lewis & Clark*: Vols. I-II, 1904.
Lewis, M. and Clark, W. *The Original Journals of Lewis and Clark, 1804-1806*: Vols. I-VIII. Edited by Reuben Gold Thwaites, reprinted New York, 1959.
Lowie, R. H. *Indians of the Plains*, New York, 1954.
Lyford, C. A. *Quill and Beadwork of the Western Sioux*, Lawrence, Kansas, 1940.
MacGregor, A. (ed.) *Tradescant Rarities: Essays on the Foundation of the Ashmolean Museum in 1863*, Oxford, 1983.
MacGregor, J. G. *Peter Fidler: Canada's Forgotten Surveyor, 1769-1822*, Toronto, 1966.
Mallery, G. *Picture Writing of the American Indians*, 10th Annual Report of the Bureau of American Ethnology, Washington D. C., 1893.
Martin, P. S., Quimby, G. I., and Collier, D. *Indians before Columbus*, Chicago, 1947.
Morrow, M. *Indian Rawhide: An American Folk Art*, Norman, Oklahoma, 1975.
Orchard, W. C. *The Technique of Porcupine Quill Decoration Among the Indians of North America*, reprinted New York, 1971.
Palliser, J. *Solitary Rambles*, Vermont, 1969.
Petersen, K. D. *Plains Indian Art from Fort Marion*, Norman, Oklahoma, 1971.
Petersen, K. D. *American Pictographic Images*, New York, 1988.
Pond, S. *The Dakota or Sioux in Minnesota As They Were in 1834*, reprinted St. Paul 1986.
Spier, L. *Plains Indian Parfleche Designs*, Publications in Anthropology, Vol. IV, No. 3. Washington D.C., 1931.
Sturtevant, W. C. and Taylor, C. F. *The Native Americans*. London, 1991.
Taylor, C. F. *Wapa'ha: The Plains Feathered Headdress*, Germany, 1994.
Torrence, G. *The American Indian Parfleche: A Tradition of Abstract Painting*, Des Moines, 1994.
Waugh, E. H. *Blackfoot Religion: My Clothes Are Medicine*. Edited by P. H. R. Stepney and D. J. Goa, Edmonton, 1990.
Webber, A. P. *North American Indian and Eskimo Footwear*, Toronto, 1989.
Weltfish, G. *The Lost Universe: Pawnee Life and Culture*, Lincoln, Nebraska, 1977.
West, G. A. *Tobacco Pipes and Smoking Customs of the American Indians*. Milwaukee Public Museum, Bulletin 17, Milwaukee, 1934.
Wildschut, W. *Crow Indian Beadwork*, New York, 1959.
Wissler, C. *Social Organization and Ritualistic Ceremonies of the Blackfoot Indians. Part II. 'Ceremonial Bundles of the Blackfoot Indians;* Anthropology Papers of the American Museum of Natural History Vol. VII, New York. 1912 (b).
Wissler, C. *Costumes of the Plains Indians*, together with *Structural Basis to the Decoration of Costumes Among the Plains Indians*, reprinted New York, 1975.
Wissler, C. *Distribution of Moccasin Decorations Among the Plains Tribes*, Anthropology papers of the American Museum of Natural History, Vol. XXIX, Part I, New York, 1927.

Other

Conn, R. 'Blackfeet Women's Clothing' in *American Indian Tradition*, Vol. 7, No. 4, 1961.
Conner, S. and B. L. 'Rock Art of the Montana High Plains' in *The Art Galleries*, Santa Barbara, 1971.
Cooley, J. 'Kiowa Tab Leggings' in *Moccasin Tracks*, June, Vol. 8, No. 10, La Patnia, California, 1983.
Dempsey, H. 'Religious Significance of Blackfoot Quillwork' in *Plains Anthropologist*, Vol. 8, Lincoln, Nebraska, 1963.
Douglas, F. H. 'American Indian Tobacco'. *Indian Leaflet Series*, No. 22, Denver, 1931.
Feder, N. 'Introduction: Crow Indian Art – The Problem' in *American Indian Art Magazine*, Vol. 6, No. 1, Scottsdale, Arizona, 1980.
Feder, N. 'Bird Quillwork' in *American Indian Art Magazine*, Vol. 12, No. 3, Scottsdale, Arizona, 1987.
Fenenga, F. 'An Early Nineteenth Century Account of Assiniboine Quillwork' in *Plains Anthropologist*, Lincoln, Nebraska, 1959.
Keyser, J. D. 'A Lexicon for Historic Plains Indian Rock Art' in *Plains Anthropologist*, Vol. 32, No. 115, Lincoln, Nebraska, 1987.
Lanford, B. 'Origins of Central Plains Beadwork' in *American Indian Art Magazine*, Vol. 16, No. 1, Scottsdale, Arizona, 1990.
Lessard, F. 'Pictographic Sioux Beadwork, A Re-Examination' in *American Indian Art Magazine*, Vol. 16, No. 4, Scottsdale, Arizona, 1991.
Libby, W. F. 'Radiocarbon Dates, II', *Science*, 114, Washington D. C., 1951.
Loud, L. L. and Harrington, M. R. 'Lovelock Cave'. *University of California Publications in American Archeology and Ethnology*, 25.1, Berkeley, California, 1929.
McClintock, W. 'Dances of the Blackfoot Indians', *Southwest Museum Leaflet*, 7, Los Angeles, 1937.
Pohrt, R. A. 'Plains Indian Riding Quirts with Elk Antler Handles' in *American Indian Art Magazine*, Vol. 3, No. 4, Scottsdale, Arizona, 1978.
Pohrt, R. A. 'Tribal Identification of Northern Plains Beadwork' in *American Indian Art Magazine*, Vol. 15, No. 1, Scottsdale, Arizona, 1989.
Ritzenthaler, R. E. 'Woodland Sculpture' in *American Indian Art Magazine*, Vol. 4, Scottsdale, 1976.
Sturtevant, W. C. 'The Sources for European Imagery of Native Americans'. Edited by R. Doggett, M. Hulvey and J. Ainsworth in *New World of Wonder, European Images of the Americas 1492-1700*, Washington D. C., 1992.
Taylor, C. F. 'The Plains Indians' Leggings' in *The English Westerners' Brand Book*, Vol. 3, No. 2, London, 1961.
Taylor, C. F. 'Early Plains Indian Quill Techniques in European Museum Collections' in *Plains Anthropologist*, Vol. 7, Lincoln, Nebraska, 1962.
Taylor, C. F. 'The *O-kee-pa* and Four Bears: An insight into Mandan ethnology', in *The English Westerners' Society Brand Book*, Vol. 15, No. 3, London, 1973.
Taylor, C. F. 'Costume with Quill-wrapped Hair: Nez Perce or Crow?' in *American Indian Art Magazine*, Vol. 6, No. 3, Scottsdale, Arizona, 1981.
Taylor, C. F. '*Wakanyan*: Symbols of Power and Ritual of the Teton Sioux', 1989 (See Introduction).
Turner. 'The Tradescant Shirt' in MacGregor. A. (ed.), 1983: 123-130.
West, I. M. 'Plains Indian Horse Sticks' in *American Indian Art Magazine*, Vol. 3, No. 2, Scottsdale, Arizona, 1978.
West , I. M. 'Tributes to a Horse Nation: Plains Indian Horse Effigies', in *South Dakota History*, Vol. 9, No. 4., South Dakota Historical Society, 1979.

PLATEAU AND BASIN

Books

Adney, E. T. and Chapelle, H. I. *The Bark Canoes and Skin Boats of North America*, Washington D. C., 1964.
D'Azevedo, W. L. (ed.) *Handbook of North American Indians, Vol. 11, Great Basin*, Washington D. C., 1986.
Devoto, B. (ed.) *The Journals of Lewis and Clark*, Boston, 1953.
Feder, N. *American Indian Art*, New York, 1973.
Gidley, M. *With One Sky Above Us*, New York, 1979.
Janetski, J. C. *The Ute of Utah Lake*, Salt Lake, 1991.
Kapoun, R. W. *Language of the Robe, American Indian Trade Blankets*, Salt Lake City, 1992.
Lomahaftewa, G. A. *Glass Tapestry*, Phoenix, 1993.
Madsen, B. D. *The Northern Shoshoni*, Idaho, 1980.
Madsen, B. D. *The Lemhi: Sacajawea's People*, Caldwell, Idaho, 1990.
Marsh, C. S. *The Utes of Colorado, People of the Shining Mountains*, Boulder, Colorado, 1982.
Morrow, M. *Indian Rawhide*, Norman, 1975.
Peterson, J. *Sacred Encounters*, Norman, 1993.
Pettit, J. *Utes, the Mountain People*, Boulder, Colorado, 1990.
Ruly, R. H. and Brown, J. A. *The Cayuse Indians*, Norman, 1972.
Schlick, M. D. *Columbia River Basketry*, Seattle, 1994.

Schuster, H. H. *The Yakima*, New York, 1990.
Smith, A. M. *Ethnography of the Northern Utes*, Albuquerque, New Mexico, 1974.
Teit, J. A. and Boas, F. *The Salishan Tribes of the Western Plateaus*, Washington D. C., 1928.
Trenholm, V. C. *The Shoshonis*, Norman, 1964.
Wheat, M. M. *Survival Arts of the Primitive Paiutes*, Reno, Nevada, 1967.
Wright, R. K. (ed.) *A Time of Gathering. Native Heritage in Washington State*, Seattle, 1991.

Other
Bernstein, B. 'Panamint Shoshoni Basketry' in *American Indian Art Magazine*, Scottsdale, Arizona, Autumn, 1979.
Chronister, A. B. 'Characteristics of Ute Beadwork 1860-1885' in *Whispering Wind*, Summer, 1992; Part 2, *Whispering Wind*, Fall-Winter, New Orleans, Louisiana, 1992.
Cohodas, M. 'Lena Frank Dick, Washoe Basket Maker' in *American Indian Art Magazine*, Scottsdale, Arizona, Autumn 1979.
Cohodas, M. 'The Breitholle Collection of Washoe Basketry' in *American Indian Art Magazine*, Scottsdale, Arizona, Autumn, 1984.
Fowler, C. and Dawson, L. 'Ethnographic Basketry' in *Handbook of North American Indians, Vol. II, Great Basin*, Washington D. C., 1986.
Gogl, J. M. 'Columbia River/Plateau Indian Beadwork' in *American Indian Basketry*, Vol. V, No. 2 (1985).
Gogl, J. M. 'The Archetypal Columbia River Plateau Contour Beaded Bag' in *Eye of the Angel*, Northampton, Massachusetts, 1990.
Lanford, B. 'Beadwork and Parfleche Designs' in *Crow Indian Art*, Mission, South Dakota, 1984.
Marr, C. J. 'Salish Baskets from the Wilkes Expedition' in *American Indian Art Magazine*, Scottsdale, Arizona, Summer, 1984.
Marr, C. J. 'Basketry Regions of Washington State' in *American Indian Art Magazine*, Scottsdale, Arizona, Spring, 1991.
Schlick, M. D. and Duncan, K. C. 'Wasco-Style Woven Beadwork, Merging Artistic Traditions' in *American Indian Art Magazine*, Scottsdale, Arizona, Summer, 1991.
Shawley, S. D. 'Hemp & Cornhusk Bags of the Plateau Indians' in *Indian America*, Tulsa, Oklahoma, Spring, 1975.
Shawley, S. D. 'Hide Tanning of the Plateau Indians' in *Indian America*, Tulsa, Oklahoma, Spring, 1976.
Slater, E. 'Panamit Shoshoni Basketry 1920-1940' in *American Indian Art Magazine*, Scottsdale, Arizona, Winter, 1985.
Whiteford, A. H. and McGreevy, S. D. 'Basketry Arts of the San Juan Paiutes' in *American Indian Art Magazine*, Scottsdale, Arizona, Winter, 1985.

CALIFORNIA

Books
Bates, C. D. and Lee, M. J. *Tradition and Innovation; A Basket History of the Indians of the Yosemite-Mono Lake Area*, Yosemite National Park, California, 1990.
Fields, V. M. *The Hoover Collection of Karuk Baskets*, Eureka, California, 1985.
Grant, C. *The Rock Paintings of the Chumash: A Study of a California Indian Culture*, Berkeley and Los Angeles, California, 1966.
Hudson, T. and Underhay, E. *Crystals in the Sky: An Intellectual Odyssey Involving Chumash Astronomy, Cosmology and Rock Art*, Santa Barbara, California, 1978.
Kroeber, A. L. *Handbook of the Indians of California*, Bureau of American Ethnology Bulletin 78, Washington D.C., 1925.
Ortiz, B. *It Will Live Forever; Traditional Yosemite Indian Acorn Preparation*, California, 1991.

Other
Bates, C. D. 'Coiled Basketry of the Sierra Miwok' in *San Diego Museum Papers, No. 15*, San Diego, California, 1982.
Bates, C. D. 'Feather Belts of Central California' in *American Indian Art Magazine*, Scottsdale, Arizonia, 1981(a).
Bates, C. D. 'Beadwork in the Far West: The Continuation of an Eastern Tradition' in *Moccasin Tracks*, La Palma, California, 1981(b).
Bates, C. D. 'Feathered Regalia of Central California: Wealth and Power' in *Occasional Papers of the Redding Museum* 2, Redding, California, 1982.
Bates, C. D. and Bibby, B. 'Collecting Among the Chico Maidu: The Stewart Culin Collection at the Brooklyn Museum' in *American Indian Art Magazine*, Scottsdale, Arizona, 1983.
Bates, C. D. and Bibby, B. 'Beauty and Omnipotence: Traditional Dance Regalia of Northern California' in *The Extension of Tradition*, Crocker Art Museum, Sacramento, California, 1985.
Dawson, L. and Deetz, J. 'A Corpus of Chumash Basketry' in *Annual Reports of the University of California Archaeological Survey* 7, Los Angeles, California 1965.
Ferris, G. J. '"Women's Money": Types and Distributions of Pine Nut Beads in Northern California, Southern Oregon and Northwestern Nevada' in *Journal of California and Great Basin Anthropology* 14(1), Banning, California, 1992.
Harrington, J. P. 'Tobacco Among the Karuk Indians of California' in *Smithsonian Institution Bureau of American Ethnology Bulletin 91*, Washington D.C., 1932.
Hudson, J. W. 'Pomo Wampum Makers' in *Overland Monthly*, August, 1897.
Kelly, I. T. 'The Carver's Art of the Indians of Northwestern California' in *University of California Publications in American Archaeology and Ethnology* 24(7), Berkeley, California, 1930.
Lee, G. 'The San Emigdio Rock Art Site' in *Journal of California and Great Basin Anthropology* 1(2), Banning, California, 1979.
McKern, W. C. 'Functional Families of the Patwin' in *University of California Publications in American Archaeology and Ethnology* 13(7), Berkeley, California, 1922.
McLendon, S. 'Pomo Baskets: The Legacy of William and Mary Benson' in *Native Peoples* 4(1), Phoenix, Arizona, 1990.
O'Neale, L. M. 'Yurok-Karok Basket Weavers' in *University of California Publications in American Archaeology and Ethnology* 32(1), Berkeley, California, 1932.
Schlick, M. D. and Duncan K. C., 'Wasco-Style Woven Beadwork: Merging Artistic Traditions' in *American Indian Art Magazine* 16 (3), Scottsdale, Arizona, 1991.
Smith-Ferri, S. 'Basket Weavers, Basket Collectors, and the Market: A Case Study of Joseppa Dick' in *Museum Anthropology* 17(2) Arlington, 1993.

THE NORTHWEST COAST

Books
Barbeau, M. *Totem Poles of the Gitksan Upper Skeena River, British Columbia*, British Columbia Bulletin No. 61, Ser. No. 12, Ottawa, 1929.
Barbeau, M. *Haida Carvers in Argillite*, National Musuems of Canada Bulletin, No. 139, 1957.
Barbeau, M. *Totem Poles*, Vols 1 & 2, Canadian Museum of Civilization: Hull, Quebec, 1990.
Barbeau, M., Garfield, V. E. and Wingert P. S., *The Tsimshian: Their Arts and Music*, New York, 1951.
Blackman, M. *During My Time: Florence Edenshaw Davidson, A. Haida Woman*, Seattle, 1982.
Boas, F. *Primitive Art*, New York, 1951.
Curtis, E. S. *The North American Indian* Vol. 10 (Kwakiutl) and Vol. 11 (Nootka), New York, 1916.
Dempsey, H. A. *Treasures of the Glenbow Museum*, Calgary, Alberta, 1991.
Duff, W. *Images Stone, B.C.: Thirty Centuries of Northwest Coast Indian Sculpture*, Saanichton, British Columbia, 1975.
Fane, D., Jacknis, I., and Breen, L. M. *Objects of Myth and Memory*, Seattle and London, 1991.
Guedon, M. F. and MacDonald, G. *'Ksan: Breath of our Grandfathers*, Ottawa, 1972.
Gunther, E. *Art in the Life of Northwest Coast Indians*, Seattle, 1966.
Hall, E. S. Jr., Blackman, M. B., and Rickard, V. *Northwest Coast Indian Graphics: An Introduction to Silk Screen Prints*, Vancouver, 1981.
Halpin, M. M. *Totem Poles: An Illustrated Guide*, Museum Note No. 3, Vancouver and London, 1981.
Hawthorn, A. *Art of the Kwakuitl Indians and Other Northwest Coast Tribes*, Seattle, 1967.
Hawthorn, A. *Kwakuitl Art*, Seattle, 1979.
Holm, B. *Northwest Coast Indian Art*, Seattle, 1965.
Holm, B. *Crooked Beak of Heaven*, Seattle, 1972.
Holm, B. *Smokey Top. The Life and Times of Willie Seaweed*, Seattle and London, 1983.
Holm, B. *Spirit and Ancestor*, Burke Museum Monograph 4, Seattle, 1987.
Holm, B., et al. *The Box of Daylight*, Seattle, 1983.
Inverarity, R. B. *Art of the Northwest Coast Indians*, Berkeley, 1950.
Jensen, D. and Sargent, P. *Robes of Power: Totem Poles on Cloth*, Vancouver, 1986.
Jonaitas, A. *Art of the Northern Tlingit*, Seattle, 1986.
Jonaitas, A. *From the Land of the Totem Poles*, Vancouver, 1988.
Jonaitas, A. *Chiefly Feasts*, Vancouver, 1991.
Kaplan, S. A. and Barsness, K. J. *Raven's Journey*, Philadelphia, 1986.
Keithahn, E. L. *Monuments in Cedar*, Seattle, 1963.
Kew, J. E. M. *Sculpture and Engraving of the Central Coast Salish Indians* Vol. 9, Vancouver, 1980.
King, J. C. H. *Portrait Masks of the Northwest Coast of America*, London, 1979.
Lobb, A. *Indian Baskets of the Northwest Coast*, Portland, 1978.
MacDonald, G. F. *Haida Monumental Art – Villages of the Queen Charlotte Islands*, Vancouver, 1983.
Macnair, P.L., Hoover, A. L., and Neary K. *The Legacy: Tradition and Innovation in Northwest Coast Indian Art*, Vancouver, 1984.
Samuel, C. *The Chilkat Dancing Blanket*, Seattle, 1982.
Samuel, C. *The Raven's Tail*, Vancouver, 1987.
Sheehan, C. *Pipes That Won't Smoke: Coal That Won't Burn*, Calgary, 1981.
Stewart, H. *Looking At Indian Art of the Northwest Coast*, Vancouver, 1979.
Stewart, H. *Cedar: The Tree of Life to the Northwest Coast Indians*, Vancouver, 1984.
Stewart, H. *Totem Poles*, Vancouver, 1990.
Sturtevant, W. C., et al. *Boxes and Bowls*, Washington D. C., 1974.
Suttles, W. *Coast Salish Essays*, Seattle, 1987.

Other
Arima, E. Y. 'A Report on a West Coast Whaling Canoe Reconstructed at Port Renfrew' in *History and Archaeology* Vol. 5, Ottawa, 1975.
Blackman, M. B., and Hall, E. S. Jr. 'The Afterimage & Image After: Visual Documents and the Renaissance in Northwest Coast Art' in *American Indian Art Magazine*, Vol. 7:2 Spring, 1982.
Dawson, G. M. 'Report on the Queen Charlotte Islands' in *Geological Survey of Canada. Report of Progress for 1878-79*, 1880.
Duff, W. 'Thoughts on the Nootka Canoe' in *The World is as Sharp as a Knife: An Anthology in Honor of Wilson Duff*. Donald N. Abbot (ed.), 1976.
Emmons, G. T. 'The Basketry of the Tlingit' in *Memoirs: American Museum of American History*, 111:3 1903.
Emmons, G. T. 'The Chilkat Blanket – With Notes on the Blanket Design by Franz Boas' in *Memoirs: American Museum of American History*, III:4, 1907.
Emmons, G. T. 'Portraiture among the North Pacific Coast Tribes,' in *American Anthropologist, n.s.* 16, 1914.
Halpin, M. M. *The Tsimshian Crest System: A Study based on Museum Specimens and the Marius Barbeau and William Beynon Field Notes*, Ph.D thesis, University of British Columbia, Vancouver, 1973.
Harris, N. 'Reflections on Northwest Coast Silver' in *The Box of Daylight*, Seattle and London, 1983.
Ryan, J. and Sheehan, C. 'Monumentality and the Peoples of the Northwest Coast' in *Canada's Native Peoples*, Canada Heirloom Series, 11: 8. Charles J. Humber (ed.), Mississauga, 1988.
Sheehan (McLaren), C. *Unmasking Frontlet Headdresses*, Masters thesis, University of British Columbia, Vancouver, 1977.
Sheehan (McLaren), C. 'Moments of Death: Gift of Life. A Reinterpretation of the Northwest Coast Image *Hawk*' in *Anthropologica*, n.s. XX, 1978.
Sheehan (McLaren), C. 'Masks of Light: Iconographic Interpretation of the Northwest Coast Raven Rattle,' unpublished paper presented to Canadian Ethnology Society, Montreal, 1980.
Suttles, W. 'The Halkomelem Sxwayxwey' in *American Indian Art Magazine*, Vol. 8:1, 1982.

THE SUBARCTIC

Books
Burnham, D. K. *To Please the Caribou: Painted Caribou-skin Coats*, Seattle, 1992.
Boudreau, N. J. (ed.) *The Athapaskans*, Ottawa, 1974.
Duncan, K. C. *Northern Athapaskan Art: A Beadwork Tradition*, Seattle, 1989.
Duncan, K. C. & Carney, E. *A Special Gift: The Kutchin Beadwork Tradition*, Seattle, 1988.
Helm, J. (ed.) *Handbook of North American Indians: Vol. 6*, Washington D. C., 1981.
Idiens, D. & Wilson, B. *No Ordinary Journey: John Rae – Arctic Explorer 1813-1893*, Edinburgh, 1993.
Jenness, D. *The Sekani Indians of British Columbia*, (National Museums of Canada Bulletin 84), Ottawa, 1937.
Leechman, D. *The Vanta Kutchin*, (National Museums of Canada Bulletin 130), Ottawa, 1954.
Mackenzie, Sir A., *The Journals and Letters of Sir Alexander Mackenzie* (W. Kaye Lamb ed.), Cambridge, 1970.
McMillan, A. D. *The Native Peoples and Cultures of Canada*, Vancouver, 1988.
Nelson, R. K. *Hunters of the Northern Forest*, 1973.
Nelson, R. K. *Make Prayers to the Raven*, Chicago, 1983.
Orchard, W. C. *The Technique of Porcupine Quill Decoration Among the Indians of North America*, New York, 1971.
Savishinsky, J. S. *The Trail of the Hare: Life and Stress in an Arctic Community*, New York, 1974.
Turner, G. *Hair Embroidery in Siberia and North America*, Oxford, 1976.

Other
De Laguna, F. 'Indian Masks from the Lower Yukon', in *American Anthropologist*, No. 38 (4), New York, 1936.
Gibbs, G. 'Notes on the Tinneh or Chipewyan Indians of British and Russian America', in *Annual Report of the Smithsonian Institution for 1866*, Washington D. C., 1872.
Osgood, C. 'The Ethnography of the Great Bear Lake Indians', in *National Museums of Canada Annual Report for 1931*, Ottawa, 1932.
Thompson, J. 'No Little Variety of Ornament: Northern Athapaskan Artistic Traditions' in *The Spirit Sings: Artistic Traditions of Canada's First Peoples*, Toronto, 1987.

THE ARCTIC

Books
Black, L. T. *Aleut Art*, Anchorage, Alaska, 1982.
Black, L. T. *Glory Remembered: Wooden Headgear of Alaskan Sea Hunters*, Juneau, Alaska, 1991.
Blodgett, J. *The Coming and Going of the Shaman*, The Winnipeg Art Gallery, Manitoba, 1979.
Boas, F. *The Central Eskimo* (1888), Lincoln, Nebraska, 1964.
Bockstoce, J. *Eskimos of Northwest Alaska in the Early Nineteenth Century: Based on the Beechey and Belcher Collections and Records Compiled During the Voyage of H.M.S.* Blossom *to Northwest Alaska in 1826 and 1827*, University of Oxford, Pitt Rivers Museum Monograph Series 1, 1977.
Collins, H. B., de Laguna, F., Carpenter, E., and Stone, P. *The Far North: 2,000 Years of American Eskimo and Indian Art*, National Gallery of Art, Washington D.C., 1973.
Damas, D., (ed.) *Handbook of North American Indians: Arctic Vol. 5*, Washington D.C., 1984.
Driscoll, B. *The Inuit Amautik: I Like My Hood to be Full*, The Winnipeg Art Gallery, Manitoba, 1980.
Fitzhugh, W. and Crowell, A. *Crossroads of Continents: Cultures of Siberia and Alaska*, Washington D.C., 1988.
Fitzhugh, W. and Kaplan, S. *Inua: Spirit World of the Bering Sea Eskimo*, Washington D.C., 1982.
Fienup-Riordan, A. *Eskimo Essays: Yup'ik Lives and How We See Them*, New Brunswick, 1990.
Fienup-Riordan, A. *Boundaries and Passages: Rule and Ritual in Yup'ik Eskimo Oral Tradition*, Norman, Oklahoma, 1994.
Hickman, P. *Innerskins/Outerskins: Gut and Fishskin*, San Francisco, 1987.
Jenness, D. *Material Culture of the Copper Eskimos*. Report of the Canadian Arctic Expedition, 1913-18, Vol. 16, Ottawa, 1946.
Jochelson, W. *History, Ethnology and Anthropology of the Aleut*, Washington D.C., 1933.
Jones, S., ed. *Eskimo Dolls*, Anchorage, Alaska, 1982.
Kaalund, B. *The Art of Greenland: Sculpture, Crafts, Painting*, Berkeley, California, 1983 (originally published in Danish, 1979).
Kaplan, S. and Barsness, K. *Raven's Journey*, Philadelphia, 1986.
Lantis, M. *Alaskan Eskimo Ceremonialism*. Monographs of the American Ethnological Society, New York, 1947.
Laughlin, W. S. *Aleuts: Survivors of the Bering Land Bridge*, New York, 1980.
Lowenstein, T. *Ancient Land: Sacred Whale. The Inuit Hunt and Its Rituals*, New York, 1993.
Nelson, E. W. *The Eskimo about Bering Strait*. Bureau of American Ethnology Annual Report for 1896-1897, vol. 18, no. 1, Washington D.C. 1899 (reprinted 1984).
Oakes, J. E. *Copper and Caribou Inuit Skin Clothing Production*. Canadian Ethnology Service Mercury Series Paper no. 118, Ottawa, 1991.
Rasmussen, K. *Intellectual Culture of the Iglulik Eskimos*, Report of the Fifth Thule Expedition 1921-24, vol. 7(1), Copenhagen, 1929.
Rasmussen, K. *The Netsilik Eskimos: Social Life and Spiritual Culture*, Report of the Fifth Thule Expedition 1921-24, vol. 8 (1-2), Copenhagen, 1931.
Ray, D. J. *Eskimo Masks: Art and Ceremony*, Seattle, Washington, 1967.
Ray, D. J. *Eskimo Art: Tradition and Innovation in North Alaska*, Seattle, Washington, 1977.
Ray, D. J. *Aleut and Eskimo Art: Tradition and Innovation in South Alaska*, Seattle, Washington, 1981.
Smith, J. G. E. *Arctic Art: Eskimo Ivory*, New York, 1980.
Spencer, R. F. *The North Alaskan Eskimo: A Study in Ecology and Society*, Bureau of American Ethnology, Smithsonian Institution, Washington D. C., 1959 (reprinted 1976).
Swinton, G. *Sculpture of the Inuit*, Toronto, 1992.
Turner, L. M. *Indians and Eskimos in the Quebec-Labrador Peninsula: Ethnology of the Ungava District*, Quebec, 1979 (originally published, Washington D.C., 1894).

Other

Ager, L. P. 'Storyknifing: An Alaskan Eskimo Girls' Game' in *Journal of the Folklore Institute* 11(3), Bloomington, Indiana, 1974.

Black, L. T. 'The Nature of Evil: Of Whales and Sea Otters' in *Indians, Animals, and the Fur Trade: A Critique of the Keepers of the Game*, Athens, Georgia, 1981.

Burch, E. S., Jr. 'The Central Yupik Eskimos: An Introduction', in *Etudes/Inuit/Studies* 8 (supplementary issue), Laval, Quebec, 1984.

Chaussonnet, V. and Driscoll, B. 'The Bleeding Coat: The Art of North Pacific Ritual Clothing' in *Anthropology of the North Pacific Rim*, Washington D.C., 1994.

Collins, H. B., Jr.; Clark, A. H.; Walker, E. H. 'The Aleutian Islands: Their People and Natural History' in *Smithsonian Institution War Background Studies*, no. 21, Washington D.C., 1945.

Driscoll, B. 'Arctic' in *The Spirit Sings*, Calgary and Toronto, 1987.

Driscoll, B. 'Pretending to be Caribou: The Inuit Parka as an Artistic Tradition' in *The Spirit Sings*.

Fienup-Riordan, A. 'The Bird and the Bladder: The Cosmology of Central Yup'ik Seal Hunting', in *Etudes/Inuit/Studies* 14(1-2), Quebec, 1990.

Hatt, G. 'Arctic Skin Clothing in Eurasia and America: An Ethnographic Study' in *Arctic Anthropology* 5(2), 1969.

Hawkes, E. W. The Dance Festivals of the Alaskan Eskimo. *University of Pennsylvania, Museum Anthropological Publications* 6(2), Philadelphia, 1914.

Hoffman, W. J. 'The Graphic Art of the Eskimos: Based Upon the Collections in the National Museum', in *Annual Report of the United States National Museum for 1895*, Washington D.C., 1897.

Holtved, E. 'Contributions to Polar Eskimo Ethnography' in *Meddelelser om Gronland* 182(2), Copenhagen, 1967.

Kroeber, A. L. 'The Eskimo of Smith Sound'. *Bulletin of the American Museum of Natural History* 12(21), New York, 1900.

Lantis, M. 'The Alaskan Whale Cult and its Affinities', *American Anthropologist* 40, Washington D.C., 1938.

Meade, M. 'Sewing to Maintain the Past, Present and Future' in *Etudes/Inuit/Studies* 14(1-2), Laval, Quebec, 1990.

Moore, R. D. 'Social Life of the Eskimo of St. Lawrence Island', *American Anthropologist*, No. 25(3), Washington D.C., 1923.

Morrow, P. 'It is Time for Drumming: A Summary of Recent Research on Yup'ik Ceremonialism' in *Etudes/Inuit/Studies* 8 (supplementary issue), Laval, Quebec, 1984.

Oakes, J. E. 'Environmental factors influencing bird-skin clothing production', *Arctic and Alpine Research* 23(1), 1991.

Stenton, D. R. 'The adaptive significance of caribou winter clothing for arctic hunter-gatherers' in *Etudes/Inuit/Studies* 15(1), Laval, Quebec, 1991.

VanStone, J. W. 'The Bruce Collection of Eskimo Material Culture from Port Clarence, Alaska' in *Fieldiana Anthropology*, vol,. 67, Chicago, 1976.

VanStone, J. W. 'The Bruce Collection of Eskimo Material Culture from Kotzebue Sound, Alaska' in *Fieldiana Anthropology*, N.S., no. 1, Chicago, 1980.

THE NORTHEAST

Books

Brasser, T. J. *A Basketful of Indian Culture Change*, Ottawa, 1975.

Coleman, B. *Decorative Designs of the Ojibwa of Northern Minnesota*, Washington D. C., 1947.

Davidson, D. S. *Decorative Arts of the Tetes de Boule of Quebec*, New York, 1928.

Feest, C. F. *Beadwork and Textiles of the Ottawa*, Harbor Springs, Michigan, 1984.

Fenton, W. N. *The False Faces of the Iroquois*, Norman, Oklahoma, 1987.

Hartman, S. *Indian Clothing of the Great Lakes: 1740-1840*, Ogden, Utah, 1988.

Lyford, C. *Iroquois: Their Art and Craft*, Surrey, British Columbia, 1989.

Mason, O. T. *Aboriginal American Basketry*, Washington D. C., 1904.

McMullen, A. and Handsman, R. G. (eds) *A Key into the Language of Woodsplint Baskets*, Washington, Connecticut, 1987.

Pelletier, G. *Abenaki Basketry*, Ottawa, 1982.

Ritzenthaler, R. E. and Ritzenthaler, P. *The Woodland Indians of the Western Great Lakes*, Milwaukee, 1983.

Skinner, A. *Material Culture of the Menominee*, New York, 1921.

Speck, F. G. *Montagnais Art in Birch-Bark, A Circumpolar Trait*, New York, 1937.

Speck, F. G. *Eastern Algonkian Block-Stamp Decoration*, Trenton, New Jersey, 1947.

Speck, F. G. *Midwinter Rites of the Cayuga Long House*, Philadelphia, 1949.

Thwaites, R. G. *The Jesuit Relations and Allied Documents: Travels and Explorations of the Jesuit Missionaries in New France 1610-1791*, New York, 1959.

Torrence, G. and Hobbs R. *Art of the Red Earth People: The Mesquakie of Iowa*, Seattle, 1989.

Turner, G. *Hair Embroidery in Siberia and North America*, Oxford, 1955.

Whitehead, R. H. *Elitekey: MicMac Material Culture from 1600 AD to the Present*, Halifax, Nova Scotia, 1982.

Other

Abbass, D. K. 'American Indian Ribbonwork' in *LORE*, No. 36 (2), Milwaukee, 1986.

Bakker, P. 'The Mysterious Link Between Basque and Micmac Art' in *European Review of Native American Studies*, No. 5 (1), Vienna, 1991.

Bardwell, K. 'The Case for an Aboriginal Origin of Northeast Indian Woodsplint Basketry' in *Man in the Northeast*, No. 31, Arlington, Virginia, 1986.

Bowdoin Gil, C. A. 'Native North American Seed Beading Techniques: Part I: Woven Items' in *Bead Journal* No. 3 (2), 1977.

Densmore, F. 'The Native Art of the Chippewa' in *American Anthropologist*, No.43, New York, 1941.

Fenton, W. N. 'Masked Medicine Societies of the Iroquois' in *Native North American Art History*. Edited by Z. P. Mathews and A. Jonaitis. Palo Alto, California, 1982.

Friedl, E. 'A Note on Birchbark Transparencies' in *American Anthropologist*, No.46, New York, 1944.

Garte, E. 'Living Tradition in Ojibwa Beadwork and Quillwork' in *Papers of the Sixteenth Algonquian Conference*. Edited by W. A. Cowan, Ottawa, 1985.

Moody, H. 'Birch Bark Biting' in *The Beaver* Outfit 287, Winnipeg, 1957.

Phillips, R. B. 'Dreams and Designs: Iconographic Problems in Great Lakes Twined Bags' in *Great Lakes Indian Art*, Edited by D. W. Penney, Detroit, 1989.

Phillips, R. B. 'Glimpses of Eden: Iconographic Themes in Huron Pictorial Tourist Art' in *European Review of Native American Studies* No.5 (2), Vienna, 1991.

Pohrt, R., Jr. 'Great Lakes Bandolier Bags in the Derby Collection' in *Eye of the Angel*, Edited by D. Wooley, Northampton, Massachusetts, 1990.

Wetherbee, M. 'Making a Basket from a Tree: Splints from black ash in the Shaker tradition' in *Fine Woodworking Techniques*, Newtown, Connecticut, 1980.

Whiteford, A. H. 'Fiber Bags of the Great Lakes Indians' in *American Indian Art Magazine* No.2 (3), Scottsdale, Arizona, 1977.

Wilson, L. A. 'Bird and Feline Motifs on Great Lakes Pouches' in *Native North American Art History*, Edited by Z. P. Mathews and A. Jonaitis, Palo Alto, California, 1982.

REFERENCES

INTRODUCTION

1 Seton, 1962:vi
2 Taylor, 1981: 42-53
3 Bourke, 1890:29
4 Kroeber, 1987: 179-205
5 Most objects herein are from the Smithsonian.
6 Stewart Culin wrote the monumental *Games of the North American Indians*.
7 The Western Apache used twining almost exclusively when making burden baskets but all their other baskets were made by coiling (see Whiteford, 1988:62-92).
8 Northwest Coast carvings and paintings, were early described as 'Art' by Franz Boas (see Boas, 1927:183).
9 Feder, 1965
10 The influential *American Indian Art Magazine* was first published in November 1975.
11 Coe, 1976:13-20
12 Taylor 1989:237-257 Such recognition is now demanding of scholars that a revaluation be made of the large number of American Indian artifacts reposing in museum and other collections.
13 There were however, men and women who excelled in their individual crafts and whose names are now renowned.
14 See Coe, 1986
15 Spinden, c.1930 in Farge, 1931:74

THE SOUTHEAST

1 Hudson, 1976:376
2 Contemporary artists and craftspeople, submitting to market demands for 'traditional' crafts, have, however, relearned old techniques.
3 Contemporary Catawba women dig clay from local clay pits noted for the purity and consistency of the clay. After the clay is prepared the potter breaks off suitable quantities and either uses them immediately or wraps them in damp cloth or leaves for storage (Fewkes, 1944:73).
4 Fewkes, 1944:113. Catawba women use ring coiling, rather than true coiling. They lay rings one on top of another to build a cylinder (Fewkes, 1944:78).
5 Fewkes, 1944:83
6 Fewkes, 1944:88
7 Fewkes, 1944:83. The Southeastern Indians did not possess the kiln. Catawba potters gradually dry their wares by placing them progressively closer to an open fire, finally placing the whole piece on the coals. (Fewkes, 1944:89).
8 Haberland, 1964:195
9 Animal effigies were representations of various animals common in the Southeastern Ceremonial Complex. It is unknown what or whom the human effigies represented.
10 Fundaburk and Foreman, 1957:168-183
11 Harrington, 1908:401-403; Speck, 1920:63. Contemporary Catawba trade pottery is especially noted for its fine craftsmanship.
12 Mississippian men usually extracted stone from local quarries by chiseling out large chunks. They then chipped them into suitable sizes.
13 Fundaburk and Foreman, 1957:116. In fashioning the rough shape of a chipped stone tool the stoneworker held the stone to be worked in a piece of buckskin in his palm and struck it with a cobble or the butt end of a length of antler.
14 Fundaburk and Foreman, 1957:116. In the grinding technique, the stone worker pecked and fractured the stone using a cobble of harder stone so that it gradually wore off the surface of the former. To refine the surface, the stoneworker used a grinding technique in which a harder stone was rubbed against the softer stone, wearing the softer stone and giving finer lines to the form and smoothing the surface. Finally, the object was polished to a high sheen using an abrader.
15 West, 1934:387-388. Mississippian men made a variety of carved effigy pipes, some in the shapes of animals, most predominantly the owl, bear, and frog. The most distinctive and outstanding Mississippian effigy pipes, however, are the human effigy pipes.
16 Brose et al., 1985:104
17 Contemporary Southeastern Indians do not practice much stonework, except in the tourist demonstration villages. But in the past few decades, the Eastern Band of Cherokee in North Carolina have revived this art form. (Leftwich, 1970:119).
18 Witthoft, 1949:54-55
19 Witthoft, 1949:47
20 Cushing, 1894:100. Copper plates were usually cut into the outline of the figure or design intended for the finished product. Southeastern Indians, up to the present day, value bilateral symmetry in their designs.
21 Haberland, 1954:200
22 Hamilton et al., 1974:5
23 Haberland, 1964:199-200
24 Hally et al., 1990
25 Hudson, 1976:372-373
26 The Creek people of Tuckabatchee owned a number of metal plates in the form of celts similar to those of the Southeastern Ceremonial Complex (Hudson, 1976:400). These plates were only brought out during the Green Corn Ceremony. They were taken to Oklahoma during Removal and have been, over the years, interred in the graves of beloved men and women (Howard, 1968:65-74).
27 Only remnants of Mississippian and early Historic Period baskets have been recovered, but these show good craftsmanship and design.
28 Choosing the right cane requires an intimate knowledge of cane and its growth patterns. Generally, basket makers choose stalks of cane about two years old, the diameter of a thumb, and with long, straight shafts between knots.
29 In recent years river cane has become scarce, forcing basket makers to use substitutes such as white oak and honeysuckle. See Leftwich, 1970.
30 Mason, 1904:221-229. Basket making has two basic techniques – weaving and coiling. In recent years some Southeastern Indian women have begun making coiled baskets out of coiled pine needles or certain types of grasses.
31 Leftwich, 1970:30
32 Speck, 1920:60
33 Dixon and Domjanovich, 1992:41; Leftwich, 1970:29. Vegetable dyes are processed by first pulverizing the roots, bark, or leaves in a mortar and pestle, and then mixing the powder with water and boiling it. Cane splints are placed in the boiling water and occasionally stirred to ensure an evenness of color.
34 Turnbaugh and Turnbaugh, 1986:102
35 Leftwich, 1970:51; Turnbaugh and Turnbaugh, 1986:106
36 Porter, 1990:84
37 Porter, 1990:86. In the 1920s and 1930s Chitimacha, Choctaw, Creek, and Cherokee women, although never having abandoned basketry altogether, began producing a variety of forms for the tourist trade.
38 Carr, 1897:401. These materials were pounded and separated and then hand spun either with a hand spindle or by simply spinning the pieces together on the knee and pulling with the other hand. European eyewitness accounts from the 18th century also describe women using suspended, two-bar looms for producing broad pieces of cloth and as using finger-weaving for narrow sashes and belts (Dockstader, 1967:54, 61).
39 Carr, 1897:401. Animal hides were soaked, scraped, and treated with pulverized animal brains to make them soft, supple, and of a uniform, desired thickness.
40 The outstanding fashion era for the Historic Southeastern Indians occurred in the late-18th, early-19th centuries, just prior to Removal. At this time, Southeastern Indian men and women reckoned fashion and clothing as a true expression of esthetics and national identity, combining colors, materials, and ornamentation in fancy wear to achieve an overall appearance of color, coordination, and elegance to their costumes.
41 Wood, 1981:52
42 Downs, 1979:38-40; Sturtevant, 1967:161
43 Sturtevant, 1967:171
44 Downs, 1979:34-35
45 Seminole men's clothing until around 1930 consisted of knee-length big shirts, which were, in effect, knee-length dresses, and Seminole men usually went bare-legged until around 1930.
46 Medford, 1975:46
47 Dockstader, 1978:57
48 Goggins, 1967:173. Interestingly, the Western style motifs closely resemble prehistoric pottery designs. It is uncertain whether these designs have been continual or were copied later.
49 Southeastern Ceremonial Complex falcon-men representations show men wearing feather capes in the form of falcon wings. A fragment of textile from the Spiro Mound in Oklahoma clearly has a wing design, but whether or not others were made of feathers is not known.
50 Part of the Mississippian ceremonial dress included feather headdresses with copper emblems. Feathers rarely preserve however.
51 Medford, 1975:42; Speck, 1951:39
52 Speck, 1951:39-44, 94
53 Gilliland, 1975:47-48
54 Speck, 1951:1-13
55 Speck, 1951:63
56 Speck, 1951:24

THE SOUTHWEST

1 Reichard, 1968:167
2 Dillingham, 1992:5
3 Cushing, 1886:511
4 Dillingham, 1992:8
5 Before the Spanish arrived in 1598, some pueblos had developed a low melting point lead glaze which was used as decoration, not as a seal. When the Spanish returned after the 1680 Revolt, the use of lead glaze disappeared and the pottery of the southern pueblos and Hopi was slipped with a clay that fired to a matte finish, and decorated with red and black which is still in use today.
6 The American entrepreneur, Fred Harvey, brought good food and quick service to the travelers on the railroads which were pushing west. He also saw that he could make money selling Indian arts and crafts. His agent, Herman Schweizer, went around the reservation buying and sometimes commissioning things which could be sold. The railroad of the late 1880s also led to a reduction in the size of many of the large vessels. Tourists wanted things of a size that they

could pack to take home.
7 Dillingham, 1992:10. This is interesting because it indicates the strong sex-linked roles in these traditional cultures, that being struck by lightning is a clear transformational experience, and that only then could one cross a sex line to perform tasks which were culturally assigned. That division, however, has broken down.
8 We believe there was a change in the shape of vessels when the Spanish introduced wheat. Bread dough needs a big open bowl to rise, and although the market for big dough bowls may have been steady under the Spanish, the American troops who arrived in 1848 were all bread, not corn tortilla, eaters, and the best known of the bread bowls, the Santo Domingo dough bowl, was probably produced to make wheat and yeast bread for the tastes of the American Army. Information from David Snow in an unpublished manuscript.
9 Margaret Harding, an anthropologist at the Lowie Museum, University of California, brought back photographs of the insides of pots to Zuni in the mid-1980s. These were pots which had disappeared from Zuni when Frank Hamilton Cushing in mid-1880 had collected almost every pot in Zuni and taken them to the Smithsonian in Washington. Verbal communication with Margaret Harding in 1985.
10 Sturtevant, 1979:517
11 Personal communication with David Snow, Southwest ceramic specialist.
12 They got control of the great turquoise mines from the pueblo of San Marcos, which emigrated to Santo Domingo when San Marcos was abandoned.
13 During the Bosque Redondo in 1864-68, one man, *Atsidi Sani*, or Old Smith, first began to work iron and fix the bridles for the soldiers and cowboys.
14 'All the smithing was done outside beside a campfire. Sometimes an apprentice would watch and help. If a young man has a father who is a silversmith, he will begin to help him with the work when he is about fourteen years old . . . As he grows older and becomes more experienced in working metal, his father gives him more to do, and within a period of a year or two he is able to make silver by himself and sell it at the trading post.' Adair, 1962:76
15 It is thought the masterful Navajo learned the craft from the Pueblos who gained it from the Spanish; there was, however, metalworking among the Athapaskan kin of the Navajo in the north, so their knowledge may predate their migration.
16 Bloom 1936:226
17 Adair, 1962:15
18 Herman Schweizer had pre-cut turquoise given to Navajo smiths who were working for traders. The Harvey company sent the material to trading posts to be made into bracelets, beads and other jewelry.
19 A second pair of horizontal beams holds the weaving. These are laid on the ground and the warp, the vertical threads, is strung continuously in a figure-eight conformation between the beams. This is then raised and fastened inside the rectangular frame. It is not attached at the top beam, but is lashed to an intermediate pole, the tension beam. This intermediate beam creates a more even tension for the warp. The lower warp is then tied directly to the bottom of the frame. Then the heddles, which are used to raise and lower the weaving, are made. They open a temporary space, or shed, between the two planes of the warp threads through which the yarn passes. After the yarn has passed, the batten – a wide flat stick – is removed, and the yarn is beaten into place with a weaving comb or a firm stroke of the batten. Berlant and Kahlenberg, 1991:41-42
20 O'Bryon, 1956:56.
21 Personal communication with Mary Hunt Kahlenberg, 1994
22 The Apache say that they use the Navajo basket because once when an Apache chief was sick, a great Navajo medicine man helped his Apache brother with the curing ceremony. The patient recovered, and when the Apache thanked his helper and asked the secret of his power, the Navajo said the basket was important.
23 The kachina is made from the dried cottonwood root, the center of which must also be the center of the kachina.

THE PLAINS

1 Pond, 1986:42
2 Waugh, 1990:70
3 Best and McClelland, 1977:4
4 Feder, 1987
5 Loud and Harrington, 1929:24. Libby, 1951:276. Martin, Quimby and Collier, 1947.
6 Some of the earliest extant examples of quillwork are to be found in the European museum collections, such as the elaborately quill-embellished shirt now in the Ashmolean Museum, Oxford (Turner in MacGregor ed., 1983:123-130) and the collection of early moccasins and headdresses in the Musée de l'Homme, Paris (Fardoulis, 1979).
7 Grinnell, 1923, Vol.I:163. Kroeber, 1902-07.
8 Ewers, 1945:29.
9 Dempsey, 1963:52.
10 Possibly the earliest account of porcupine quillwork from the Plains region was by Dr. Samuel Lathan Mitchell, who has described in great detail an Assiniboin quilled *wapiti* skin collected before 1817. (Fenenga, 1959:19-22. Orchard, 1926:64).
11 Taylor, 1962, 1981. Quillwork on bark, very common among the Micmac and Ojibwa, was not found on the Plains; however, the use of moosehair while firmly associated with Woodland tribes was, on occasions, also utilized by the Plains Cree.
12 Bebbington, 1982:30
13 The pony bead still continued to be used in Idaho, northwest Montana, and eastern Washington even as late as 1900.
14 Lanford (1990) has recently put forward ideas relating to the origins and precursors of symbolic and decorative beadwork motifs among the central Plains groups.
15 Pohrt (1989) has further references relating to North Plains beadwork.
16 Ewers, 1945:38
17 Lyford, 1940:71
18 Lessard (1991) has a detailed discussion of pictographic Sioux beadwork which includes identification of the producers.
19 Lowie, 1954:143
20 A discussion of the origins of Crow Indian beadwork designs appears in Wildschut, 1959 and more recently in Feder, 1980.
21 MacGregor, 1966:116
22 Robert Ritzenthaler's survey (1976) of Woodland sculpture demonstrates that carved objects were rarely more than a foot in length and that woodworking was carried out by men. Several parallels have been found between Woodland carving and that from the Plains (Ewers, 1986:11).
23 Ewers, 1986:12 and 15
24 Ewers, 1986:41.
25 Ewers, 1986:18 pictures a human effigy Tree-Dweller Medicine, said to have been for some 200 years in the Wabasha (Santee Sioux) family. It is 6in (15cm) high and of painted wood.
26 McClintock, 1937:13
27 West, 1978:64.
28 West, 1979:295 and 299.
29 Pohrt, 1978:63.
30 Pohrt, 1978:63
31 Ewers, 1986:177.
32 Palliser, 1969:146-47.
33 From time immemorial, the area was considered to be neutral ground and anyone could visit the quarry in peace and mine the stone (Catlin, 1841, Vol.II:169). The pipestone and finished product was widely traded, pipe bowls of catlinite having been found in 17th century Iroquoian sites. The Pipestone National Monument was established in 1937 and the exclusive right to the use of the quarry by Native Americans only was established.
34 Douglas, 1931.
35 Ewers, 1986:50.
36 Catlin, 1841, Vol.I:334. Experiments show that such work was very time-consuming. To drill a cone-shaped hole some 25mm (1in) deep into catlinite employing the method described by Catlin took one hour. (West, 1934, Vol.I:341-42).
37 Ewers, 1963:42 and 50.
38 Sturtevant, 1992:28.
39 Golden or 'calumet' eagle feathers were the most prized for headdresses. These came from the immature bird and were white with dark brown or black tips. Such feathers were considered exceedingly valuable. (See Denig, 1930:589).
40 Ewers reported that when the Sioux-style bonnet was introduced among the Blackfeet in about 1895, it became so popular as to replace the traditional Blackfeet style almost entirely. (Ewers, 1945:61)
41 Ewers, 1945:61.
42 Taylor, 1994:23.
43 Fletcher and La Flesche, 1911:447. (See Taylor, 1994:91-99 for a more detailed discussion relating to the symbolism).
44 The cutting, lacing, and beadwork embellishment associated with the Blackfeet woman's dress has been considered by Conn (1961:114-117). See also Ewers (1945:42).
45 Lewis and Clark, 1904, Vol.II:129. Further descriptions and a discussion of the various styles of leggings used on the northern and central Plains are in Taylor (1961).
46 Cooley, 1983.
47 Weltfish, 1977:375.
48 Wissler, 1912(b):40.
49 Taylor, 1989:247.
50 238 human hair and 68 horsehair locks embellish this shirt which is now in the collections of the Buffalo Bill Historical Center, Cody, Wyoming.
51 Mallery, 1893:31.
52 Petersen, 1971 and 1988.
53 Conner, 1971 and Keyser, 1987. In pre-reservation times, petroglyph sites were regarded as special places and imbued with spiritual power.
54 Some petroglyphs were colored with earth paints enhancing the image but unless the petroglyph was protected this coloring faded.
55 A number of bone 'paint brushes' have been found in early Pawnee and Mandan sites (Ewers, 1939:36).
56 Ewers, 1939:9-10.
57 Hail, 1983:40.
58 Ewers, 1939:19-21.
59 Taylor, 1973.
60 Arni Brownstone has recently compared traditional Blackfeet pictography and 19th century European painting, identifying two distinct pictorial systems. See Brownstone, 1993:29.
62 A favored source for making metal defleshers was the sawn-off end of the old northwest gun.
63 The term 'parfleche' is of doubtful origin but it appears in French narratives as early as 1700 and is probably from some old French root, possibly from *parer* 'to parry', *fleche* 'arrow' in reference to the shield or body armor of rawhide.
64 See Spier, 1931:82 for a definition of the parfleche.
65 A beaver tail was often boiled to make a sticky glue. (See Ewers, 1945:17).
66 Morrow, 1975:78. Torrence, 1994.
67 Webber, 1989:4 considers the theories of the development of the moccasin.
68 Larocque, 1910:27.
69 Clark, 1885:259. For a detailed analysis of Crow, Sioux and Arapaho moccasins, see Wildschut 1959; and Kroeber 1902.
70 Wissler's (1927) studies of moccasin decorations covers the 25-year period 1890-1915 and considers both partially and fully quilled and beaded moccasins and their distribution.

PLATEAU AND BASIN

1 Devoto, 1953:246
2 In 1805 Lewis and Clark recorded that the people along the Columbia River were very eager to trade for blue and white beads. However, surviving pieces of beadwork reliably dated to before 1850 are very rare today.
3 Rev. Spalding, quoted in Wright, 1991:36.
4 While the popularity of seed beads increased as the 19th century progressed, they never completely replaced the earlier pony beads. In the 1840-70 period Plateau women often incorporated both in the same piece of beadwork.
5 The development of curvilinear beadwork on the Plateau may have been influenced by the beadwork worn by eastern Indians who participated in the fur trade in the west as early as the 1820s.
6 Elk, deer, horses and even fish were most common in the earlier part of the period.
7 The Transmontaine style is characterized by the use of a wide range of bead colors to produce large diamond, hourglass and triangular design motifs in a flat stitch. Major design elements were often outlined in a single line of white beads or by a lane of dark blue beads or both, set against a light field. The Transmontaine style also makes extensive use of red wool cloth as a background.
8 Another distinctive beadwork style was produced by a small group of Wasco/ Wishram women on the western edge of the Plateau. Usually found on small flat bags, this work appears to be 'loomed' but was woven with a loose warp technique. Bead colors were usually very simple, with designs in one color of dark beads on a white background. Distinctive animal, human, and skeletonal human 'X-ray' designs were popular.
9 Classic Ute blocky-design seed beadwork after about 1870 is virtually indistinguishable from Jicarilla beadwork of the same period.
10 Experts disagree whether quill-wrapped horsehair was produced exclusively by Plateau women, by Crow women or both.
11 The natural range of the buffalo extended into the southern Plateau and northern Great Basin areas. Buffalo were found there in small herds until they were killed off in the 1830s.
12 One of the earliest surviving pieces of Plateau art is a painted, flat, fringed parfleche envelope collected in 1841 and now in the Smithsonian.
13 Liquid paint was made from powdered natural or trade pigments mixed with a medium such as glue. It was usually applied to the hide with a porous bone 'brush' or stylus. Alternatively, powdered pigments were mixed with a glue medium and allowed to dry into small cakes, which were used to draw directly on to the damp hide.
14 Parfleches filled with food, clothing and other articles were commonly given away in large numbers during inter-tribal events on the Plateau, such as marriages. This factor, plus the fact that many Plateau tribes have shared reservations for over a hundred years sometimes make distinct tribal styles of parfleche design hard to differentiate.
15 Shoshoni men also practiced the Plains tradition of realistic paintings on soft hides, depicting their war exploits.
16 The Southern Paiutes may have made some parfleches, but parfleche use was not prevalent among non-horse people.
17 Mats were made from tule stems twined and sewn together side by side with hemp cordage. These mats were used primarily for longhouse coverings, as well as for a variety of other household purposes.
18 Cornhusk bags filled with roots were common gifts at both inter- and intra-tribal occasions on the Plateau so it is difficult to identify a particular cornhusk bag design with any particular tribe. The same materials and weaving techniques were used to produce a wide variety of other objects such as horse gear (saddle drapes and martingales), belt pouches and occasionally clothing.
19 Fowler and Dawson, 1986:705
20 Those people, principally the northern and eastern Shoshoni, Bannock and Ute, adopted Plains-style parfleche and tanned hide containers for transport and storage.

CALIFORNIA

1 Kroeber, 1925:194
2 For perhaps the most complete discussion of ethno-esthetics among Yurok and Karok basket weavers, see O'Neale, 1932.
3 For a discussion on the use of a variety of baskets in processing acorns for food, see Ortiz, 1991.
4 Bates, 1982:33-34 and Bates and Lee, 1990:39-40.
5 Harrington, 1932:128.
6 O'Neale, 1932.
7 Mrs. Hickox was actually the daughter of a Wiyot woman and a non-Indian man, although she identified as Karok. See Fields, 1985.
8 Their lives are detailed in McLendon, 1990.
9 For more on Joseppa Dick see Smith-Ferri, 1993.
10 Bates and Lee, 1990.
11 Dawson and Deetz, 1965.
12 Bates and Bibby, 1985.
13 These belts continued to be produced into the first quarter of the 20th century. Belts made in the late-19th century often used commercial cordage for the weft and glass beads for decoration. For additional information on the belts, see Bates, 1981a, Bates and Bibby, 1983 and McKern, 1922.
14 This style of headpiece was commonly used by Yokuts people, by people as far north as the Coast Miwok of the Bodega Bay region, and by people as far east as the Paiute of western Nevada. The use of these magpie headpieces does not seem to have spread farther south than the Chumash.
15 A discussion of the manufacture and use of pine nut beads is in Ferris, 1992.
16 For clamshell disc and magnesite bead manufacture among the Pomo, see Hudson, 1897.
17 There is very little published on the spread of glass beadwork to California. Most of the known primary sources are cited in Bates, 1981b.
18 These octopus bags among the Wasco were probably produced in imitation of Cree-Meti bags, brought west during the fur trade in the 1830s and 1840s. See Schlick and Duncan, 1991.
19 For a lengthy discussion see Kelly, 1930.
20 Grant, 1966; Hudson and Underhay, 1978.
21 Lee, 1979.
22 L. Frank Manriquez uses these village names to identify herself, rather than the Spanish names of Gabrielino and Juaneño.
23 Bates and Lee, 1990:171.

THE NORTHWEST COAST

1 Duff, 1975.
2 Ryan and Sheehan, 1988.
3 Blackman (1982) records that Florence Davidson painted canoes carved by her husband Robert.
4 Sometimes plant, insect, celestial phenomena, tides and even the wind were represented; frequently they were given personified forms, though pure formline design elements could be used to portray their natural forms.
5 Frank Boas was one of the first ethnographers to publish the vocabulary of visual forms enabling Euro-Americans to 'read', at a pre-iconographic level, the fundamental images in Northwest Coast art, 1951:183-298. For a contemporary version of his interpretations see Stewart, 1979.
6 Fortunately, there were a few such as Marius Barbeau who made a special effort to identify artists not only by name, but by their works. Barbeau, 1929 and 1957.
7 Three-dimensional design of the north is strongly

two-dimensional in concept: in some works, essentially flat design was wrapped around a form, and carved in high relief. Some objects were more sculptural in concept, though still decorated with formline designs. Southern Kwakiutl and Bella Coola artists used a somewhat more flamboyant version of the northern formline design system. Holm, 1965 has the most in-depth analysis.

8 Again, Holm and his students have been at the forefront in the identification of individual Northwest artists through their stylistic signatures. Holm, 1983.

9 Some Haida named the individual beams and posts as well; in some instances a house could have more than one name.

10 For house types see Stewart, 1984:60-75

11 Sometimes the Tsimshian houses used the slotted plank technology to create horizontal house planking between vertical squared timber posts.

12 The antiquity of crest poles has long been debated. Scholars do know that the early European visitors to the coast recorded the presence of large house frontal poles and massive free standing carved poles, though their mention is sporadic. It is likely that with increased contact, and access to technology and wealth, there was a flourishing of crest pole carving. Barbeau, 1929 and 1990; Inverarity, 1950; Keithahn, 1963; Halpin, 1981; Macdonald, 1983.

13 The concept of *totemism* acknowledges a special relationship between humans and animals marked by an avoidance of the animal for food, or even for interactions. Totemism implies animal worship by humans. This cultural practice was not found on the Northwest Coast.

14 Physically the undertaking was complex and required the services of many experienced men to harvest a 60-80ft (18-24m) red cedar. The trees most suitable for poles (as well as houses and canoes) were deep in the forest, straight and free from knots. Stewart, 1990.

15 Selection of the artist alone was a complicated matter. Initially a family member (usually from another lineage) might be given the hereditary honor of carving the pole though his involvement was nominal and in fact the actual carving was carried out by a professional artist. Maquettes or miniatures of the pole were sometimes carved and submitted to the patron for approval. Given artistic license in interpreting the crests, the artist nonetheless followed the conventions of three-dimensional representation and formline design.

16 Particularly if the sculpture was to be a house frontal or portal pole, the log's heartwood was excavated from the back of the pole, leaving it 'C'-shaped in the cross-section. This made it possible to use very large logs for poles, as they were considerably lighter without the heartwood and moreover, were less likely to rot, split or check.

17 House planks were adzed in a similar manner, the builders claiming that the long parallel rows of adze marks gave a 'finished' appearance.

18 The northern artists, maintaining a traditional restraint, were far less flamboyant than their southern colleagues who sometimes painted rather than carved some of the crest details.

19 The method of raising a pole has not changed over the centuries – even contemporary poles are raised in the age-old manner. The heel of the pole was placed into the hole and ropes tied to the upper portion were strung over a crossbar supported by sturdy scaffolding. Under the direction of an experienced person counting time with a drum, the pole was slowly raised by dozens of people hauling and pulling.

20 Few poles ever fell, but if they did, they were left where they lay, for to raise the pole again would require the same level of potlatching it would take to raise a new pole. Economics and practical wisdom opted for the new pole.

21 Smaller canoes were constructed using the same methods as the larger ones, but were not steamed and usually lacked prow and stern additions.

22 Holm notes that there is considerable debate on whether or not Northwest Coast mariners 'sailed' before Euro-American contact. He believes the debate is a matter of semantics. Holm, 1987:98

23 Stewart, 1984:52-60. Duff, 1976; Arima, 1975.

24 Small holes were drilled in the roughed out hull and filled with measured pegs of darkened wood or lighter yellow cedar. The carver then removed wood from the inside of the hull to the uniform depth of the pegs, creating an even thickness.

25 An operculum is the small white shell 'trap door' on the opening of the red turban snail.

26 Sturtevant, 1974.

27 Gender bias in traditional ethnographies has perhaps robbed women of full credit for this ingenious and elegant art which was as prevalent as men's woodworking arts and just as highly prized by their society.

28 Cooking baskets were woven with such tight construction methods that they could be used for stewing and steaming in much the same way as bent wood boxes.

29 Holm, 1987:222

30 Stewart, 1984:128

31 Cherry bark, horsetail fern roots, cattail leaves, leaves of beargrass, reed canary grass and swamp grass, to name a few, were employed in the construction and embellishment of baskets.

32 All of these techniques and materials are discussed with photographs in Lobb, 1978.

33 Emmons, 1903; Kaplan, 1986; Holm, 1987.

34 In the spring, after the offering of appropriate prayers, long strips of bark were taken from tall, living trees. (Taking the strips did not kill the tree.) The inner bark was separated from the outer, and beaten to soften and separate layers.

35 Early mariners reported that the people wore two pieces of bark clothing, loose blankets or capes about the shoulders covering a blanket or skirt belted on the lower body.

36 A splendid painted cedar bark robe is in the British Museum. Likely Nuu-chah-nulth, it was collected by Capt. Cook in 1780. See King (1979).

37 Chilkat weaving was also used to produce tailored sleeved or sleeveless tunics, dance aprons, leggings and shamans' headgear.

38 See Dawson, 1880:120; 127-128. Samuel's monumental work *The Chilkat Dancing Blanket* remains the authority on the history and construction techniques, Samuel 1982.

39 Holm notes that 'Classic Chilkat blankets date only to the beginning of the 19th century. Their predecessors were geometrically patterned tined robes of which only a handful have survived.' Holm, 1987:182. Samuel, 1987.

40 'The blanket is shaped like a house worn upside down. Metaphorically, the house-shaped blanket which engulfs the dancer is *GonaquAde'ts* underworld house.' Sheehan, 1977:226-227.

41 In Tsimshian, all the words connected with this dancer have the same root word, *halait*, which roughly translates as 'dancer', 'shaman' 'power' and 'sacred'; the dancer is *Wihalait*; the blanket, *Gweshalait*; the frontlet headdress, *amhalait*; and the Raven rattle as *Hasem semhalait*. All are stored in a Chief's box or *'anda amhalait*. Halpin, 1973:213

42 Holm, 1984:182

43 Fane, et al, 1991; Holm, 1987; Gunther, 1966; Kaplan, 1986; Dempsey, 1991; Jonaitas, 1988.

44 Jonaitas, 1986.

45 Emmons, 1914, was one of the first to discuss 'portraiture' on the coast, though the Euro-American concept of portraiture may not have the same connotation. See also the discussion of portrait 'masks' by Haida artist Charles Gwaytihl in Macnair, et al. 1984:70-71; and King, 1979.

46 Halpin, 1973:75

47 Holm, 1984:89

48 A photographed account of a 20th century *Hamatsa* ceremony may be seen in Macnair, 1984.

49 For descriptions of the Kwakiutl masks see Hawthorn, 1967 and 1979; and Holm 1972.

50 The nose of the *Sxwayxwey* was either a head of a bird or it merely had skeletal nasal passages; two birds with elongated necks rose over the forehead of the *Sxwayxwey*. A wide ruff circled the mask and long reeds with tips of downy feathers bobbed from the perimeter. The four dancers, on a healing mission, carried hooped rattles hung with huge Pacific sea scallop shells. Salish art is described in Kew, 1980, and Suttles, 1982 describes the masks of the Halkomelem (Coast Salish) *Sxwayxwey*.

51 In the early-19th century, the hereditary right to this headdress was passed by marriage to a Kwakiutl family, the Hunts, where it is worn to this day. Later, it was also obtained by some Northern Wakashan and Bella Coola tribes.

52 Sheehan, 1977.

53 Duff, 1975:12

54 Euro-American motifs such as floral patterns and the American eagle were used along with traditional formline designs prior to 1900. Harris, 1983: 132-136.

55 Holm, 1983:106

56 Holm, 1984:186.

57 Jensen 1986. Innovating on appliqued blankets, Haida artist Dorothy Grant has created contemporary fashions. Blackman, 1992.

58 Hall, et al 1981.

59 Blackman & Hall, 1982:30-39

60 Guédon and MacDonald, 1972.

THE SUBARCTIC

1 Mackenzie, 1970:133

2 Many explorers and traders found, often after initial scepticism, that native technology had much to commend it. Dr John Rae, who explored the western shores of Hudson Bay in the 1840s, wrote: 'At first I could not be persuaded that a person could walk better with such great clumsy looking things as snowshoes on his feet crunching knee deep in snow, but it did not require very long practice to decide this question in favour of the snowshoes'. Quoted in Idiens & Wilson, 1993:80

3 It has been suggested that the decoration of ritual equipment with incised lines (for example, items used during periods of puberty seclusion or mourning) may imply that at least some of this was more than merely decorative. (Thompson, 1987:146)

4 None of the native peoples lived in isolation prior to European contact. All were part of an elaborate and long-established inter-tribal trading network.

5 According to the archeologist J. V. Wright, 'It has been somewhat of a problem to determine from where this pottery came. It is not part of any of the ceramic complexes to the south, and there exists a broad zone to the northwest completely lacking in and thereby precluding a possible Asiatic origin. The only reasonable alternative is that the idea of pottery was adopted from the south via stimulus diffusion and that the Archaic populations of the Shield evolved a distinctive ceramic complex after they had acquired the essential techniques of manufacture.' (Helm, 1981:89)

6 Koyukon and Ingalik continued to make clay lamps and cooking pots into the Historic Period and into the 20th century.

7 The effect of Europeans was felt long before they actually appeared and western manufactured goods were traded through the existing aboriginal networks to become part of the cultural inventory of groups far from the point of source.

8 Mackenzie, 1970:133

9 Mackenzie, 1970:291 A traditional method of cooking was to fill a container with food and water and drop in heated stones until the water boiled.

10 It has been suggested that this style of decoration may in fact pre-date European contact because of its similarity to the earliest known woven quill-work, although the few bark trays so far recovered are undecorated. (Duncan, 1989:26)

11 Perhaps the most unusual method of decorating bark is that still practiced today by Cree women in Manitoba and Saskatchewan. By folding a piece of bark and biting it, a skilled worker can create a range of intricate patterns which is revealed when the bark is unfolded.

12 Quoted in McMillan, 1988:219-220

13 Savishinsky, 1974:21

14 Eyed needles for sewing appear to have been unknown in the Subarctic until introduced by traders, although eyed needles for lacing snowshoes have been recovered from prehistoric sites.

15 Whole rabbit skins were too flimsy for clothing

16 Quoted in Duncan, 1989: 38 It was, of course, in the trader's interest that people should bring him their furs and dressed skins rather than turn them into clothing for themselves. When Alexander Murray established Fort Yukon in 1847, he reported, 'Blankets, axes, knives, powder horns and files went off rapidly enough, but it was hard to dispose of the clothing as they consider their own dresses much superior to ours both in beauty and durability, and they are partly right, although I endeavoured to persuade them to the contrary.' Quoted in Nelson, 1973:205

17 There are still certain areas where traditional materials triumph. The anthropologist Joel Savishinsky records a Hare hunter comparing the skin slippers made by his wife with a pair of store-bought woolen socks: 'Two weeks ago all I had were those lousy woolen ones from the store, but they weren't worth a damn. It was forty or fifty below and my feet were freezing. Then I had Lena make me these. That's some difference I'll tell you. I put these on and I don't care if it's sixty below – it's like I don't feel anything and my feet never hurt.' Quoted in Savishinsky, 1974:21

18 Quoted in Thompson, 1987:147

19 Because the style and decoration of these painted coats proved attractive to travelers and collectors, a number have survived from quite an early date. Several of those now in European museums have been dated as early as 1700 – largely on stylistic grounds, since documentation is often lacking.

20 While the designs clearly had very powerful symbolic meaning for the hunter who dreamed them and had them painted on his coat, it is impossible at this remove even to guess what that meaning might have been. (Burnham,1992:59)

21 It has been noted that, in general, the earlier coats display finer, more detailed painting. Dorothy Burnham has suggested that, before the arrival of Christian missionaries, when hunters were able to have several wives, one might have been released from her other duties to concentrate on painting her husband's coat. (Burnham, 1992:3)

22 While in coats of similar European cut, gussets are introduced to give added fullness to the skirts, this is not necessarily the case with these painted skin coats. On some of the later coats, the insert is actually narrower than the piece it replaced. Thus, the influence of contemporary European fashion, although strong, is more visual than structural. (Burnham, 1992:11-12)

23 Mackenzie, 1970:184

24 The floral designs which have dominated Subarctic art since the mid-19th century are entirely European in origin.

25 National Museums of Scotland L.304.127

26 National Museums of Scotland 563:1

27 White women who exerted influence on native communities – nuns, schoolteachers, the wives of clergymen and traders – actively encouraged Indian women to learn European domestic crafts such as embroidery and lace-making, which they regarded as having a civilizing effect.

28 Quoted in Duncan, 1989:38 Zagoskin is of course describing ceremonial or 'dress' clothing. Everyday wear in this area, as elsewhere, was not decorated apart from a few fringes and perhaps a patterned belt. Because such costume was everyday, it was rarely commented on or collected.

29 Venice had the monopoly of glass bead production until the 1880s, when Bohemian (Czech) beads became available and were imported.

30 The shells mentioned by Zagoskin were almost certainly dentalia or 'tooth shells', which were widely traded from the Pacific coast all over the interior. They were highly prized as decoration and as a form of currency and conspicuous wealth.

31 Quoted in Duncan & Carney, 1988:34

THE ARCTIC

1 Kay Hendrickson, Nunivak Island, as quoted in Morrow, 1984:124

2 For a full discussion of the prehistoric and historical development of Arctic cultures, see Damas (ed.), 1984

3 Burch, 1984:5

4 Lantis, 1947; Lowenstein, 1993; Spencer, 1959: 332-353; Fitzhugh and Crowell, 1988.

5 Rasmussen, 1929; Fitzhugh and Kaplan, 1982; Fienup-Riordan, 1990:167

6 Meade, 1990:230

7 Driscoll, 1987: 176-187

8 For a description of gutskin parkas and treatment, as well as examples of extant garments, see: Nelson (1983); Turner, 1976 (1894):56-58; Moore, 1923; Jochelson, 1933; Collins, et al., 1973; Fitzhugh and Kaplan, 1982; Hickman, 1987; Bockstoce, 1977; Black and Liapunova in Fitzhugh and Crowell, 1988; Chaussonnet in Fitzhugh and Crowell, 1988

9 Morrow, 1984:125, 137

10 Meade, 1990:231

11 Meade, 1990:231-234

12 Fitzhugh and Kaplan, 1982:220; Nelson, 1899: 228-232

13 Driscoll, 1987: 176-182

14 See Stenton, 1991 for an excellent description of the hypothermal qualities of caribou clothing.

15 Driscoll, 1987

16 Turner, 1976 (1884):49

17 Driscoll, 1980, 1987

18 For artifact examples, see: Ray, 1977, 1981; Fitzhugh and Kaplan, 1982; Driscoll, 1987 (Vol. 2)

19 Driscoll, 1987:193-199

20 Aleutian women were especially known for their production of finely woven grass baskets, an area outside the scope of this chapter. See, for example, Ray, 1981; Black, 1982.

21 Fitzhugh and Kaplan, 1982:56, 107

22 Fienup-Riordan, 1994:168

23 Morrow, 1984:124

24 See Morrow quoted in Fienup-Riordan, 1990:53; see also Fitzhugh and Kaplan, 1982:166

25 Ager, 1974; Fitzhugh and Kaplan, 1982:156-159

26 See also Laughlin, 1980; Fienup-Riordan, 1994.

27 See, especially, Black, 1991 for analysis of the symbolic implications of hunting hat decoration

28 Morrow, 1984 offers an excellent summary of Yup'ik ceremonialism based on research among elders collected by Elsie Mather, a native Yup'ik speaker.

29 Morrow, 1984:124

30 Morrow, 1984:123-127

31 Hawkes, 1914

32 Fitzhugh and Kaplan, 1982:202-205

33 Fienup-Riordan, 1990:49-67

34 Hawkes, 1914

35 Boas 1964:197

36 For a comprehensive discussion of the development of Inuit art in the Canadian Arctic, see Swinton, 1992; for an exceptional analysis of a specific theme in contemporary Canadian Inuit art, see Blodgett, 1979.

37 Morrow, 1984; Fienup-Riordan, 1990, 1994

38 Black, 1981

THE NORTHEAST

1 Torrence and Hobbs, 1989:19
2 In the autumn of 1687, Jesuit Father Beschefer sent 'Pieces of bark, on which figures have been marked by the teeth' to France (Thwaites 1959:287).
3 For example, Friedl, 1944:150
4 See Speck 1937:74-80. He also suggests that these dental pictographs might have been a source for what he calls 'phytomorphic' (literally, plant forms) art decorations (Speck, 1937:77-78).
5 Davidson, 1928, Moody, 1957, Speck, 1937 and innumerable others have suggested this and yet there is no concrete evidence.
6 For instance, William H. Holmes as cited by Densmore 1941:679
7 Densmore, 1941:679 (emphasis added). A number of other sources reinforce this ability.
8 Bardwell, 1986:54
9 Wetherbee, 1980:197
10 Speck (1947:22) lists several individuals and their rights to specific resorts in New England. Mason (1904: Plate 120) provides a photograph of Caroline Masta, an Abenaki who made baskets at

Belmar, New Jersey from splints and sweet grass supplied by her family in Quebec (Canada). These she sold at Asbury Park and Boardwalk in New Jersey (Pelletier, 1982:6).
11 R. H. Whitehead (1982) provides the definitive study and analysis of Micmac quillwork from the historical evidence to the current situation.
12 If the bark is removed properly at the correct time, the tree is not killed.
13 When possible, the quills were taken during the spring before they became filled with an oily fluid as the summer progressed.
14 The burning of the barbed end turns the quill into ash effectively removing it from being caught on the hands or bare feet (Whitehead, 1982:100n3).
15 Whitehead suggests that this might have been considered a conventionalized representation of a fir tree (1982:146n304).
16 Whitehead (1982:193) uses this term to distinguish the motif from the right-angled swastika. However, linguist Peter Bakker (1991:21) recognizing the motif as identical to the Basque national symbol, calls it by the Basque term *lauburu*.

17 It is important to note here that Ursuline nuns located in Quebec convents are known to have produced similar quillwork from circa 1773 until the 1830s. Poor quality and differences in motifs serve to differentiate these from the work of the Micmac.
18 Once a hide had been scraped, it was soaked overnight in a solution of butternut shells or alder bark before tanning. Although there are some indications that this was done for 'special' garments, it was most assuredly an esthetic intent.
19 Native people first taught the nuns how to work in birch bark and moosehair. However, not only did the nuns utilize these materials to provide instruction in European methods of embroidery, they also commercially exploited this bark and moosehair art form by producing and selling similar wares themselves for a brief period of time (Phillips, 1991:22).
20 Forest Faces were mythological semi-human beings appearing as disembodied heads with long, snapping hair who darted from tree to tree in the forest. They are constantly hungry for tobacco.
21 Fenton (1987) has suggested a classification

scheme which not all Iroquoianists accept.
22 Another set of wooden masks represents a variety of forms from pigs to clowns and for specialized societies.
23 Fenton, 1987:177-178
24 This replicates the action of the Great Doctor who scraped his rattle on the cosmic (World) tree to absorb its strength.
25 Fenton, 1987:54-59
26 Bowdoin Gil, 1977:50
27 Pohrt, 1990:25
28 Whiteford, 1977:52
29 See for example, Feest 1984; Phillips 1989; Whiteford 1977; Wilson 1982.
30 One species used is the Spreading Dogbane (A. androsaemi folium) and the other, Indian Hemp (A. cannibinum).
31 Skinner, 1921:260n3.
32 Feest, 1984:15
33 Abbass, 1986
34 Hartman, 1988:41; Torrence and Hobbs, 1989:18
35 Skinner, 1921
36 Torrence and Hobbs, 1989:19
37 Torrence and Hobbs, 1989:49.

INDEX

PICTURE CREDITS

With the exception of those items listed below, all the artifact photography was shot by Don Eiler with the cooperation of the Department of Anthropology at the National Museum of Natural History, Smithsonian Institution, Washington D.C., and most of the black-and-white prints were supplied by the National Anthropological Archives (NAA), Smithsonian Institution. The publishers are grateful to the Smithsonian Institution for the opportunity to photograph artifacts and offer thanks to Deborah Hull-Walski, Collections Manager, and her staff at the Museum Support Center in Suitland, Maryland, for all their help. A special thank you to Deborah A. Wood, Museum Consultant, who organized things so efficiently and whose contribution was vital to the project.

Front Endpaper: Jim Winkley; **Page 1:** Stark Museum of Art (SMA), ref 22.900/16; **7:** (left) NAA 81-13443; **8:** (right) NAA 86-4103; **9:** (right) NAA 1102-B-13; **13:** Salamander Books Ltd/American Museum of Natural History (AMNH), New York, ref 2298; **14:** (right) NAA 1033; **19:** (left) Historical Association of Southern Florida, ref 1973.29X.1; **21:** (left) NAA 44368-I, (right) Cranbrook Institute of Science (CIS), ref 1360; **24:** NAA 4561; **26:** (top) NAA 4571, (bottom) Salamander/AMNH, ref 9218; **27:** (right) SMA, ref 42.900/42; **28:** (top) SMA, ref 42.900/30; **30:** (bottom) Library of Congress (LoC), ref USZ-62-99573; **33:** (left) Milwaukee Public Museum (MPM), ref 44528; **34:** (center) LoC, ref USZ-62-99569; **39:** (top) SMA, ref 62.900/24, (bottom) Salamander/AMNH, refs (left to right) 8890, 8688, 8690, 8763, 8767, 8703, 8694, 8956; **40:** NAA 4543; **41:** (right) SMA, ref 22.900/27; **44:** Colin F. Taylor; **45:** (top) NAA 3184-A; **49:** (top) NAA 1775-A; **52:** (top) Salamander/Buffalo Bill Historical Center; **53:** NAA 75-11151; **55:** Salamander/Buffalo Bill Historical Center; **57:** (left) NAA 1459-B, (right) SMA, ref 82.900/332; **58:** Colin F. Taylor; **61:** (top) Salamander/AMNH, ref 5365; **65:** (top) MPM; **65:** (top) Montana Historical Society (MHS), ref 954-554; **66:** NAA 46786-B; **69:** (right) Salamander/AMNH, ref 3737; **74:** NAA 75-16219; **78:** (right) NAA 79-4322; **81:** Santa Barbara Museum of Natural History, photo – Tom Haci; **87:** (bottom) Alaska State Library (ASL), ref PCA 87-13; **88:** National Museums of Canada (NMC), ref 243; **89:** American Museum of Natural History (AMNH), New York, ref 42288; **91:** Royal British Columbia Museum (RBCM), ref PN 12217; **93:** (inset) NMC, ref 242; **95:** (top) NAA, ref 62.900/52A&B, (bottom) ASL, ref PCA 87-106; **96:** (bottom) RBCM, ref PN 1543; **97:** (right) Salamander/AMNH, ref 8184; **98:** (bottom) RBCM, ref PN 9197; **101:** (bottom) courtesy John W. Heintz via Carol Sheehan; **103:** Salamander/AMNH, ref 5105; **105:** (bottom) NAA 10455-N-1; **106:** (top left) NAA 75-5350; **107:** (top) courtesy The Field Museum, neg A-62082; **113:** SMA, ref 62.900/53; **115:** LoC, ref USZ-62-101243; **117:** (left) NAA 44826-C; **120:** (right) Smithsonian Institution, neg 77-5634; **121:** Sheila Spence, Winnipeg Art Gallery, © Indian and Northern Affairs Canada, courtesy Inuit Art Section; **123:** Cranbrook Institute of Science (CIS), ref 1625; **126:** (right) NAA 84-10788; **131:** CIS, ref 3754; **132:** (top) Rochester Museum and Science Center, ref RM 2088, (bottom) CIS, ref 3040; **133:** (top left) CIS, ref 1259, (top right) NAA, ref 56826; **back endpaper:** Jim Winkley.

The selection and captioning of all illustrations in this book have been the responsibility of Salamander Books Ltd and not of the individual contributors.